URBAN IMAGINARIES IN NATIVE AMAZONIA

URBAN IMAGINARIES IN NATIVE AMAZONIA

TALES OF ALTERITY, POWER, AND DEFIANCE

EDITED BY

FERNANDO SANTOS-GRANERO AND EMANUELE FABIANO

THE UNIVERSITY OF
ARIZONA PRESS
TUCSON

The University of Arizona Press
www.uapress.arizona.edu

We respectfully acknowledge the University of Arizona is on the land and territories of Indigenous peoples. Today, Arizona is home to twenty-two federally recognized tribes, with Tucson being home to the O'odham and the Yaqui. The University strives to build sustainable relationships with sovereign Native Nations and Indigenous communities through educational offerings, partnerships, and community service.

ISBN-13: 978-0-8165-4967-2 (hardcover)
ISBN-13: 978-0-8165-5662-5 (paperback)
ISBN-13: 978-0-8165-4968-9 (e-book)

Cover design by Leigh McDonald
Cover illustration: *Shamans visiting the underwater city of the Anaconda People* by Elena Valera (Bawan Jisbe), 2009
Typeset by Sara Thaxton in 10/14 Warnock Pro with Payson WF and Helvetica Neue LT Std

Publication of this book is made possible in part by the proceeds of a permanent endowment created with the assistance of a Challenge Grant from the National Endowment for the Humanities, a federal agency.

Library of Congress Cataloging-in-Publication Data
Names: Santos-Granero, Fernando, 1955– editor. | Fabiano, Emanuele, editor.
Title: Urban imaginaries in native Amazonia : tales of alterity, power, and defiance / edited by Fernando Santos-Granero and Emanuele Fabiano.
Description: [Tucson] : The University of Arizona Press, 2023. | Includes bibliographical references and index.
Identifiers: LCCN 2022031513 (print) | LCCN 2022031514 (ebook) | ISBN 9780816549672 (hardcover) | ISBN 9780816549689 (ebook)
Subjects: LCSH: Indians of South America—Amazon River Region—Social conditions. | Urban Indians—Amazon River Region. | City and town life—Amazon River Region. | Urbanization—Amazon River Region. | Rural-urban migration—Amazon River Region.
Classification: LCC F2230 .U73 2023 (print) | LCC F2230 (ebook) | DDC 305.898081/1—dc23/eng/20220928
LC record available at https://lccn.loc.gov/2022031513
LC ebook record available at https://lccn.loc.gov/2022031514

Printed in the United States of America
♾ This paper meets the requirements of ANSI/NISO Z39.48-1992 (Permanence of Paper).

CONTENTS

Part III. Urban Imaginaries Through Time

URBAN IMAGINARIES IN NATIVE AMAZONIA

Amerindian Urban Imaginaries

A Double-Mirror Reality

FERNANDO SANTOS-GRANERO AND EMANUELE FABIANO

Although urbanization is an ancient phenomenon, going back in time at least nine thousand years (P. Taylor 2012), for most of human history people lived in dispersed, low-density rural settlements. This began to change as a consequence of the Industrial Revolution (1760–1840), when, due to technological changes in production and manufacturing, rural emigration increased and urban populations began to grow rapidly. In 1800, only 10 percent of the world's population lived in urban areas. Today, 55 percent of the world's population (according to the United Nations) or as much as 85 percent (according to the European Commission) live in urban settings (Ritchie and Roser 2019), the discrepancy deriving from different definitions of *urban*—an issue that will be discussed in more detail below. Regardless of these differences, however, what the above figures indicate is that urbanization has not only accelerated sharply in the past two hundred years but has, in the process, become a global phenomenon.

This rapid process of urbanization has had significant social, economic, and political impacts. On the positive side, high population density (and the concentration of resources in cities) has fostered technological advancements, economic specialization, higher productivity, and lower costs of production. It has promoted new forms of connectedness, political activity, and social solidarity, and it has encouraged creativity and the development of a broad range of cultural activities and forms of entertainment. On the negative side, it has deepened social inequalities, leading to the emergence of slums, overcrowding, and an urban underclass. It has promoted individualism and anonymity, thus weakening traditional family networks and forms of cooperation. And it has increased pollution, waste production, environmental degradation, and crime. In brief, although urbanization has generally led to higher standards of living, it has also condemned a large proportion of urban dwellers to a life of poverty and squalor.

Despite lingering perceptions of Amazonia as a wild, remote, mostly rural space, the region has not escaped this global trend. Thanks to the building of a large network of roads and the development of better means of transportation, since the 1960s Amazonia has experienced a rapid process of urbanization. By 1985, with over 50 percent of the population of Amazonia living in urban areas, Bertha K. Becker (1985) had already described it as an "urbanized forest." Today, almost forty years later, with approximately 70 percent of the Amazonian population living in cities (Becker 2013, 310; Chaves et al. 2021, 1187), urbanity has become hegemonic, and Amazonia is now an urban forest. The appeal of cities and urban lifeways has extended to the region's every corner, including its three million Indigenous people belonging to some 350 ethnic groups (Charity et al. 2016, 26). As a result, by 2010, 36 percent of Brazil's Amazonian Indigenous population lived in urban settings (Santos et al. 2019). Although the pace of Indigenous urbanization has varied in other Amazonian regions, it is safe to assume that between 30 and 40 percent of Amazonia's Indigenous population now lives, more or less permanently, in cities. The urbanization of Amazonia has neither been the result of a unidirectional process nor been limited to the Indigenous people living closest to cities. Migrants to Amazonian cities often originate from the rural and urban areas of the Andes or the coastal regions of Brazil (Emlen 2020; Ødegaard 2010). In some cases, they are international migrants coming from neighboring countries (Aragón 2011). It is therefore appropriate to consider Amazonian cities and their current population as the result of complex demographic flows between rural and urban areas, often leading to the multisite household pattern that characterizes Amazonian populations nowadays (Padoch et al. 2008).

The Causes of Urban Migration

The pull factors of rural-to-urban Indigenous migration vary greatly from case to case. A few elements, however, are common throughout Amazonia. Access to secondary and college education for one's children is one of the most common. Whereas elementary education is nowadays available in most Indigenous settlements, higher education is still mostly confined to cities. As the aspiration to follow high school and college studies increases, more and more Indigenous young men and women move to cities to make their dreams possible. Proximity to better health services and salaried work opportunities is equally common, as Indigenous people have become increasingly dependent on the market for the satisfaction of their needs. There are, however, other, less obvious factors. Indigenous leaders often move to regional cities to be closer to government agencies and engage in lobbying activities on behalf of their people (McSweeney and Jokisch 2007, 2015). Shamans move to cities to seek a broader clientele or to represent their people in regional and national events (Conklin 2002; Coutinho 2016; Perruchon 2002). And Indigenous artists settle in cities to take advantage of the opportunities provided by galleries, art dealers, and a larger audience (Feldman 2018).

More generally, as several contributors to this volume point out, Indigenous Amazonian people seem to be attracted to the wealth, technological wonders, entertainment possibilities, and many comforts offered by urban centers. Thus, electricity, gas, running water, home appliances, paved streets, public transportation, hospitals, pharmacies, supermarkets, malls, cinemas, clubs, and stadiums exert a strong allure to reside in the city. However, Indigenous urban migration cannot be understood simply as a definitive, unidirectional process. As Daniela Peluso (2015a, 58) has argued, these migrations "rarely signify full-time absences or dislocations from communities of origin," and they do not "necessarily entail a permanent moving to towns." Rather, they often constitute transitory phenomena that promote "a wide series of active links between cities and communities of origin," as well as a constant flux of people in both directions. Indeed, as Raymond Williams (1973) asserts in his renowned book *The Country and the City*, between the rural and the urban there are regular, necessary, and functional ties. This is even more evident in contemporary Amazonia, a space of interaction and articulation of complex social, cultural, and economic realities, whose interdependence demonstrates the inconsistency of a dichotomous stance according to which greater social complexity leads inevitably to a modern and civilized "urban" model detached from the "rural" (Browder and Godfrey 1997; Tritsch et al. 2015).

Urban Indigenous populations are thus composed of a diversity of people living under a diversity of conditions. Men and women who move perma-

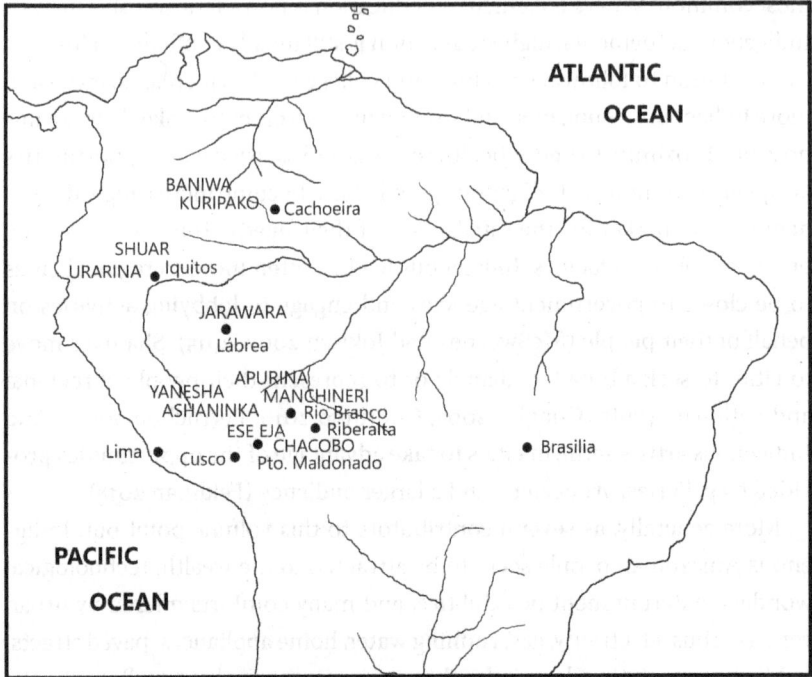

MAP I.1 Location of Indigenous peoples and urban centers mentioned in this volume. Crafted by Fernando Santos-Granero.

nently to the city with their families in search of better job opportunities. Leaders of regional and national ethnopolitical organizations who spend long periods of time in the city with or without their families. Community leaders of all sorts, who move to the city temporarily to participate in political meetings, training courses, or specialized workshops. Youngsters who visit the city in search of adventure and as part of the rite of passage of becoming an adult. Young women working as maids for white-mestizo families, who often marry non-Indigenous urban dwellers and stay in the city as cultural mediators. High school students living with relatives in the city, far from their families, for the better part of the year. College students living in pension rooms or college dorms with other students, who often engage in odd jobs to supplement the stipend provided by their families or communities. And men and women who visit the city periodically to call on relatives, seek medical attention, sell their products, or make purchases. In fact, with increasing frequency, migration does not end in the urban centers of the migrants' region of origin, but extends much farther, encompassing not only large urban centers at the national level, but also cities in close or faraway countries (Davis et al. 2017; Eloy, Brondizio, and Pateo 2015). This trend subverts the stereotypical image of Indigenous people as naturally rooted to their places of origin, images that regard sedentary life as a necessary condition for Indigenous people not to lose their "indigeneity" (Forte 2010, 2; Chernela 2015; Yagüe 2014).

For some of these people, visiting the city is the first step of a process leading to a permanent move. For others, visiting the city is part of a new way of life in which community and city are regarded not as opposite realities but as integral parts of their everyday lives. For still others, however, the city is still a remote, extraneous space, little known and mostly experienced through the tales and anecdotes of relatives and friends. In brief, there is no single Indigenous urbanization process. Rather, there are many different Indigenous urbanization processes, since the different causes for moving to the city and the different conditions under which Indigenous people live in the city determine very different ways of experiencing, using, adapting to, and contesting urban spaces.

Indigenous Urbanization in Amazonian Studies

The growing presence of Indigenous Amazonian people in regional and extraregional cities in the past decades has prompted Amazonianist anthropologists to pay more attention to this kind of population. In the late 1990s, some scholars had already noted that many Amazonian Indigenous people were migrating to the cities on a more or less permanent basis (González 1997). However, it was only some years later that the first ethnographic works on the process of Indigenous urbanization in Amazonia appeared. Among these, notable studies include those of Roberto Jaramillo (2003) on the reconfiguration of the ethnic identities of Indigenous migrants in the city of Manaus; Cristiane Lasmar (2005, 2008) on the marriage strategies of Tukano and Tariana women settled in the city of São Gabriel da Cachoeira; Daniela Peluso and Miguel N. Alexiades (2005) on the influence that environmental organizations have had on the processes of urbanization and urban ethnogenesis among the Ese Eja; Geraldo Andrello (2006) on the lives of Indigenous migrants in the multiethnic and highly urbanized mission post of Iauaretê; and Pedro de Niemeyer Cesarino (2008a) on the ways that

Marubo people mobilize mythological and shamanistic discourses to make sense of the city and develop strategies for the occupation of urban spaces.

By then it was clear that Indigenous urbanization was not a phenomenon unique to Brazilian Amazonia but had acquired a pan-Amazonian character. In view of this, Alberto Chirif and Pedro García Hierro (2007) pointed out in their book *Marcando territorio* that, in contrast to the central importance that the struggle for land had had for the Indigenous movement since the 1960s, there were now important processes of "deterritorialization" by which many Indigenous people were abandoning their lands of origin to go to live in the city. At the same time, they noted the need for regional and national ethnopolitical organizations to incorporate into their agendas the issue of urban Indigenous people: people who no longer "depend on the territory or face the same problems as their countrymen who have remained in the rivers" (Chirif and García Hierro 2007, 311). For their part, geographers Kendra McSweeney and Brad Jokisch (2007) argued that urbanization processes should not be regarded as opposed to Indigenous struggles for land or the preservation of Indigenous identities. On the contrary, they claimed, through the political action of urban Indigenous people in coordination with local and regional leaders, these processes could present a unique opportunity to promote collective objectives such as territorial struggle, autonomous development, and the strengthening of ethnic identities.

It was only in the past decade, however, that interest in the urban Indigenous phenomenon has thrived. Based on a preliminary study of four Indigenous urban populations in Peru, Oscar Espinosa (2009, 52) argued that not all Amazonian Indigenous peoples relate to the urban in the same way. While some urban migrants attempt to disguise their Indigenous identity, others reaffirm it through political action, and still others, instead of migrating to cities, tend to urbanize their communities, bringing the city to the forest. In the following years, several works were published analyzing the causes of the growing urbanization processes (Arcila 2011), the participation of Amazonian Indigenous people in the construction of urban territorialities (Peña Márquez 2011), the phenomenon of urban *malocas* (communal dwellings) (Sánchez 2010), and the "hypermarginalization" to which Amazonian Indigenous people are subjected when they migrate to the city (Bessire 2014).

Especially instructive among these early contributions are Pirjo Kristiina Virtanen's (2006, 2010, 2012) works on how Manxineru (Manchineri) youths living in the city of Rio Branco adapt creatively to their new setting, experience their ethnicity, and deal with the twin problems of discrimination and exploitation. In the same line, Ismael Vega Díaz (2014) analyzes the social insertion strategies of native Amazonians living in Lima, including the preservation and reinvention of their ethnic identities, the re-creation of their cultural customs, and the maintenance of permanent relationships with their communities of origin using various means and especially the new digital technologies. The complex interrelation between urban Indigenous people and their counterparts in their communities is also one of the main lines of research in a set of articles published by the *Journal of Latin American and Caribbean Anthropology* in a special issue edited by Daniela Peluso (2015b).

All these authors note that Indigenous urbanization processes raise the question of the survival and continuity of native Amazonian peoples. However, whereas some think that these processes undermine Indigenous identities and promote acculturation (Mayor Aparicio and Bodmer 2009, 64), others affirm that urban Indigenous people are not necessarily condemned to stop being Indigenous, since being Indigenous is a "way of being" (*forma de ser*) rather than a "way of being in a place" (*forma de estar*) (Santos-Granero 2007, 16), and they call for "urban Indigenous people to be recognized as Indigenous with the same rights as their counterparts living in rural communities" (Espinosa 2009, 57). In fact, contrary to those who claim that urban Indigenous people are no longer Indigenous, some urban native Amazonians claim that the city has made them "more Indigenous" and see themselves as pioneers building a "city of Indians" within the white city (Sánchez 2010, 146, 150).

Object of this Volume

Adopting Alexiades and Peluso's (2015, 5) cogent assertion that "urbanization often begins in people's minds," we propose in this volume to analyze not the material or sociological aspects of Amazonian Indigenous urbanization processes, but their ideational dimension as it finds expression in their "urban imaginaries." A summary review of the ethnographic literature shows that urban life has long intrigued Indigenous Amazonians, who regard white people's cities as the locus of both extraordinary power and unusual danger. The powerful allure that these cities have held, and continue to hold, over the imaginaries of native Amazonian peoples has transformed these places into models for the representation of extreme alterity under the guise of extraordinary, urbanized, other-than-human worlds. Indigenous mythical and cosmological discourse has peopled the land with underground cities (Whitten 1976, 41; Kohn 2007, 112; Feather 2010, 284), subaquatic metropolises (Murphy 1958, 128; Narby 1989, 23–24; Chaumeil 2002, 41; Uzendoski 2009, 155; Pitarch 2012, 76; Hugh-Jones 2018, 218–19), remote forest cities (Hill 2009, 116; Brabec de Mori 2005; Da Silva, Shepard, and Carmo 2017, 118), arboreal cities (Brown 1986, 61; Lagrou 1998, 22, 39, 254), and celestial towns (Maybury-Lewis 1974, 289; Cesarino 2008b, 219; Morin 2015, 361; Walker 2012, 151) that are normally invisible to lay people. These ubiquitous enchanted cities are sometimes represented as hypervillages, but most often they are endowed with the symbols of the highly urbanized and industrial national societies that Indigenous Amazonian peoples are a part of. Thus, they often include elements regarded as being emblematic of city life: streets, cars, motorcycles, lampposts, stores, banks, hospitals, and high-rises. They are places characterized by an abundance of consumer goods, money, and complex technologies, but also of bizarre alimentary customs, and of alien (often contrary) social and political forms of organization; places whose urban structure, architecture, and metropolitan practices are not mere narrative props, but the means to convey Indigenous concerns about the nature of power, alterity, and domination as well as the need for resistance and defiance.

This volume seeks to analyze and explore the ambivalent nature of native Amazonian urban imaginaries and the extent to which they reflect as well as influence Indigenous people's urban experiences. This topic is particularly relevant since, as we have seen, in the past decades Indigenous Amazonians have been moving in large numbers to cities and large towns within and without Amazonia. In such a juncture, the study of native Amazonian urban imaginaries is no longer a mere exoticizing ethnographic endeavor; it is an academic imperative.

Contributors to this volume address this subject from a variety of viewpoints and methodological approaches in order to answer a set of key questions: Are these urban imaginaries a means of experiencing the lifeways of white and mestizo people by temporarily adopting their points of view? Do they respond to a mimetic process through which Indigenous Amazonians seek to appropriate the power of white people's cities without relinquishing their own identity? Are they the result of an attempt to construct Indigenous utopias or dystopias, that is, alternative realities derived from a radical process of social inversion or the exacerbation of the negative aspects of urban life? Or are they simply an epiphenomenon of the long history of contact with their respective national societies, a brave attempt to reflect on their own history by reconstructing the meaning of past experiences in the light of present events?

Contributors analyze these issues from historical, ethnographic, and philosophical perspectives. They inquire about the meaning of native Amazonian urban imaginaries, their structure and content, their social purpose, and their fit with other aspects of Indigenous ontologies and cosmologies. Above all, they seek to analyze how these ambiguous urban imaginaries express a singular view of the cosmos and cosmopolitical relations, how they inform and shape forest-city interactions, and what the historical processes were through which they came into existence. In brief, through the systematic analysis of the urban imaginaries of eleven Indigenous Amazonian peoples as represented in myths, cosmological discourse, and narratives of personal experiences, contributors seek to understand the reasons for their widespread diffusion, as well as their influence in rural-to-urban migration and processes of urbanization (map I.1).

Imaginaries and the Urban

The notion of imaginary has been the object of much interest in the past decades, having been applied to a broad range of social phenomena and fields of research: modern national societies (Perreault and Valdivia 2010; C. Taylor 2002, 2004; Gaonkar 2002), science and technology (Eaton, Gasteyer, and Busch 2014; Jasanoff and Kim 2013; Fortun and Fortun 2005), environmental studies (Davis and Burke 2011; McGregor 2004; Nesbitt and Weiner 2001), queer studies (Tongson 2011), tourism (Salazar 2011), and, of course, urban studies (Millington 2012; Huyssen 2008; Prakash and Kruse 2008). As is usually the case, despite its widespread use, there seems to be little agreement as to the meaning of this notion, which ranges from a "symbolic matrix within which a people imagine and act as world-making collective agents" (Gaonkar 2002, 1) to "the cognitive and somatic images" that people carry within them to make sense of different situations, peoples, and places (Huyssen 2008, 3).

The broad and often divergent scope of these definitions originates in part from the etymology of this notion. As an adjective, *imaginary* derives from the Latin *imaginarius*, "that which exists only in the imagination" (Lewis and Short 1879, s.v. "imaginarius"). As a noun, it is closer to the Latin *imago*, meaning "an imitation, copy of a thing, an image, or likeness." The range of meanings of *imago* is, however, much broader and includes the notions of apparition, semblance, and appearance, but also conception, thought, and depiction. In this latter sense, *imago* can be defined as "an image or likeness of a thing formed in the mind, a conception, thought, imagination, idea" (Lewis and Short 1879, s.v. "imago"). Here we propose to use the term *imaginary* not in the sense of an imagination, as a mental product lacking factual reality, but in this latter sense, as a representation or complex understanding of a particular dimension of existence that functions as a cognitive tool. From this point of view, imaginaries are mental constructs founded on information derived from a variety of sources: empirical observation and other forms of perception, such as dreams, visions, and revelations, but also oral traditions, received wisdom, third-party reports, and even rumors and hearsay. They differ, however, from theories and other kinds of intellectual formulations in that they are mostly unstructured and inarticulate (C. Taylor 2002, 105).

Imaginaries are, nonetheless, much more than simple sets of ideas about a given aspect of lived experience. They constitute a means to apprehend, comprehend, and make sense of complex actualities and practices. As such, they play a central role in contexts of interface with novel, unknown, or little-known peoples, places, or social practices. In such contexts, imaginaries become heuristic devices that facilitate exploration of the differences between the "imaginers" (those who imagine) and the "imagined." They are concerned with attaching meaning to otherwise ungraspable situations or realities. Although based on individual perceptions and understandings, imaginaries are always collective representations, shared by a group of people as the result of prolonged social and historical interaction. As such, they are not only "socioculturally sedimented" but also "historically inflected" (Fortun and Fortun 2005, 50).

Here we are interested in both individual perceptions and collective representations, since we believe that they are mutually constitutive. In effect, as Noel B. Salazar (2011, 864), citing Paul Ricoeur, has argued, "The imaginary is both a function of producing meanings and the product of this function." As collective imaginaries are shaped by individual experiences, so individual understandings are informed by the imaginaries of the collectivity to which they belong. In what until recently were largely oral societies, these mental constructs find expression in highly structured oral narratives—myths, songs, and chants—but also in less formalized first- or third-person oral accounts.

From this perspective, the ordinary or extraordinary experience of urban life reveals its constructed nature through a changing mosaic of elements whose combination does not produce a fixed and invariable entity, that is, a universal form, a type of prototypical settlement or a delimited spatial unit identifiable with the city model (Brenner and Schmid 2015, 165). On the contrary, such experience corresponds to a process, an operation of production and updating of the diverse urban perspectives, leading to the construction of an imaginary that makes the city both a theoretical category and an empirical object. In this sense, as Andreas Huyssen (2008) indicates, urban imaginaries are more concrete and have a much more profound effect than they appear to have, insofar as they are the reality of any city, rather than simple products of the imagination, and differ depending on a multitude of perspectives and positions adopted by the subjects who create or inhabit them.

Whereas it is true that urban imaginaries, like any other inhabited space, are based on preexisting sociabilities, geographies, and ideologies and are the product of a slow accumulation process, it is also true that they in turn impose forms of sociability, subjectivity, and intersubjectivity, sharing with real cities the fact of existing simultaneously within and without their inhabitants. Indeed, as Rolf Lindner (2016) indicates in his discussion on the importance of the urban imaginary as an anthropological subject, it is impossible to reduce the life of a city or understand it adequately by focusing exclusively on its material aspects. On the contrary, it can be argued that the images and symbols that accompany the physical space make it even more "real," since the imaginary is not opposed to reality, but is nourished by it and "deepens" it in a very specific way (Lindner 2016, 114). If the city is "a state of mind" and the result of people's attempts "to grasp the meaning of its complexity in an imaginative and symbolic way"—as Richard Wohl and Anselm Strauss (1958, 523) point out in a foundational work on the importance of the symbolic representation of the urban—then urban imaginaries can be said to be "effective realities that shape the behaviour, cosmologies and desires of people in cities, or of those who visit them, imagine them, or describe them in narrative or imagery" (Hansen and Verkaaik 2009, 5).

Given that native Amazonian urban imaginaries generally refer to objects, customs, and facilities characteristic of contemporary urban centers, it would be tempting to attribute their origin to the cities that cropped up throughout Amazonia during the rubber boom era (1870–1910). This would be an error. As Peter Gow (2011) has noted, the origin of such urban imaginaries may go as far back in time as 1300 CE, when the first large settlements began to coalesce in the Upper Xingu region. Those protocities— structured around a central plaza, surrounded by palisades and defensive ditches, connected by a series of raised roads to satellite villages or other similarly large settlements, and inhabited by thousands of people (Heckenberger 2003, 2005)—constituted a new architectural and residential development that must have impressed the minds of those non–urban dwellers who saw them or heard about them. More recent research has demonstrated that early urbanism in Amazonia may be even older, going as far back as 800 BCE, in which case the model for native Amazonian urban imaginaries could have been the Upper Xingu "galactic polities" (Heckenberger et al. 2008), the Marajoan mounds (Schaan 2012), the Mojos earthworks (Walker 2008), or, as Virtanen argues in this volume, the geometric earthwork structures found in the Upper Purus region (see also Saunaluoma, Pärssinen, and Schaan 2018). In fact, as Santos-Granero claims in this volume, the origin of these urban imaginaries may even be much older, being modeled on the Andean cities of the Initial Period (1800–900 BCE), and those of Chavín, Wari, Inca, and colonial times. In brief, native Amazonian urban imaginaries are not a recent development and may have sprung up thousands of years ago through contact with early urban peoples living in large cities within and without the Amazon region.

But what exactly is understood by *urban*, and what qualifies as a *city*? These notions are intimately connected, to the point of seeming almost synonymous. As we shall see, this is not necessarily true. Whereas the term *city* refers to the material dimension (the setting) of large human residential agglomerations, the term *urban* alludes to a certain way of life (a condition) characteristic of that kind of large and socially complex settlement. For this reason, the two terms are not necessarily synonymous or coterminous: declining cities may no longer have an urban way of life, whereas large settlements that do not qualify as cities may have urban attributes and practices.

Although we agree with archaeologist Michael E. Smith (2020, 15) in that "there is no 'best' definition of terms like city or urban," we believe that it is impossible to discuss urban imaginaries without at least an operational definition of such terms. In an early work, Louis Wirth (1938, 8) defined city "as a relatively large, dense, and permanent settlement of socially heterogeneous individuals." More than a decade later, in his foundational work "The Urban Revolution," archaeologist V. Gordon Childe (1950) presented a more detailed definition of the city, which, despite numerous criticisms, is still influential in present-day understandings of urban settings. He defined cities as large settlements with a population in the thousands, displaying a complex division of labor, social stratification, payment of surpluses to a central authority, large-scale public works, methods of recording, exact sciences, systems of writing, higher forms of art, foreign trade, and a social organization based on residence rather than kinship. As Smith (2009, 10) has noted, however, Childe's definition is "not so much about cities or urbanism per se as it is about the series of interrelated social, economic, political, and cultural changes that led to the earliest states and cities." It is probably due to this particular approach that Childe's definition includes some traits that, although generally associated with state formations, are not necessarily defining of cities or city life. This is the case, for instance, with methods of recording, systems of writing, and higher forms of art, which are accessory rather than definitory traits. Wari and Inca cities sprang in the absence of writing systems, and many of the earliest cities lacked recording systems or the kind of sophisticated forms of art mentioned by Childe. In addition, Childe's definition omits an important aspect of the urban phenomenon, to wit, that cities are not autonomous and self-sufficient entities, but are part of a larger system that includes people living in its rural peripheries.

While there is some agreement as to what qualifies as a city, there is no universal definition of what constitutes an urban area. Nowadays, countries tend to apply different criteria—settlement size, population density, or economic advancement, for example—to define urban areas, and even within the same country definitions of the urban have varied through time. Thus, for instance, according to the 1950 U.S. Census "urbanized areas" were continuously built-up areas with a population of 50,000 or more, whereas "urban places" were densely settled population centers with at least 2,500 inhabitants. This distinction was abandoned by the 2020 U.S. Census, which defined as urban areas all settlements that "encompass at least 4,000 housing units or at least 10,000 persons" (U.S. Bureau of the Census 2021). In stark contrast, according to the 2017 Peruvian Census, an urban area is every settlement containing at least 100 contiguous houses and an average of 500 inhabitants (INEI 2018). The only factor that seems to be common to the various definitions of city and the urban condition is that they are phenomena tightly linked to the development of social complexity. Given the lack of consensus, for the purpose of this volume, we understand *city* to be a large agglomeration of nonrelated people living in a hierarchically structured space, articulated by a central authority, that depends for its subsistence on its relationship with people living in its rural peripheries under less dense settlement arrangements. *Urban*, in contrast, we understand as the complex social interactions and lifestyles characteristic of life in cities.

Based on the above considerations, we define *urban imaginaries* as the collective representations or mental constructs informed by individual experience and perceptions that refer to cities and urban lifeways and serve as both cognitive tools and blueprints for social action. In Indigenous Amazonia urban imaginaries consist of images and understandings about the urban reality of extraordinary and potentially dangerous Others—from terrestrial, aquatic, and heavenly spirits to pre- and postcolonial urban peoples—that emerge through a double-mirror process, known in Western art history as *mise en abyme* (Reinhardt 2012). Through this game of parallel mirrors, the elements of the urbanity of Amazonian, Andean, and European peoples are attributed to the worlds of other-than-human beings (which are imagined filled with streets, stone buildings, factories, and automobiles), whereas the characteristics of the beings that inhabit the supernatural worlds are attributed to the human Others living in urban spaces, who are conceived of as endowed with extraordinary and often nefarious powers.

Urban realities and urban imaginaries are thus infinitely reflected. They are not only mutually constitutive but historically constructed, changing through time in response to the experience of new forms of urbanity and urban lifeways. In painting and literature, the mise en abyme may take the form of an image that contains a smaller copy of itself, like Jan van Eyck's 1434 painting *Portrait of Giovanni Arnolfini and His Wife*, or of a story within a story, like André Gide's 1925 novel *The Counterfeiters* (Reinhardt 2012, 86). In such cases, as Lucía Tena Morillo (2019, 483) argues, the double image or the secondary story may reflect the entire work, or it may instead focus on a particular aspect, whose refraction is not evident and which may even seem at first sight insignificant, but which becomes fundamental for the interpretation of the whole. This latter possibility, as we shall see, is particularly true of Indigenous Amazonian urban imaginaries, which often place emphasis on a few urban features to express—in a synecdochic manner—the urban reality of dangerous or ambiguous Others. Although there is no doubt, as Sylvia Caiuby Novaes (1997) has argued in relation to the Bororo, that such play of mirrors can be regarded as a metaphor that facilitates exploration of the self as reflected in the Other, here the emphasis is not so much on Indigenous Amazonian "self-images" but on the "Other-images" that have historically developed as the result of contact with urban peoples. Interestingly enough, as Philippe Erikson and Robin M. Wright demonstrate in this volume, Indigenous Amazonians often claim that modern white people's cities were founded on the sites of old Indigenous settlements, in which case Indigenous urban imaginaries seem to comprise diverse layers of self- and Other-images.

In the following pages, we discuss some of the central themes that emerge from a reading of the chapters included in this volume, with the aim of characterizing Indigenous Amazonian urban imaginaries, as well as advancing new questions and suggesting new lines of research.

The Urban Nature of Other-Than-Human Worlds

As contributors to this volume argue, cities and urbanity are not recent phenomena in the lives of Indigenous Amazonian peoples. Knowledge of ancient cities and large settlements has, directly or indirectly, left a deep impression on native Amazonians, to the point of shaping their ontological and cosmological conceptions. The influence of these early experiences of urban centers and unprecedented forms of urban life has been so pervasive that even when interaction with city dwellers was openly hostile, as in the case of the Chacobo, it significantly marked their ritual life, as well as their understandings of interethnic relations and ways of engaging with urban spaces (see Erikson, this volume).

The spatial, architectural, and sociopolitical characteristics of the invisible cities of other-than-human worlds clearly not only reflect the experience of living in present-day urban centers, but also evoke ancient connections with pre-Columbian urban centers (see Santos-Granero, this volume). As Virtanen argues in this volume, archaeological excavations in the Purus region suggest the existence of urban centers utilized for large-scale ceremonies in which rulers made food offerings to their followers, while at the same time marriages were arranged, commercial exchanges were made, and political alliances established. This indicates a pattern of temporal habitation and exchange between people and their leaders that may have functioned in the

Purus region in much the same way as it did in the Andes under Inca rule. Rulers fed arriving visitors, who then contributed with their labor to building the city and its structures. The morphology of these places thus embodies the values of their inhabitants, the generosity of their rulers, and the integration of different peoples within an ecology of relationships involving both humans and other-than-humans.

It is likely, as Santos-Granero suggests in this volume, that all native Amazonian peoples living along the Andean foothills of Peru, Ecuador, Bolivia, and Colombia had similar encounters with neighboring urban civilizations. The effects of these contacts are still inscribed in their urban imaginaries. Even if these imaginaries rarely incorporate elements related to the experience of urbanity of Amazonian peoples' ancestors, such ideas are clearly present in Indigenous peoples' relationship with the spirit worlds. Thus, even if it is not possible to reconstruct the earliest Indigenous experiences with urban centers, contemporary descriptions of other-than-human cities make it possible to understand how Indigenous peoples have experienced those processes.

Enchanted cities seem to subvert the common notion of temporality—as something homogenous, continuous, and clearly directed—since within their confines time and space are sometimes compressed and sometimes extended. This allows for the superimposition of elements from a distant past with the latest technological novelties and elements of contemporary urban life, including the presence of institutions and governing bodies characteristic of the human world. One of the earliest recorded Southern Arawak urban imaginaries describes a fabulous Amazonian city ruled by a powerful Inca (see Santos-Granero, this volume). With the passage of time the elements of this imaginary have been updated: the palaces and golden objects present in this early account have become the hospitals, cars, and shops of the most recent narratives, while the despotism of Inca rulers has become the duplicity of conquerors, viceroys, and presidents. Similarly, the tree cities evoked by Urarina shamanic discourse incorporate some of the emblematic elements of the experiences of evangelization and life in the eighteenth-century Jesuit missions, but this time in the context of a noisy and overpopulated megalopolis (see Fabiano, this volume).

As the examples cited above demonstrate, being historical constructs, urban imaginaries have changed through time, mirroring changes in the encounters with and experience of urban centers. In general terms, however, native Amazonians assimilate other-than-human worlds to non-Indigenous urban lifestyles and perceive enchanted cities as hierarchical and oppressive places. Indigenous descriptions of other-than-human urban worlds often present qualities antithetical to those that define the typical Amazonian village, suggesting an intense identification with Western culture, the non-Indigenous world, and associated lifestyles (see, among others, Homan 2018, 159–60; Lagrou 2013, 250; Calavia Sáez 2007, 170). The layout and architecture of such urbanized other-than-human worlds also mirror those of contemporary human cities (see Fabiano and Maizza, this volume).

Southern Arawak urban imaginaries have incorporated impressions of the urbanized world of white and mestizo people, whose cities are regarded as places of material wealth, abundance, and technological innovations (see Santos-Granero, this volume). Enchanted cities are often described as monumental places where space is organized and used in ways radically different from life as experienced in Indigenous communities. Their topography contains lavishly decorated buildings constructed of nonperishable materials and wide-open spaces where people gather in large numbers for social, religious, or commercial purposes. Most importantly, cities often have facilities that make life easier: water channels, fountains, sewage systems, gas, and electricity.

If cities are the expression of the creativity, knowledge, and inventiveness of the white or mestizo Others, it is not surprising, then, that the inhabitants of the urbanized other-than-human worlds—spirit owners of animals or spirits of the dead—often play the role of rulers or masters. In Shuar urban imaginaries a motley crew of spirits and monsters thrive in characteristically urban habitats (see Buitron, this volume). Manxineru and Apurinã oral history and myths share similar ideas about the urban nature of animal- and plant-owning spirits, who often appear in human form in dreams and visions (see Virtanen, this volume). Among the Ese Eja, the spirits of the defunct (*emanokwana*) live, as do white people (*deja*), in a large city called Kweijana (see Peluso, this volume). Densely populated, Kweijana is the place where the dead live and thrive in a variety of increasingly large towns and villages.

The other-than-human entities that inhabit these cities—located within hills or caves, or in underwater and chthonic realms—conduct their activities in streets, buildings, and plazas. According to the Baniwa, the urbanized other-than-human worlds consist of multiple interconnected levels (see Wright, this volume). These enchanted cities do not exist on the same spatiotemporal plane as do the cities in which many Baniwa live today, but rather in another, transcendental reality that interacts directly with the present. On one level, there are the cosmogonic cities, spaces where the immutable ancestral identities were produced. These cities are the ultimate source of why things are the way they are in the world, and they contain places where the primordial powers were transformed into the present-day landscape, places understood as the primordial and perennial sources of all life and death in the world. On another level, there are the colonial towns mentioned in the clan histories, spaces characterized by identity loss, ethnic transformation, or assimilation into "white" society. Finally, on the vertical planes of the cosmos, there are the shamanic places of healing, also conceived of as cities.

For the Manxineru and Apurinã, the urban worlds in which spirits dwell are located in different venues (see Virtanen, this volume). The spirit world can be understood as a galactic system with its own special entry points, composed of various units comprising the domains of different master spirits. The interconnections that exist between these worlds and the places inhabited by humans allow spirits to move between them, appearing to humans as animals and plants, while living as humans in the spirit world. The entrances to these worlds can be physical places, such as holes or elevations in the earth, as well as metaphysical places. These latter entrances, for example, take the form of geometric images that appear in ayahuasca healing ceremonies, which allow access to the worlds of the master spirits. In addition to possibly moving between different realities and interacting with the human world, the other-than-human inhabitants of these places adopt the same patterns of consumption that Indigenous people regard as a distinctive feature of humans living in large urban centers. These become places where goods or objects mediate relationships between people, further strengthening individualism and continually creating new needs (see Fabiano, this volume).

Despite the emphasis these imaginaries place on the industrialized and technological world of white people, there are cases in which the enchanted cities present diametrically opposed characteristics. Moreover, some features attributed to these places subvert the ethical or political norms of the ordinary non-Indigenous world, to the point of bringing to paroxysm, as Peluso argues in this volume, some of the emblematic characteristics of Indigenous rural life. By accentuating the expressions of solidarity and friendship that characterize community living, and by encouraging complicity, companionship, and proximity among their inhabitants, these enchanted cities take on the appearance of hyper–Indigenous villages: alternate realities to the non-Indigenous world that incorporate the benefits of a modern, urban lifestyle without substituting them for Indigenous forms of sociality. Thus, among the Jarawara, it is believed that the souls (*abono*) of plants, which have a human appearance, leave their bodies to be elevated (*nayana*) to the upper layer (*neme*) by other plant beings (see Maizza, this volume). The *neme*, both a hyper–Indigenous village and a hyper–white city, resembles a large, modern city, but with a much better standard of living. In effect, in the villages of the upper layer everyone is young, there are no diseases, hunters are stronger, plants are larger and more beautiful, and rivers teem with fish. Food is plentiful, and no one ever goes hungry. Moreover, the inhabitants of the *neme* can obtain anything they desire: there are plenty of goods and they are easy to buy; no one must pay exorbitant prices or carry their weight. The inhabitants of the *neme* spend a lot of time together, celebrating feasts. In addition, there are many people, but everything is clean and there is no garbage. In other words, the *neme* is a Jarawara reading of non-Indigenous cities, a reading of how these cities could be good if they were conceived through the Indigenous imagination.

Cities as Places of Hierarchy and Coercion

Indigenous Amazonian depictions of urbanized other-than-human worlds tend to share a hierarchical and oppressive nature that likens them to contemporary non-Indigenous cities. According to Indigenous understandings, by reaffirming the subject position of white or mestizo people, the city— with its spatial logic, the behavior of its inhabitants, and the institutions it houses—reinforces the subaltern place assigned to Indigenous peoples. For the Urarina, the notion of the urban is strongly linked to the dynamics of assimilation to the non-Indigenous world (see Fabiano, this volume). This is also a clear indication of how the city embodies the authoritarianism and coercion that the Urarina recognize as structural components of their past relations with non-Indigenous *patrones* or bosses.

As some contributors suggest, from an Indigenous point of view, the institutions that govern both human and other-than-human cities are entities that seem to obey their own laws and rules, the result of a social force of separation and disjunction that is radically opposed to the connectedness and attachment that guarantee Indigenous Amazonian social well-being (see Buitron, this volume). Sometimes they appear as agencies or bureaucracies that act arbitrarily and brutally or specialize in the use of violence as a coercive strategy. For the Southern Arawak, cities are the loci of despotic and abusive power, expressed in their prisons, military bases, and police barracks (see Santos-Granero, this volume). Likewise, for Shuar people, the city is a place of domination and anonymity, of disaffection and deprivation, since it embodies a sociopolitical order contrary to Indigenous life. An inescapable reference to the dominant character of these places is military power, which Indigenous people unfailingly associate with the coercive power of city dwellers (see Buitron, this volume). The Urarina, for instance, assert that as soon as human spirits are brought as captives to the arboreal megalopolises of the tree spirits, they experience a drastic reduction of their subjectivity (see Fabiano, this volume). Human spirits are enslaved, organized in a military fashion according to a hierarchical and oppressive order that finally imprisons them within a binary logic in which beings are either producers or consumers of goods.

If there is a clear analogy between the authoritarian institutions that govern both human cities and other-than-human urbanized worlds, the same is true of their inhabitants. For native Amazonians, city dwellers often exercise power over all those who pass through or spend time in their urban centers. According to the Southern Arawak, they are greedy people always in search of material gain (see Santos-Granero, this volume). They try to impose their domination through lies and deceit, and do not hesitate to send their soldiers, police, and engineers to invade, measure, and colonize Indigenous lands. Worse, non-Indigenous people seek to deprive Indigenous people of their vitality. Although city rulers may make great displays of generosity to their allies and friends, they may just as easily turn against them. This is also the case of other-than-human cities, in which depersonalized individuals often face an authority that cannot be opposed. Power in these cases is always visible in its effects—the hierarchical imposition of a certain order and the punishment of those who transgress it—often taking the form of a monstrous and predatory entity (see Buitron, this volume), an authoritarian sovereign (see Santos-Granero, this volume), or a "spirit president" (see Fabiano, this volume).

Urban Centers as Sources of Power

Cities are not only regarded as seats of coercive authority, but also conceived of as important sources of power. Regardless of how these various urban worlds are described, a recurring feature in Indigenous narratives regarding these sites is the way that humans strive to appropriate their power or that of their inhabitants. Indigenous leaders often gain power through their visits to cities and their encounters with high state authorities (see Santos-Granero, this volume), or they acquire new technical skills, access to jobs, or influential positions (see Virtanen, this volume). Likewise, a long stay in the city allows them to develop better skills in the national language or to complete a period of formal education, thus acquiring useful abilities that allow them to return to their villages of origin and play important roles in the local education and health sectors (see Erikson, this volume).

These are not, however, the only examples of how cities are viewed as sources of power. Discourses on contemporary and enchanted cities are nourished by the same logic of negotiation with the Other and subsequent incorporation of the Other's power, the purpose of which is to secure access to sources of vital force, acquire knowledge, fabricate socially adept people, and sustain life (Overing 1983–84). As Aparecida Vilaça (2007, 186) notes, it could be argued that traveling to "white people's cities" and experiencing their food, bodies, and worldviews is like a shamanic journey. Baniwa shamans claim that among the cities found in the celestial and subterranean layers of the cosmos there are two that are the sources of antidotes to the negative powers originating from both witchcraft and colonial cities (see Wright, this volume). Similarly, Manxineru and Apurinã people often associate shamanic journeys to obtain power from various other-than-human agents with their ongoing efforts to understand and control the political institutions and sources of knowledge of contemporary white-mestizo cities (see Virtanen, this volume). Analogous to shamanic initiation, visiting— even if for a limited time—or simply getting to know the urban world can provide the necessary experience to master relationships with the Other, such as representatives of state institutions and various non-Indigenous actors. It is evident, then, that in addition to positing a critical understanding of the contemporary urban world—the world of white-mestizo people and non-Indigenous institutions—Indigenous urban imaginaries contribute to experiencing those worlds in advance, enabling, in the future, the acquisition of new powers, skills, and knowledge.

Besides providing critical insight into a wide range of Amazonian practices, this notion, central to Indigenous thought and profusely documented in anthropological literature (Viveiros de Castro 2002; Barcelos Neto 2008; Cesarino 2008b; Lima 2005; Vilaça 1992; Gow 1991, among others), is in line with Indigenous peoples' openness to the Other and their deep interest in foreign goods and ideas. This would explain not only their interest in modern and technologically advanced cities, but also the relevance attributed to knowledge emanating from the urban world, be it human or other-than-human. Through the adoption of foreign ways of dressing, adorning, and treating or caring for the body, but also forms of building houses and organizing villages, Amazonian Indigenous people seek to adopt the perspective of their more powerful social Other in the hope that, by becoming like the Other—even if only partially and temporarily—they will be better able to understand them, establish peaceful social relations with them, or obtain powers and knowledge to control them (see Santos-Granero 2009; Gow 2007; Vilaça 2006, 2007; Erikson 2009). Thus, in perspectivist terms, one could argue that large urban centers represent the locus of knowledge of the non-Indigenous world (Nunes 2010a, 24).

This does not mean, however, that the strong attraction exerted by cities leads inevitably to abandoning Indigenous identities and ways of life. It simply means that Indigenous people are willing to continue to experience difference as a survival strategy. This attitude is particularly evident in Shuar communities, among which the seemingly paradoxical act of "urbanizing the forest" is a way of capturing the power of cities and Ecuadorian mestizos (*apach*) to improve their living conditions (see Buitron, this volume). In attempting to establish symbolic equality with the *apach*, Shuar seek not to look like them or to be equal to them, but rather to control their sources of power so as to be able to compete with them on a equal footing (see also Vilaça 2006, 514). If human cities allow access to different perspectives—the perspectives of white and mestizo people—then the exploration of other-than-human cities is the most intense form of experiencing the Other, a privileged point from which to acquire, experiment with, and attempt to control the Other's knowledge.

The Transformative Dimension of Urban Lifeways

Contact with human and other-than-human urbanized worlds is always transformative in its effects. This is manifested in the way cities affect the bodies of those who inhabit or visit them. Such transformations depend on the degree of exposure to the Other and its knowledge, and thus on the risks involved in the various forms of acquisition and (attempted) control of such knowledge. In this sense, the urbanity of human beings can be as dangerous as the urbanity of the spirit world, since in both cases the visitor is exposed to their transformative powers. Like sociality, commensality, and consubstantiality, sharing cities is also a way of becoming, maintaining, or transforming people and kin (see Peluso, this volume). As Wright contends in this volume, all cities are places of transformation, but unlike shamanic cities, in which shamans transform into spiritual Others to harness the powers of the spirit world, historical and contemporary cities are places of alterity in which there is always the risk of undergoing irreversible transformations. While cities offer new skills and sources of knowledge that can be turned into new forms of power, the acquisition of these skills is not a process without consequences, insofar as it imposes changes that require considerable effort.

Thus, whereas cities can be important sources of power, their transformative nature can also turn them into places of danger and disempowerment. As we have seen, staying in a human city is similar to experiencing urbanized extraordinary realities. In both cases, the urban experience affects the lives of those who inhabit or pass through the place, often resulting in a process of metamorphosis or bodily transformation and, in some cases, illness. Urarina shamans' descriptions of the densely urbanized places that exist within trees emphasize their noxiousness and relation to illness and death (see Fabiano, this volume). There is also a certain analogy between these arboreal metropolises and the urban spaces experienced in ordinary contexts. Such similarities suggest the existence of a strong contrast between the practices and behaviors that ensure a healthy and productive life, which the Urarina associate with the safe and familiar space of the community, and those of the city, regarded as a space of illness and death.

In some cases, cities are considered to be the very origin of the afflictions that affect humanity. In Baniwa shamanic discourse it is claimed that everything that exists in the city, including industrial goods, has been produced by the factories of the white people's world, which supply the urban centers where Indigenous people also live (see Wright, this volume). According to Baniwa cosmogonic narratives, in these factories, located on the periphery of the white world, the first Amaru woman settled and became the "Mother of White People." She is a powerful sorceress who sends the smoke and fumes from white people's factories to the land of the Baniwa. These fumes cause illness and fever, "white people's diseases" usually associated with respiratory sickness.

Unlike shamanic transformations, which are commonly associated with strange and spectacular contexts, such as rituals or healing activities, city-induced transformations do not necessarily occur in a spectacular way (Nunes 2013, 44). Oral accounts of these experiences emphasize the feelings of debilitation in the city and the gradual return to a state of well-being upon moving back to the village. For Shuar people, the suffering experienced while living in urban settings is manifested in a weakening of their bodies because it negates the personalized and contentious ways in which they typically understand and deal with conflict (see Buitron, this volume). In the city, Shuar individuals experience a form of vulnerability derived from impersonal and threatening situations, a debilitating deprivation of vital force usually associated with a state of illness. This is also the case with Apurinã and Manxineru leaders and spokespeople, who, after spending long periods in urban areas, affirm that the experience dangerously weakened their bodies (see Virtanen, this volume).

Indigenizing the City, Urbanizing the Forest

Despite the potential risks, experiencing the city confers value and prestige insofar as, for many, urbanity represents an ideal of progress and development worth aspiring to. In this sense, the search for real or symbolic proximity to the city not only feeds the aspirations and expectations of obtaining the benefits associated with modernity, but often leads to the adoption of an urban style of life. For Indigenous Amazonians, moving to the city, idealized as a place of success and prosperity, becomes a means to overcome the limitations of life in their communities of origin and obtain new and valuable resources (in this volume, see Santos-Granero; Fabiano; Wright; Erikson).

The increased Indigenous presence in Amazonian cities, their growing participation in urban activities, and the accelerated processes of urbanization of rural realities have had important implications for Indigenous Amazonian populations. Frequent contacts with the city have contributed to redefining how Indigenous people think, act, speak, work, construct their homes, and give meaning to daily life, and have transformed their dreams and aspirations (Pereira and Torres 2008, 26). This has led some to assert that when living in cities, Amazonian Indigenous people cease to be Indigenous, a false perception that, however, remains deeply rooted in popular conceptions. Such a perception derives from an essentializing and reductive vision of contemporary Indigenous Amazonian societies, conventionally thought of as traditional, rural, and generally antithetical to urban realities.

A closer look at the lives of urban native Amazonians provides a different reading. Indigenous urbanization in Amazonia depends on a set of multidirectional processes that are often highly contingent and situational. As we have seen, it does not always entail a permanent move to the city; rather, urbanization is a circulatory dynamic that continuously connects cities with different communities and villages, giving rise to multisite dwellings (see Peluso, this volume). Likewise, even when the urban experience seems to foster homogenization and acculturation, the daily lives of Indigenous families residing permanently or temporarily in cities demonstrate their exceptional capacity for adaptation, resignification, negotiation, and cultural reworking (see, e.g., Nunes 2010b; Trivi 2010; Horta 2017; Melo 2013).

This creative force, which enables the cultural reproduction of Indigenous Amazonian societies—and, sometimes, the replication of traditional social relations in the city—is associated, according to Virtanen in this volume, with a conscious effort to domesticate urban spaces. This attitude is also a clear example of defiance of the white-mestizo world, as it is an expression of Indigenous people's refusal to submit to the norms of city life. By maintaining their own social and cultural practices, Indigenous urban dwellers not only promote the creation of more complex and pluricultural urban spaces, but also redefine the social practices and identification processes of local groups, producing specific places for different types of coexistence, diversifying them, and creating new territories. This gives rise to a dialectical process between the local and the global, the village and the city, in which Indigenous populations diversify globalizing flows according to their own cultural schemes (Sahlins 1999), and thanks to which, instead of adapting their bodies and practices to the urban space, they have turned urban areas into familiar places.

There are other forms in which Indigenous Amazonians defy the urban white-mestizo world. Among Shuar people, attempts to "urbanize the forest" are also acts of rebellion, insofar as they are a refusal to submit to the hierarchies and impositions of city life, without losing the possibility of enjoying its advantages (see Buitron, this volume). Despite having a negative image of cities, Shuar people do not dislike urbanity in general. On the contrary, urban life exerts a strong attraction on them, so that they often extol the riches and technological wonders of cities, places where people have uninterrupted access to hospitals, electricity, running water, paved streets, and televisions—all the things that the *apach* can manufacture, thanks to their entrepreneurial skills. Shuar people desire to take advantage of these foreign capabilities and to enjoy the goods available in the city, so they seek new ways of connecting their forest communities with the life of the city. The Chacobo seem to share the same ideal; namely, to bring the comforts of city life to their own villages instead of migrating permanently to the city (see Erikson, this volume).

Such attempts at urbanizing the forest continue the subtle process of appropriating and incorporating urban powers and aim at turning villages into semiautonomous zones of refuge and well-being. This is, in many cases, an aspiration that translates into changes in the traditional architecture and materials used to construct dwellings, the construction of infrastructure for common use, or increased access to services, which are often offered to promote "inclusion" by regional and national institutions (see Fabiano, this volume). In this sense, what is produced is not really a continuum from oppressive white-mestizo cities to improved Indigenous forest cities, but a continuum from cities as sites of exploitation, disease, and deprivation to cities as sites of empowerment, well-being, and abundance (see Buitron, this volume).

Ambivalence Regarding City Life

It is clear from the above that native Amazonian peoples have ambivalent feelings about contemporary urban centers and their inhabitants. As we have seen, however, a large proportion of today's Indigenous population has ties to or resides in urban centers. Although in some cases this dynamic has favored the emergence of Indigenous urban communities, life in the city is difficult, often driving Indigenous people to hide their most visible forms of indigeneity to avoid discrimination by their neighbors or potential employers (Espinosa 2009). This form of marginalization is fueled by the national governments, which devote very few institutional initiatives and public policies to recognizing the existence of urban Indigenous communities, thus hindering access to their basic rights.

Despite the perceived advantages of an urban lifestyle, many Indigenous people believe that living in urban spaces has negative consequences, particularly in terms of personal health and the quality of social life (see Wright, this volume). Even though cities continue to be strong poles of attraction, the conviction persists that life in the city does not offer opportunities for a real improvement of living conditions or, at least, that the advantages it offers are inferior to those that could be derived from a more flexible link with their communities of origin (see Fabiano, this volume). From this point of view, the city acts as a social force of separation and disjunction that contradicts in every way the social connections and links that, from an Indigenous perspective, ensure human well-being (see Virtanen and Buitron, this volume). The violence, marginality, food scarcity, and pollution that native Amazonians experience in urban spaces engender feelings of fear, anxiety, and, ultimately, rejection. Fostering anonymity and disaffection, cities thus represent places of suffering, where the Indigenous sociopolitical order is inverted, and where despotic and abusive power prevails (see Santos-Granero, this volume).

Even in those cases where there is a long history of interaction with urban centers and this link is recognized as a condition for access to better living conditions, the city is seen, at most, as a necessary evil, something to be endured temporarily in the hope of a better future (see Erikson, this volume). This view of urban life challenges the notion that the city allows access to prosperity and better living conditions. Unlike village life, the city engenders new needs, such as money and the accumulation of goods, which not only alienate families from traditional productive practices but also lead to a loss of autonomy and the acceptance of a social hierarchy mediated by power over things.

The city is also the root of serious social problems among young people because adolescents no longer receive instruction in the "traditional" ways, and social norms associated with village life are difficult, if not impossible, to maintain in the new urban contexts. This results in less control by the older over the younger generation and, consequently, favors the emergence of intergenerational conflicts. Among the Baniwa, for instance, this has resulted in a higher incidence of disease and suicides among urban Indigenous adolescents, often associated with the appearance of a "being of darkness" responsible for haunting the young and driving them to end their lives (see Wright, this volume).

Final Remarks

Today, Amazonian Indigenous people find themselves at a juncture where they have adopted an urban lifestyle that often clashes with their traditional way of life. Faced with this situation, they have developed a variety of strategies to resolve this dilemma, such as the indigenization of cities or the urbanization of the forest, but also the construction and deployment of rich imaginaries in which countless urbanized worlds coexist. The powerful attraction that large cities have exerted on the imaginaries of Indigenous Amazonian peoples has transformed these places into models for the representation of extreme otherness under the appearance of extraordinary, alien worlds. As the contributors to this volume argue, these urban scenarios are characterized by a strong identification with the symbols of the highly urbanized and industrial national societies that native Amazonian peoples are part of. The experience of these other-than-human worlds is always multidimensional. It is susceptible to change and has a transformative character, both corporeal and incorporeal.

Given these characteristics, there can be no doubt that native Amazonian urban imaginaries arise from the direct or indirect experience of past and present Indigenous and non-Indigenous urban centers, thus incorporating the historical and contingent aspects of that experience. As mentioned above, with our present knowledge of Amazonian history, it is not too far-fetched to claim that many Indigenous peoples were cognizant of urban spaces and urban lifestyles way before the arrival of European conquerors in the region.

Amazonian cities, however, are not always visible to the human observer. Certain types of cities are part of the nonvisible spirit world, and they shape and are shaped by the Amazonian rural-urban imagery, the narratives of creation, and the sociospatial knowledge of terrestrial and transversal realities (see Peluso, this volume). Indigenous urbanized multiverses are composed of a series of dimensions or planes inhabited by beings living in large cities, a situation that contrasts with the Indigenous reality, which until quite recently was characterized by life in relatively small and dispersed settlements.

The cities depicted in these urban imaginaries subvert phenomenal reality, not only exacerbating the morphological and structural characteristics of contemporary, non-Indigenous urban spaces, their technological modernity, and their hierarchical and oppressive features, but also idealizing the beneficial and life-giving features of the Indigenous world and its rural lifestyle. In these urban imaginaries Amazonian Indigenous peoples see their own way of life as the ideal form of existence, while the Others (human or other-than-human) live an urban existence that is presented as antagonistic to their way of life.

Even when these cities appear opposed to the dystopian technological and oppressive cities built in the image of the white world, they do not always embody an Indigenous ideal of well-being. In other words, their qualities are not normative in character: they do not refer to an axiological dignity that must be sought in order to achieve some kind of perfection and, therefore, do not necessarily represent Indigenous utopias in the face of the decadence of everyday reality.

By interweaving symbolic, social, and ideological systems, the Indigenous notion of city not only describes a complex process through which representations and abstractions that reflect and translate the real are articulated, but also makes possible the construction of and experimentation with "subject-places" that are inscribed in a geography whose components are alive, mobile, and endowed with intentionality (Calavia Sáez 2004, 126). Since Indigenous Amazonian urban imaginaries are not a flat representation of an ordinary urban reality, it is clear that they are not simply the result of recent urbanization processes. While we can affirm that the historical experience of urban centers has nurtured Indigenous urban imaginaries, our findings allow us to question the simplistic idea that this derives exclusively from processes of acculturation brought about by proximity to the Western, white world. In other words, we reject the notion that native Amazonian urban imaginaries are mere narrative accessories resulting from an elaborate process of integration of foreign or distant elements into Indigenous discourse. Rather, the creativity and broad diffusion that characterize native Amazonian urban imaginaries suggest that they constitute a means of conveying Indigenous concerns about the nature of power, alterity, and domination, but also a means of expressing Indigenous endurance and defiance.

Thus, the memory of events that have had a profound impact on Indigenous peoples survives and is constantly re-actualized in a complex urban multiverse that, through contact with its inhabitants and the appropriation of their knowledge and objects, produces tangible effects on the ordinary human world. The appropriation of non-Indigenous societal structures, institutions, norms, and knowledge of the world, on the one hand, and the strategies of resistance and defiance developed in the face of the subordination imposed by urban life, on the other, have produced social transformations that go far beyond a simple reaction to the traumatic impact of urban modernity. In this sense, besides being instruments of political subjectivity and manifestations of a collective ethical maturity, Indigenous urban imaginaries also provide a space for social action and a variety of strategies to confront the processes of domination and exploitation that Indigenous Amazonian peoples face nowadays.

In short, from the authors' contributions we can conclude that although urban imaginaries are a historical construction, they are hardly a simple epiphenomenon of the long history of contacts with the non-Indigenous world. In addition to representing an attempt to reflect on their own history, these urbanized other-than-human worlds create realities to be interpreted, known, and/or manipulated. At the same time, like modern cities, these places allow Indigenous Amazonians to experience the ways of life of white and mestizo people, temporarily adopting their points of view. This urban perspectivism is associated with a mimetic process that acts both as a relational strategy and a means through which Indigenous people strive to appropriate the power of white people and their cities. This process invariably implies a transformation—often transitory and reversible—but one that does not necessarily lead to the loss of their Indigenous identity. Undoubtedly, by embodying a reality that has practical consequences for the lives of the human beings who inhabit or visit them, urbanized other-than-human worlds do not constitute a fiction or a false perception. In this sense, even when urban imaginaries appear to be an attempt to construct alternate realities derived from a radical process of social inversion that denies the existing social order or exacerbates the negative aspects of urban life, they do not constitute a mere abstract exercise. The experience of enchanted cities induces different ways of acting and thinking, and its influence goes far beyond the borders of the urbanized other-than-human worlds, often affecting people's life strategies, courses of action, and decisions.

References

Alexiades, Miguel N., and Daniela Peluso. 2015. "Introduction: Indigenous Urbanization in Lowland South America." In Peluso 2015b, 1–12.

Andrello, Geraldo. 2006. *Cidade do índio: transformações e cotidiano em Iauaretê*. São Paulo: Editora da Universidade Estadual Paulista.

Aragón, Luis E. 2011. "Introduction to the Study of International Migration in the Amazon." *Contexto Internacional* 33:71–102.

Arcila, Oscar H. 2011. *La amazonía colombiana urbanizada: un análisis de sus asentamientos urbanos*. Bogotá: Instituto Amazónico de Investigaciones Científicas-Sinchi.

Barcelos Neto, Aristóteles. 2008. *Apapaatai: rituais de máscaras no Alto Xingu*. São Paulo: Editora da Universidade de São Paulo.

Becker, Bertha K. 1985. "Fronteira e urbanização repensadas." *Revista Brasileira de Geografia* 47 (3–4): 357–71.

Becker, Bertha K. 2013. *A urbe amazônida: a floresta e a cidade*. Rio de Janeiro: Editora Garamond.

Bessire, Lucas. 2014. "The Rise of Indigenous Hypermarginality: Native Culture as a Neoliberal Politics of Life." *Current Anthropology* 55 (3): 276–95.

Brabec de Mori, Bernd. 2005. "The Most Powerful Shaman: About Creation and Transformation of Mythology in Native Societies on the Ucayali River (Peruvian Amazon)." Paper presented at the international interdisciplinary conference Globalisation and Representation, Brighton, United Kingdom, March 12, 2005.

Brenner, Neil, and Christina Schmid. 2015. "Towards a New Epistemology of the Urban." *CITY* 19 (2–3): 151–82.

Browder, John O., and Brian J. Godfrey. 1997. *Rainforest Cities: Urbanization, Development, and Globalization of the Brazilian Amazon*. New York: Columbia University Press.

Brown, Michael F. 1986. *Tsewa's Gift: Magic and Meaning in an Amazonian Society*. Tuscaloosa: University of Alabama Press.

Calavia Sáez, Óscar. 2004. "Mapas carnales: el territorio y la sociedad yaminawa." In *Tierra adentro: territorio indígena y percepción del entorno*, edited by Alexandre Surrallés and Pedro G. Hierro, 121–36. Copenhagen: International Work Group for Indigenous Affairs.

Calavia Sáez, Oscar. 2007. "Viajeros, extraños, extraviados: los Yaminawa y sus muertos." In *Etnografías de la muerte y las culturas en América Latina*, edited by Juan Antonio Flores Martos and Luisa Abad González, 165–81. Cuenca, Spain: Universidad de Castilla–La Mancha.

Cesarino, Pedro de Niemeyer. 2008a. "¿Babel da floresta, cidade dos brancos? Os Marubo no trânsito entre dois mundos." *Novos Estudos* 82:133–48.

Cesarino, Pedro de Niemeyer. 2008b. "Oniska: a poética da morte e do mundo entre os Marubo da Amazônia occidental." PhD diss., Universidade Federal do Rio de Janeiro.

Charity, Sandra, Neil Dudley, Denise Oliveira, and Sue Stolton, eds. 2016. *Living Amazon Report 2016: A Regional Approach to Conservation in the Amazon*. Brasília: World Wildlife Foundation Living Amazon Initiative.

Chaumeil, Jean-Pierre. 2002. "Ciudades encantadas y mapas submarinos: redes transnacionales y chamanismo de frontera en el Trapecio amazónico." In *Lo transnacional: instrumento y desafío para los pueblos indígenas*, edited by Françoise Morin and Roberto Santana, 25–49. Quito: Ediciones Abya-Yala.

Chaves, Willandia A., Denis Valle, Aline S. Tavares, Thais Q. Morcatty, and David S. Wilcove. 2021. "Impacts of Rural to Urban Migration, Urbanization, and Generational Change on Consumption of Wild Animals in the Amazon." *Conservation Biology* 35 (4): 1186–97.

Chernela, Janet M. 2015. "Directions of Existence: Indigenous Women Domestics in the Paris of the Tropics." *Journal of Latin American and Caribbean Anthropology* 20 (1): 201–29.

Childe, V. Gordon. 1950. "The Urban Revolution." *Town Planning Review* 21 (1): 3–17.

Chirif, Alberto, and Pedro García Hierro. 2007. *Marcando territorio: progresos y limitaciones de la titulación de territorios indígenas en la amazonía.* Copenhagen: International Work Group for Indigenous Affairs.

Conklin, Beth A. 2002. "Shamans Versus Pirates in the Amazon Treasure Chest." *American Anthropologist* 104 (4): 1050–61.

Coutinho, Tiago. 2016. "Forest Shamanism in the City: The Kaxinawá Example." *Sociologia and Antropologia* 6 (1): 159–79.

Da Silva, Vera M. F., Glenn Shepard, and Nívia A. S. do Carmo. 2017. "Os mamíferos aquáticos: lendas, usos e interações com as populações humanas na Amazônia brasileira." In *Olhares cruzados sobre as relações entre seres humanos y animais na Amazônia (Brasil, Guiana francesa)*, edited by Guillaume Marchand and Felipe Vander Velden, 115–37. Manaus: Editora da Universidade Federal do Amazonas.

Davis, Diana K. and Edmund Burke III, eds. 2011. *Environmental Imaginaries of the Middle East and North Africa.* Athens: Ohio University Press.

Davis, Jason, Samuel Sellers, Clark Gray, and Richard Bilsborrow. 2017. "Indigenous Migration Dynamics in the Ecuadorian Amazon: A Longitudinal and Hierarchical Analysis." *Journal of Development Studies* 53 (11): 1849–64.

Eaton, Weston M., Stephen P. Gasteyer, and Lawrence Busch. 2014. "Bioenergy Futures: Framing Sociotechnical Imaginaries in Local Places." *Rural Sociology* 79 (2): 227–56.

Eloy, Ludivine, Eduardo S. Brondizio, and Rogerio do Pateo. 2015. "New Perspectives on Mobility, Urbanisation and Resource Management in Riverine Amazonia." *Bulletin of Latin American Research* 34 (1): 3–18.

Emlen, Nicholas Q. 2020. *Language, Coffee, and Migration on an Andean-Amazonian Frontier.* Tucson: University of Arizona Press.

Erikson, Philippe. 2009. Comments to "Hybrid Bodyscapes: A Visual History of Yanesha Patterns of Cultural Change," by Fernando Santos-Granero. *Current Anthropology* 50 (4): 497.

Espinosa, Oscar. 2009. "Ciudad e identidad cultural: ¿cómo se relacionan con lo urbano los indígenas amazónicos peruanos en el siglo XXI?" *Bulletin de l'Institute Français d'Études Andines* 38 (1): 47–59.

Fausto, Carlos, and Michael Heckenberger, eds. 2007. *Time and Memory in Indigenous Amazonia: Anthropological Perspectives.* Gainesville: University Press of Florida.

Feather, Conrad. 2010. "Elastic Selves and Fluid Cosmologies: Nahua Resilience in a Changing World." PhD diss., University of St. Andrews.

Feldman, Nancy Gardner. 2018. "Shipibo-Conibo Textiles 2010–2018: Artists of the Amazon Culturally Engaged." *Textile Society of America Symposium Proceedings*

2018, Vancouver, September 19–23, 2018. https://doi.org/10.32873/unl.dc.tsasp .0029.

Forte, Maximilian Christian. 2010. "Introduction: Indigeneities and Cosmopolitanism." In *Indigenous Cosmopolitans: Transnational and Transcultural Indigeneity in the Twenty-First Century*, edited by Maximilian Christian Forte, 1–16. New York: Peter Lang.

Fortun, Kim, and Mike Fortun. 2005. "Scientific Imaginaries and Ethical Plateaus in Contemporary U.S. Toxicology." *American Anthropologist* 107 (1): 43–54.

Gaonkar, Dilip Parameshwar. 2002. "Toward New Imaginaries: An Introduction." *Public Culture* 14 (1): 1–19.

González, Jesús Manuel. 1997. "Indian City: To Be Urban and Indian in Venezuela; Assimilation or Cultural Reaffirmation?" *Abya Yala News* 10 (3): 20–21.

Gow, Peter. 1991. *Of Mixed Blood: Kinship and History in Peruvian Amazonia*. Oxford: Clarendon Press.

Gow, Peter. 2007. "La ropa como aculturación en la amazonía peruana." *Amazonía Peruana* 15 (30): 283–304.

Gow, Peter. 2011. "Rethinking Cities in Peruvian Amazonia: History, Archaeology, and Myth." In *The Archaeological Encounter: Anthropological Perspectives*, edited by Paolo Fortis and Istvan Praet, 174–203. St. Andrews: Centre for Amerindian, Latin American and Caribbean Studies.

Hansen, Thomas Blom, and Oskar Verkaaik. 2009. "Introduction: Urban Charisma; On Everyday Mythologies in the City." *Critique of Anthropology* 29 (1): 5–26.

Heckenberger, Michael J. 2003. "The Enigma of the Great Cities: Body and State in Amazonia." *Tipití: Journal of the Society for the Anthropology of Lowland South America* 1 (1): 27–58.

Heckenberger, Michael J. 2005. *The Ecology of Power: Culture, Place, and Personhood in the Southern Amazon, AD 1000–2000*. New York: Routledge.

Heckenberger, Michael J., Christian Russell, Carlos Fausto, Joshua Toney, Morgan Schmidt, Edithe Pereira, Bruna Franchetto, and Afukaka Kuikuro. 2008. "Pre-Columbian Urbanism, Anthropogenic Landscapes, and the Future of the Amazon." *Science* 321 (5893): 1214–17.

Hill, Jonathan D. 2009. *Made-from-Bone: Trickster Myths, Music, and History from the Amazon*. Urbana: University of Illinois Press.

Homan, Joshua. 2018. "Inga Rimakkuna: Indigenous Frontiers in the Pastaza Basin, Peru." PhD diss., University of Kansas.

Horta, Amanda. 2017. "Indígenas em Canarana: notas citadinas sobre a criatividade parque-xinguana." *Revista de Antropologia* 60 (1): 216–41.

Hugh-Jones, Stephen. 2018. "Su riqueza es nuestra riqueza: perspectivas interculturales de objetos o gaheuni." In *Objetos como testigos del contacto cultural: perspectivas interculturales de la historia y del presente de las poblaciones indígenas del Alto Río Negro (Brasil/Colombia)*, edited by Michael Kraus, Ernst Halbmayer, and Ingrid Kummels, 197–226. Berlin: Ibero-American Institute.

Huyssen, Andreas. 2008. "Introduction: World Cultures, World Cities." In *Other Cities, Other Worlds: Urban Imaginaries in a Globalizing Age*, edited by Andreas Huyssen, 1–25. Durham, N.C.: Duke University Press.

INEI (Instituto Nacional de Estadística e Informática). 2018. *Perú: perfil sociodemográfico, 2017*. Chap. 1, "Características de la Población." https://www.inei.gob .pe/media/MenuRecursivo/publicaciones_digitales/Est/Lib1539/.

Jaramillo, Roberto. 2003. "Indiens urbains: processus de reconformation de l'identité ethnique indienne à Manaus." PhD diss., École des Hautes Études en Sciences Sociales.

Jasanoff, Sheila, and Sang-Hyun Kim. 2013. "Sociotechnical Imaginaries and National Energy Policies." *Science and Culture* 22 (2): 189–96.

Kohn, Eduardo. 2007. "Animal Masters and the Ecological Embedding of History Among the Ávila Runa of Ecuador." In Fausto and Heckenberger 2007, 106–29.

Lagrou, Els. 1998. "Cashinahua Cosmovision: A Perspectival Approach to Identity and Alterity." PhD diss., University of St. Andrews.

Lagrou, Els. 2013. "Chaquira, el inka y los blancos: las cuentas de vidrio en los mitos y en el ritual kaxinawa y amerindio." *Revista Española de Antropología Americana* 43 (1): 245–65.

Lasmar, Cristiane. 2005. *De volta ao Lago de Leite: gênero e transformação no Alto Rio Negro*. São Paulo: Editora da Universidade Estadual Paulista.

Lasmar, Cristiane. 2008. "Irmã de índio, mulher de branco: perspectivas femininas no alto rio Negro." *Mana* 14 (2): 429–54.

Lewis, Charlton T., and Charles Short. 1879. *A Latin Dictionary*. Oxford: Clarendon Press.

Lima, Tânia Stolze. 2005. *Um peixe olhou para mim: o povo Yudjá e a perspectiva*. São Paulo: Editora da Universidade Estadual Paulista.

Lindner, Rolf. 2016. "The Imaginary of the City." In *Sensing the City: A Companion to Urban Anthropology*, edited by Anja Schwanhäußer, 114–20. Berlin: Birkhäuser.

Maybury-Lewis, David. 1974. *Akwẽ-Shavante Society*. New York: Oxford University Press.

Mayor Aparicio, Pedro, and Richard E. Bodmer. 2009. *Pueblos indígenas de la amazonía peruana*. Iquitos, Peru: Centro de Estudios Teológicos de la Amazonía.

McGregor, Andrew. 2004. "Sustainable Development and 'Warm Fuzzy Feelings': Discourse and Nature Within Australian Environmental Imaginaries." *Geoforum* 35 (5): 593–606.

McSweeney, Kendra, and Brad Jokisch. 2007. "Beyond Rainforests: Urbanisation and Emigration Among Lowland Indigenous Societies in Latin America." *Bulletin of Latin American Research* 26 (2): 159–80.

McSweeney, Kendra, and Brad Jokisch. 2015. "Native Amazonians' Strategic Urbanization: Shaping Territorial Possibilities Through Cities." In Peluso 2015b, 13–33.

Melo, Juliana G. 2013. "Dimensões do urbano: o que as narrativas indígenas revelam sobre a cidade? Considerações dos Baré sobre Manaus, AM." *Teoria e Cultura* 8 (1): 115–26.

Millington, Nate. 2012. "Post-Industrial Imaginaries: Nature, Representation, and Ruin in Detroit, Michigan." *International Journal of Urban and Regional Research* 37 (1): 279–96.

Morin, Françoise. 2015. "Résilience et flexibilité du chamanisme Shipibo-Konibo (Pérou)." *Anthropologica* 57 (2): 353–66.

Murphy, Robert E. 1958. *Mundurucu Religion*. Berkeley: University of California Press.

Narby, Jeremy. 1989. "Visions of Land: The Ashaninca and Resource Development in the Pichis Valley in the Peruvian Central Jungle." PhD diss., Stanford University.

Nesbitt, J. Todd, and Daniel Weiner. 2001. "Conflicting Environmental Imaginaries and the Politics of Nature in Central Appalachia." *Geoforum* 32 (3): 333–49.

Novaes, Sylvia Caiuby. 1997. *The Play of Mirrors: The Representation of Self Mirrored in the Other*. Austin: University of Texas Press.

Nunes, Eduardo Soares. 2010a. "Aldeias urbanas ou cidades indígenas? Reflexões sobre índios e cidades." *Espaço Ameríndio* 4 (1): 9–30.

Nunes, Eduardo Soares. 2010b. "'O pessoal da cidade': o conhecimento do mundo dos brancos como experiência corporal entre os Karajá de Buridina." In *Conhecimento e cultura: práticas de transformação no mundo indígena*, edited by Marcela Coelho de Souza and Edilene Coffaci de Lima, 205–28. Brasília: Athalaia Gráfica e Editora.

Nunes, Eduardo Soares. 2013. "O território das onças e a aldeia dos brancos: lugar e perspectiva entre os Karajá de Buridina (Brasil Central)." *Journal de la Société des Américanistes* 99 (2): 35–64.

Ødegaard, Cecilie Vindal. 2010. *Mobility, Markets, and Indigenous Socialities*. London: Routledge.

Overing, Joanna. 1983–84. "Elementary Structures of Reciprocity: A Comparative Note on Guianese, Central Brazilian, and North-West Amazon Socio-Political Thought." *Antropológica* 59–62:331–48.

Padoch, Christine, Eduardo Brondizio, Sandra Costa, Miguel Pinedo-Vasquez, Robin Sears, and Andrea Siqueira. 2008. "Urban Forest and Rural Cities: Multi-Sited Households, Consumption Patterns, and Forest Resources in Amazonia." *Ecology and Society* 13 (2). https://ecologyandsociety.org/vol13/iss2/.

Peluso, Daniela. 2015a. "Circulating between Rural and Urban Communities: Multisited Dwellings in Amazonian Frontiers." In Peluso 2015b, 57–79.

Peluso, Daniela, ed. 2015b. "Indigenous Urbanization: The Circulation of Peoples Between Rural and Urban Amazonian Spaces." Special issue, *Journal of Latin American and Caribbean Anthropology* 20 (1).

Peluso, Daniela, and Miguel N. Alexiades. 2005. "Indigenous Urbanization and Amazonia's Post-Traditional Environmental Economy." *Traditional Dwellings and Settlements Review* 16 (2): 7–16.

Peña Márquez, Juan Carlos. 2011. *Mitú: ciudad amazónica, territorialidad indígena*. Leticia: Universidad Nacional de Colombia.

Pereira, Hamida, and Iraildes Caldas Torres. 2008. "A imagem da cidade: cotidiano, sonhos e utopias dos moradores do Cacau Pirêra-Iranduba (AM)." *Somanlu: Revista de Estudos Amazônicos* 8 (1): 25–42.

Perreault, Tom, and Gabriela Valdivia. 2010. "Hydrocarbons, Popular Protest, and National Imaginaries: Ecuador and Bolivia in Comparative Context." *Geoforum* 41 (5): 689–99.

Perruchon, Marie. 2002. "Magia en camino: chamanismo entre los Shuar de la Amazonía del Oeste." *Anales* 5:143–64.

Pitarch, Pedro. 2012. "La ciudad de los espíritus europeos: notas sobre la modernidad de los mundos virtuales indígenas." In *Modernidades indígenas*, edited by Pedro Pitarch and Gemma Orobitg, 61–87. Madrid: Iberoamericana.

Prakash, Gyan, and Kevin M. Kruse, eds. 2008. *The Spaces of the Modern City: Imaginaries, Politics, and Everyday Life*. Princeton, N.J.: Princeton University Press.

Reinhardt, Dagmar. 2012. "Shifts in Code: Performative Geometries in Alice's Wonderland." In *Youtopia, a Passion for the Dark: Architecture at the Intersection Between Digital Process and Theatrical Performance*, edited by Dagmar Reinhardt, 65–90. Melbourne: Freerange Press.

Ritchie, Hannah, and Max Roser. 2019. "Urbanization." *Our World in Data*. Revised November 2019. https://ourworldindata.org/urbanization.

Sahlins, Marshal. 1999. "What Is Anthropological Enlightenment? Some Lessons of the Twentieth Century." *Annual Review of Anthropology* 28 (1): i–xxiii.

Salazar, Noel B. 2011. "Tourism Imaginaries: A Conceptual Approach." *Annals of Tourism Research* 39 (2): 863–82.

Sánchez, Luisa Fernanda. 2010. "Paisanos en Bogotá: identidad étnica y migración indígena amazónica." In *Perspectivas antropológicas sobre la amazonía contemporánea*, edited by Margarita Chaves y Carlos del Cairo, 129–52. Bogotá: Instituto Colombiano de Antropología e Historia.

Santos, Ricardo, Bruno Nogueira Guimaraes, Alessandra Traldi Simoni, Leandro Okamoto da Silva, Marta de Oliveira Antunes, Fernando de Souza Damasco, Rosa Sebastiana Colman, and Marta Maria do Amaral Azevedo. 2019. "The Identification of the Indigenous Population in Brazil's Official Statistics, with an Emphasis on Demographic Censuses." *Statistical Journal of the International Association for Official Statistics* 35 (1): 29–46.

Santos-Granero, Fernando. 2007. Prólogo to Chirif and García Hierro 2007, 12–17.

Santos-Granero, Fernando. 2009. "Hybrid Bodyscapes: A Visual History of Yanesha Patterns of Cultural Change." *Current Anthropology* 50 (4): 477–512.

Saunaluoma, Sanna, Martti Pärssinen, and Denise Schaan. 2018. "Diversity of Pre-Colonial Earthworks in the Brazilian State of Acre, Southwestern Amazonia." *Journal of Field Archaeology* 43 (5): 362–79.

Schaan, Denise. 2012. *Sacred Geographies of Ancient Amazonia: Historical Ecology of Social Complexity*. Walnut Creek, Calif.: Left Coast Press.

Smith, Michael E. 2009. "V. Gordon Childe and the Urban Revolution: A Historical Perspective on a Revolution in Urban Studies." *Town Planning Review* 80 (1): 3–29.

Smith, Michael E. 2020. "Definitions and Comparisons in Urban Archaeology." *Journal of Urban Archaeology* 1:15–30.

Taylor, Charles. 2002. "Modern Social Imaginaries." *Public Culture* 14 (1): 91–124.

Taylor, Charles. 2004. *Modern Social Imaginaries.* Durham, N.C.: Duke University Press.

Taylor, Peter. 2012. "Extraordinary Cities: Early 'City-ness' and the Origins of Agriculture and States." *International Journal of Urban and Regional Research* 36 (3): 415–47.

Tena Morillo, Lucía. 2019. "Sobre la *mise en abyme* y su relación con la écfrasis y la intertextualidad: aproximación a una tipología." *Actio Nova: Revista de Teoría de la Literatura y Literatura Comparada* 3:481–505.

Tongson, Karen. 2011. *Relocations: Queer Suburban Imaginaries.* New York: New York University Press.

Tritsch, Isabelle, Cyril Marmoex, Damien Davy, Bernard Thibaut, and Valery Gond. 2015. "Towards a Revival of Indigenous Mobility in French Guiana? Contemporary Transformations of the Wayãpi and Teko Territories." *Bulletin of Latin American Research* 34 (1): 19–34.

Trivi, Nicolás A. 2010. "Territorialidad mbyá-guaraní en el espacio urbano en la comunidad de Lomba do Pinheiro, Porto Alegre: una experiencia de investigación en la Tekoá Anhetenguá." *Geograficando* 6 (6): 119–45.

U.S. Bureau of the Census. 2021. "Urban Areas for the 2020 Census: Proposed Criteria." *Federal Register* 86 (32): 10237–43.

Uzendoski, Michael A. 2009. "La textualidad oral Napo Kichwa y las paradojas de la educación bilingüe intercultural en la Amazonia." In *Repensando los movimientos indígenas,* edited by Carmen Martínez Novo, 147–71. Quito: FLACSO-Sede Ecuador/Ministerio de Cultura.

Vega Díaz, Ismael. 2014. *Buscando el río: identidad, transformaciones y estrategias de los migrantes indígenas amazónicos en Lima Metropolitana.* Lima: Terra Nuova.

Vilaça, Aparecida. 1992. *Comendo como gente: formas do canibalismo Wari' (Pakaa-Nova).* Rio de Janeiro: Editora da Universidade Federal do Rio de Janeiro.

Vilaça, Aparecida. 2006. *Quem somos nós: os Wari' encontram os brancos.* Rio de Janeiro: Editora da Universidade Federal do Rio de Janeiro.

Vilaça, Aparecida. 2007. "Cultural Change as Body Metamorphosis." In Fausto and Heckenberger 2007, 169–93.

Virtanen, Pirjo Kristiina. 2006. "The Urban Manchinery Youth and Social Capital in Western Amazonian Contemporary Rituals." *Anthropos* 101 (1): 159–167.

Virtanen, Pirjo Kristiina. 2010. "Amazonian Native Youths and Notions of Indigeneity in Urban Areas." *Identities* 17 (2): 154–75.

Virtanen, Pirjo Kristiina. 2012. *Indigenous Youth in Brazilian Amazonia: Changing Lived Worlds.* New York: Palgrave Macmillan.

Viveiros de Castro, Eduardo. 2002. *A inconstância da alma selvagem.* São Paulo: Cosac Naify.

Walker, Harry. 2012. "Demonic Trade: Debt, Materiality, and Agency in Amazonia." *Journal of the Royal Anthropological Institute* 18:140–59.

Walker, John H. 2008. "Pre-Columbian Ring Ditches Along the Yacuma and Rapulo Rivers, Beni, Bolivia: A Preliminary Review." *Journal of Field Archaeology* 33 (4): 1–15.

Whitten, Norman E., Jr. 1976. *Sacha Runa: Ethnicity and Adaptation of Ecuadorian Jungle Quichua*. With the assistance of Marcelo N. Naranjo, Marcelo Santi Simbaña, and Dorothea S. Whitten. Urbana: University of Illinois Press.

Williams, Raymond. 1973. *The Country and the City*. London: Chatto and Windus.

Wirth, Louis. 1938. "Urbanism as a Way of Life." *American Journal of Sociology* 44: 1–24.

Wohl, Richard, and Anselm Strauss. 1958. "Symbolic Representation and the Urban Milieu." *American Journal of Sociology* 63 (5): 523–32.

Yagüe, Blanca. 2014. "'Hacer comestible' la ciudad: Las redes como estrategias alimentarias de los indígenas urbanos de Leticia, Amazonia colombiana." *Revista Colombiana de Antropología* 50 (2): 141–66.

PART I

Enchanted Cities and
Urban Cosmopolitics

CHAPTER 1

Cities of Transformation and Power in the Baniwa and Kuripako Cosmos

ROBIN M. WRIGHT

Nearly fifty years ago, when I began working with the Baniwa of the Upper Aiary River in Brazil, they had a much more limited notion of the Brazilian *cidade* (city) than they do today. Much of the elder generation knew better the towns and urban centers where they had worked during the second rubber boom (1940s): Leticia, Miraflores, and Mitú in the Vaupés region of Colombia, and San Fernando de Atabapo in Venezuela. Slightly less did they know of the only town on the Brazilian side, São Gabriel da Cachoeira, which was at that time a mission center and military base, with a community of local merchants and Indigenous families. Those who had experience in the *cidades* spoke in ambivalent terms as they both marveled at the merchandise, and warned of the confusion, violence, and disease prevalent in the cities, and the ease with which hard-earned money could be lost.

Today, however, many Baniwa and Kuripako families live in or around the city of São Gabriel, capital of the municipality of the same name and largest city in the Northwest Amazon, though they also keep houses in their villages and shelters in local garden sites near the city. For the younger generations, downriver cities are regarded as sources of opportunity in education, politics, and social and religious networking, among others. More Baniwa youth than ever before are now living in numerous cities in Brazil, pursuing their education while being exposed to the transformations that living in cities can bring. Shamans, too, have long worked in the urban context, as they see they have an important and difficult job of keeping under control the prevalent sicknesses associated with city living.

The notion of *cidade* has a complex history for the Baniwa and Kuripako, as well as having an important place in shamanic discourse about the other world and in mythic discourse about the primordial world. I explore in this chapter the urban imaginary in the Baniwa and Kuripako notions of cities as spaces of transformation and power. In particular, I focus on Baniwa values distinguishing collective identity from alterity—otherness—as these play out in the various contexts in which an urban imaginary has developed.

Baniwa urban imaginaries consist of multiple, interconnected conceptual levels. First, for the Baniwa and other Indigenous inhabitants of São Gabriel, the capital of the municipality, the city is a place both of potential opportunities and of malignant and predatory spirits that persecute all humans, and especially the youth. These spirits exist in an other, parallel reality alongside that of humans and are associated with physical spaces in the urban environment. When humans invade their spaces, they are believed to retaliate with sickness, predating on these intruders.

Second, colonial cities, named in clan histories, are remembered as spaces of loss of Baniwa identity and ethnic transformation, or assimilation into the white people's (*yalanawinai*) society. They are spaces of violence, peril, and disease. Yet, they are spaces that hold a piece of the clans' historical identities. Colonial cities are also seen as the source of the white man's knowledge and power, against which visionary shamans have defiantly demonstrated the greater power of their shamanic spirits.

Third, there are shamanic healing places, also called cities, in the vertical planes of the cosmos. These sacred spaces, which only the shamans can attain, are the source of powerful medicine for reversing the disastrous effects of sorcery. They do not exist on the same spatiotemporal plane as the actual cities where many Baniwa live today, or on that of the historical cities. They exist in an other, transcendent, sacred reality but one that directly interacts with the present.

And fourth, there are what I call the cosmogonic cities, the "world centers" that many Baniwa and Kuripako communities believe are the ultimate source of life and death in the world. Like shamanic healing places, these cities exist on a different spatiotemporal plane. The sacred places I discuss here are what the Baniwa understand to be "eternal places, not made by man" (*midzakakwa*).[1] The power in these places (river rapids, mountains, caves) resides in the fact that they are understood as the primordial and perennial source of all life and death in the world. They are spaces where unchanging ancestral identities were produced. These "cities" contain *spaces of transformation*, places where the cosmos came into being as a set of transformations that the creator demiurge realized.[2] These powers have the potential to affect anyone who enters the space, transforming them into Others.

I use a variety of sources to discuss these themes: contemporary experiences (my own and those of Baniwa friends) in the city of São Gabriel; clan oral histories representing colonial cities; shamanic discourse about cosmological cities as spaces of healing powers or as spaces of predatory spirits coexisting with humans in the terrestrial cities; and lastly shamanic discourse about cosmogonic cities and sacred geographies that provide visible representations (petroglyphs, in particular) of primordial transformations as remembered in the sacred narratives.

One of my principal sources on shamanic discourse is a Baniwa jaguar shaman of the Hohodene clan who was born in the village of Wapui on the Upper Aiary River in 1933 (according to the Salesian birth register). Manuel da Silva was a renowned shaman who migrated to São Gabriel around the turn of the century for health treatment and later was hired as a shaman in the Brazilian Army Hospital in the city. Finally, he decided to take up permanent residence there with his wife and daughter, and he lived and continued his practice in São Gabriel even at an advanced age, until his passing in late 2020.

I worked with Manuel over a period of forty years. One of the earliest stories he told me was of a forty-five-day-long canoe trip he and a friend made (probably in the 1950s–1960s) down the Rio Negro, starting from the Upper Aiary, to Manaus, the capital city of the State of Amazonas in Brazil. What they saw became one of the few sources of information at that time for the villagers back home about the "big city." As a shaman and political leader, he would later claim this as a unique, long-distance journey to a city on the edge of the known world. His use of the term *cities*, discussed here, is often associated with places in the cosmos and powerful spirits.

In this chapter, I discuss two cosmogonic cities. During my first fieldwork trip, in the late 1970s, I lived in the village of Wapui, on a river bluff in front of the great rapids and sacred city called Hipana on the Aiary River. Years later, Brazilian anthropologist Carlos Xavier (2008) would document a "Great City" on the Upper Içana River in Colombia. I rely heavily on interviews with several elders and shamans to discuss these cities.

The Northwest Amazon

The Northwest Amazon region is home to Northern Arawakan–, Eastern Tukanoan–, and Naduhup-speaking peoples. The Baniwa, Kuripako, and Wakuenai are three of the numerous Northern Arawakan–speaking peoples who live in the area, along the borders of Brazil, Colombia, and Venezuela (map 1.1; Hill 1993; Journet 1995; Wright 1998). In Brazil, the Baniwa and Kuripako live primarily in over ninety-three multifamily communities on the Içana River and its tributaries, notably the Aiary. Many Baniwa and Kuripako also live in the towns and urban areas of the Rio Negro (Instituto Socioambiental, n.d.).

Their societies are traditionally organized according to a system of patriclans associated with territories where the multiple communities belonging to each clan live by swidden agriculture, fishing, hunting, and foraging. Large and important clans among the Baniwa include the Hohodene, Walipere-dakenai, and Dzawinai, which are exogamous and have long histories of intermarriage. Each clan's communities consider themselves to be the descendants of heroic ancestors, organized according to a hierarchical model of agnatic siblings differentiated by relative age (senior/junior brothers) and ceremonial roles (chiefs, shamans, dancers, and servants).

Each clan is owner of ceremonial property that includes an "animal ancestor" (Fontes 2018) in the form of a sacred flute or trumpet, the clan's first ancestor; a set of ceremonial chants sung during the rites of initiation called Kuwaipan (Kwepani among the Wakuenai of the Guainía River in Venezuela); ceremonial dance-songs; orations to heal; and oral histories of warfare, contact with the white people, and visionary prophets. Each Baniwa clan also has its own set of sacred places in a territory defined by the cosmogonic narratives, a sacred geography that I have called a mythscape (Wright 2013): the Kuripako clans of the Upper Içana have distinct mythscapes from the Baniwa of the Içana and its tributaries; and the Wakuenai of the Guainía have others. These mythscapes define cosmogony; they are interconnected, sacred spaces that define life cycles in the cosmos.

Beginning in the late 1940s and early 1950s, North American Protestant evangelical missionaries crusaded among the Baniwa, provoking a major condemnation of traditions such as shamanism, dance festivals, and sacred landscapes. Most Baniwa and Kuripako communities at that time were desperately seeking refuge from the destruction of the second rubber boom,

MAP 1.1 The Northwest Amazon region. Instituto Socioambiental.

which seriously distorted the integrity of many communities, given the ambulatory nature of the labor. And, as Márcio Meira (2018) traces in a history that spans from colonial times to the present along the Rio Negro, many communities were brutalized by a predatory system of *aviamento* (borrowing on credit).

Consequently, the Baniwa and Kuripako converted to evangelicalism in the late 1940s in search of relief from this oppressive system and the possibility of reconstructing their communitarian values and ways of life. Only a few communities on the Upper Aiary River succeeded in defending their shamanic traditions against the evangelical campaigns to eradicate them. The converted Baniwa pastors, urged by the missionaries, turned against the shamans, threatening them with propaganda and abusive campaigns. Had it not been for the resistance of a group of shamans of the Upper Aiary, there would likely be no more Baniwa shamans left today. Fortunately, one powerful shaman and prophet named Kudui urged his apprentices and followers to resist the imposition of evangelicalism and to prepare for the "coming of the whites." He instructed the communities of the Upper Aiary not to repress their traditional culture, but rather to forge a different relation to the Christian Bible, one that included both the shamans as spiritual intermediaries and the ancient, cosmogonic traditions.

Baniwa and Kuripako conversion to evangelicalism produced in many communities a deliberate avoidance of the urban environment as a place of potential spiritual danger, although aspiring Baniwa pastors frequently visited the city of São Gabriel to receive instruction from American missionaries. By the late 1980s, however, major transformations began in the city, dramatically changing Indigenous perceptions of it.

São Gabriel da Cachoeira: "The Most Indigenous City in Brazil"

São Gabriel da Cachoeira is located on the banks of the Upper Rio Negro at its confluence with the Uaupés River, in the frontier region of the Brazilian Northwest Amazon (figure 1.1). Numerous Baniwa and other Northern Arawakan–, Eastern Tukanoan–, and Naduhup-speaking peoples live in and around the city, along with a sizable migrant population and a constant turnover of outside researchers and tourists. São Gabriel has today a population of approximately thirteen thousand people in a municipality of forty-five thousand people, mostly Indigenous (IBGE, 2019). The city was built on Northern Arawakan Baré people's land, and it has had a long history of geopolitical interests establishing a presence there. São Gabriel today is a majority-Indigenous city consisting of speakers of at least four different Indigenous language families, along with Brazilian and other languages (see Eloy, Le Tourneau, and Hervé 2005).

In 1764, the Portuguese built a large stone fortress on top of a hill overlooking the rapids of the Rio Negro to defend their colonial interests against Spanish pretensions in the region. For generations, the colonial town was involved in economic cycles of production for export to emerging cities on the Lower Rio Negro. Throughout colonial history, the Northwest Amazon became increasingly compromised by the global expansion of capitalist interests, as demonstrated extensively in recent studies by Paraense historians Márcio Meira (2018) and Décio de Alencar Guzmán (2021).

FIGURE 1.1 Aerial view of downtown São Gabriel da Cachoeira, 2019. Photo by IBGE.

In the mid-nineteenth century, the newly formed state government of Amazonas attempted to impose programs of conscripted labor on the Indigenous population. Against these the Indigenous inhabitants of the Upper Rio Negro revolted in various ways, including through prophet movements led by Baniwa and Tukano shamans who foretold the overturning of colonial domination through cataclysmic change (discussed below). Throughout the latter half of the nineteenth century and the first half of the twentieth, the ancestors of the Baniwa knew the city of São Gabriel as a place where they could get access to work for rubber and *piaçaba* (palm) bosses, and acquire merchandise such as salt, matches, cloth, and soap.

In the late 1970s, when I first stayed in the city, the population was calculated to be around 6,000 people, swollen by a transient group of workers involved in the construction of the Northern Perimeter Highway, which would integrate regions of the Northern Amazon. In the mid-1980s, when I visited again, the population was 4,500 and rigidly controlled by the presence of the Salesian missions and the Brazilian military. Between the mid-1980s and 2002, the population more than tripled in size, as waves of migrants came to the city from rural areas seeking jobs, education for their children, and health services (see Brandhuber 1999; Lasmar 2005). With such a rapid agglomeration of people, issues peculiar to city life began to emerge: health concerns, food insecurity, housing insecurity, and others.

For the Baniwa, the city is known as Hiipanako, or Dzakale Makakoe (Great "City"). São Gabriel is traditionally in the territory of their affines the Northern Arawakan Baré. In Baniwa stories, São Gabriel is remembered as a place where a predatory water serpent from the Uaupés River was trapped by the Baré and then killed and cut into pieces, its body parts transformed into various water animals (turtles, dolphins, large fish) of the Rio Negro and Amazon. The city is thus conceptualized by the Baniwa as a *space of alterity and transformations*. I will return to this story later in the text.

There is, according to shamans and incantation specialists, an invisible, nonhuman side to the city, one that shamans can actually see and that, it is widely believed, directly affects humans. Isaias Fontes, Hohodene Baniwa leader of the Federation of Indigenous Organizations of the Rio Negro,[3] explained to me that "in the eyes of the *pajé* [shaman], when he is in a trance with *pariká* [shaman's psychoactive snuff made from the bark of *Virola* trees], instead of what ordinary people see as benches of stone he *sees the epicenter of a city that is the fortress of the Yoopinai spirits, a great imaginary city seen by the pajé.* This is the importance of São Gabriel da Cachoeira" (pers. comm., July 31, 2020). The "fortress" refers to an actual historic landmark, the five-pointed stone fort that the Portuguese built in 1764 atop the Morro da Fortaleza to defend their colonial interests against the Spanish. One of its main attractions is the Anta [Tapir] stone, with its high relief pictographs of animals and other drawings. These, in the Baniwa shamans' perspectives, are transformations of powerful, predatory spirit beings known as the Yoopinai, which hold a central place in Baniwa cosmogony.

As one incantation specialist described to me in detail:

They are dangerous places because they are the cities of Invisible People, cities of the Yoopinai. . . . In the vision of a Shaman, knowledgeable about sacred places, these enchanted beings are people like we humans, so I call them Invisible People. Here I will mention some sacred places: there is a stone that resembles an animal which is untouchable, it is the hill of the Fortaleza. There is also a "pot of malaria" [which] is an invisible pot, but in the view of a shaman, it is a pot of the daughter of Maliweko, the ancient spirit owner of lightning and thunder. . . . Nowadays, many drownings are happening mainly among the whites and people who do not know or no longer believe in these sacred places. There is also a stone with the image of a water monster called Inirriwheri, where people are attacked invisibly, causing symptoms of muscle pain in their knees until people become paralyzed. [These stones and others] are alive and very dangerous to humanity. They're dangerous to this town. It's the Yoopinai. They once existed alongside [the demiurge] Kuwai and humanity, they were people like us, so they are living beings. In the eyes of most people, they are only stones, but in the view of the shamans these stones are alive.

The Yoopinai spirits are believed to prey on humans, giving them sickness, or even abducting them (see Estorniolo 2020). Humans have the obligation to respect physical and spiritual boundaries separating them from the Yoopinai spirits, including their known spaces in and around the city. Unfortunately, with the rapid advance of population settlement, the aggregation of so many distinct peoples around São Gabriel, and the rise in tourism, it becomes a challenge to sustain the respect for and avoidance of these spaces. The situation has become—in the eyes of many—chaotic, with many people subsequently becoming afflicted with new and exogenous illnesses.

Hohodene Baniwa shamanic discourse adds to the urban imaginary of São Gabriel by affirming that all merchandise circulating in the city is produced by the *fábricas* (factories) in the "cities of the whites," which provide merchandise to the urban populations. These *fábricas* are located in a large ring around the periphery of this world. There are places where, according to cosmogonic narratives, the first woman, Amaru, settled and became the primordial "Mother of the White People," that is, the Spaniards and Portuguese. She is considered to be a powerful sorceress who, shamans state, sends smoke and fumes from the *fábricas* back to the lands of the Baniwa. These fumes give people sicknesses and fever, known as the "sicknesses of the whites," mostly respiratory diseases (flu, colds, tuberculosis, whooping cough, and, most recently, COVID-19). The fumes take the form of smells associated with the white man's world, such as gasoline, machine oil, and oil-based paint, which circulate throughout the city.[4]

That São Gabriel is a place of inordinate sickness and violence has been discussed in studies by health professionals at the Fundação Oswaldo Cruz.

Maximiliano Loiola Ponte de Souza and Jesem Douglas Yamall Orellana (2012, 36), for example, observed that "the average rate of suicide mortality in São Gabriel da Cachoeira from 2000 to 2007 was three times higher than the registered rate for the general Brazilian population from 2001 to 2003" (see also Souza 2016). Similar observations regarding suicide were made several years later by Aloízio Cabalzar, anthropologist of the Instituto Socioambiental (Socio-Environmental Institute), who has lived for twenty-five years in São Gabriel. According to him, the only certainty among the families of the Upper Tiquié River (a tributary of the Lower Uaupés, with predominantly Eastern Tukano communities, which migrated in large numbers to São Gabriel; see Brandhuber 1999) is that the suicides by hanging began in the city of São Gabriel, not in the villages: "There is a bit of this idea that disease in the Amazon, in general, by the very history of contact with the whites, has always moved upriver from a city toward the headwaters. Suicide, too, is a contagious disease that is entering the communities coming from São Gabriel." Along with the suicides, he explained, there were reports of a mysterious, hooded figure who tormented adolescents, "a being of darkness" that followed them around until finally they put an end to their lives (Cabalzar, cited in Viana 2015). Some reports speak of satanic rituals performed at the city cemetery, with the hooded entity holding the "book of magic of São Cipriano."

This demonic figure resonates, I believe, with Baniwa beliefs in Yoopinai and Inyaime spirits, which persecute humans for transgressions against them, the places where they dwell, or the moral order humans are expected to observe. Shamans have also described a malignant sorcerer that seemed to have descended on the city. In 2012, Manuel da Silva reported that he had seen the demonic figure, tall and strong, carrying a mesh fishnet that he placed over his victims to drag them away to their deaths (Viana 2015).

Medical anthropologist Luiza Garnelo suggested that youth suicides were due to "inter-generational conflict," the youth being "out of control" of the elder generation (Garnelo and Wright 2001). The adolescents were no longer receiving instruction in the traditional ways, as Baniwa social norms and cultural ways were difficult if not impossible to maintain in the urban context. As a result, sicknesses, social ills (alcoholism, depression, violence), and adolescent suicides in the city seemed to be spiraling out of control.

Researchers see these ills as the product of multiple factors that have produced serious alienation: a long history of missionary boarding schools, intergenerational trauma, and the repression of traditional knowledge (what has been called epistemicide). Perhaps with the flourishing of interest since the early twenty-first century in new and exciting projects of sustainable development and artistic creativity, new vistas are being opened for other forms of revitalizing and affirming traditional culture.

The COVID-19 pandemic, however, has had a devastating impact on the city of São Gabriel, which has mourned the loss of hundreds of Indigenous people, including several important and knowledgeable elders, such as the acclaimed Dessano artist Feliciano Lana, the Tuyuka elder Higino Tenório, and the writer Aldevan Baniwa. The demands placed on medical professionals and Indigenous leaders working in the city during the pandemic have been unbelievably harsh, and these professionals have been heroic in ensuring that support and medical assistance have reached the communities. Indigenous healing specialists (shamans, incantation specialists, and herbalists) have also been hard at work, along with nongovernmental institutions and the federal government's Special Secretariat of Indigenous Health, to control its spread. One highly respected incantation specialist, who lives in São Gabriel, attributed the pandemic to the predatory Yoopinai spirits, saying that they were, "strangely attacking, as sparks of fire, in the lungs of people."

Colonial Cities as Spaces of Ethnic Transformation

We turn our attention to the colonial cities of the Rio Negro and their place in the memories and oral histories that clan members have of their ancestors. Distinct from the sacred stories, oral histories refer to a time within direct genealogical distance from the narrator. These stories are like protohistories, at the end of which a genealogy connects the stories with living elders, usually the eldest "brother" of a clan. As I have argued (Wright 2005), they are clearly within the time frame of the earliest recorded contact between Baniwa clans and the colonial authorities, from the second half of the eighteenth century on. Colonial cities in the clan histories are imagined as spaces of *ethnic displacement and transformation from Indigenous into white people.*

The oral histories I discuss here are from two of the largest Baniwa clans, the Hohodene and the Walipere-dakenai (for comparable stories among Kuripako clans, see Journet 1995). Both stories recount periods of conflict, violence, flight, and loss during the colonial period. There are parallels that can be drawn between these clan histories and cosmogonic stories in which primordial conflicts between enemy tribes and the first ancestors of humans resulted in irreversible losses, followed by recovery and regeneration.

In the Hohodene story, following a war on the Upper Uaupés River, their ancestor and his people were forcibly taken downriver to the colonial town of Barcelos on the Lower Rio Negro (though other narrators say it was the town of Barra, precursor to the present-day city of Manaus; see Wright 1998). Barcelos was the late eighteenth-century capital of the Portuguese captaincy of the Rio Negro. At that time, the Portuguese policy of *descimentos* (relocation from the *sertão* [backland] to the towns) was in effect, by which Portuguese troops would "persuade" natives, often by force, to "descend" the rivers from their villages to work in the colonial towns. Many Baniwa were taken in slavery in the mid-eighteenth century to distant cities such as Belém do Pará (Meira 1993). It is plausible that the story of the Hohodene ancestor refers to this same period. The Hohodene narrative shows, as Fernando Santos-Granero argues in this volume, that the Indigenous Amazonian experience of cities and urban lifeways goes back deep in time.

Their experience in the town of Barcelos/Manaus did not last for more than a generation, for there were "diseases" and "wars" from which several clan ancestors fled and returned home to the Içana River. All the sons of these ancestral chiefs, it is said, remained in Barcelos/Manaus and "became soldiers," that is, they "became white" ("transformed," "became other," *na-padámakawa*). Consequently, the continuity between generations was broken, making Hohodene society inviable since the ancestor returned home alone, childless, and wifeless.

The ancestors of the Walipere-dakenai clan then offered to make an alliance with the Hohodene warrior-chief through intermarriage and, eventually, to share the riverine territory along the Aiary. In Baniwa cosmogonic stories, a single survivor from the destruction of the enemy tribes, a warrior-hero, regenerates society and creates the conditions for the production of new generations of descendants.

A later attempt to urge the Hohodene to descend the Rio Negro met with a defiant refusal by the clan brothers. Remembering how they had lost their villages in their forced descent to colonial towns, they responded that their work on gardens and houses was more important. The story remembers the downriver space as one of loss of identity, intergenerational loss, and permanent ethnic transformation into "whites." Identity was regenerated through a return upriver to the homeland. (A similar kind of capture-and-flight story is told in the Baniwa narrative discussed below related to a healing chant for victims of sorcery.)

The Walipere-dakenai tell a slightly different version, which states that the hero-ancestor, along with many other clan "brothers," descended the Rio Negro fleeing from wars, and went to live in the place where the city of Manaus is nowadays, but before there were any white people there at all (see Wright 2005, 98ff.). After a while, the white people came and brutally expelled the Walipere-dakenai. They relocated upriver and founded another town, Barcelos, living there until the white people came and forced them again to relocate upriver, this time to São Gabriel da Cachoeira. Again, the white people came and made war against them. Many Walipere-dakenai died in these wars, until they revolted against the hero-ancestor and eliminated him. After this, the clans dispersed.

Here, the drama of Indigenous history is posed in starkly simple terms: the Indigenous people were the first settlers in the areas of the Rio Negro cities but were later violently expelled by the white people. This is similar to what Philippe Erikson argues in this volume in relation to the Chacobo, namely, that from a Chacobo point of view, white-mestizo cities are an outgrowth of ancient Chacobo villages.

Baniwa memories of their historical, visionary shamans and prophets around the mid- to late nineteenth century and early twentieth highlight how they led antisorcery movements and were seen by state government authorities in Brazil and Venezuela as threats to borderland security. In these stories, *doutores* (learned men, sometimes "authorities"), having knowledge and power, came from the city of Caracas, Venezuela, to the region and challenged the prophets to survive being sealed in a coffin and submerged repeatedly in the Orinoco River (see Wright and Hill 1986; Wright 2005). The coffin can be understood as the death-dealing stranglehold the white people imposed on Indigenous peoples through the systems of conscripted labor and repression of Indigenous political mobilization. The prophets not only survived the submersion tests but also challenged the *doutores* to take their own medicine (be submerged), which, of course, they did not survive, demonstrating the greater power that the visionary prophets had over the white authorities—the sort of power alluded to in messianic myths.

Despite all the challenges and potential threats to health and well-being that the cities represent, many young Baniwa today have taken up permanent residence in cities as far away as Rio de Janeiro, Brasília, Belém, Campinas, and São Paulo, in pursuit of higher education, job opportunities, and political purposes. For a great many of them, shamanic protection, especially through oration, is important for "turning away" the negative powers circulating in these cities. Celestial, shamanic cities afford powerful protective spaces for recovery from the ills of these urban environments.

Cosmological Cities as Spaces of Shamanic Healing Power

For Baniwa and Eastern Tukano shamans, incantation specialists, and herbal specialists, the cities of São Gabriel and Manaus are places where their services are in high demand. Most especially, they are sought for protection against sorcery (*marecaimbara*), the sicknesses of the Yoopinai spirits, and innumerable other sicknesses and social ailments that arise from the urban and peri-urban environments. Baniwa shamans and chanters have access to cosmological sources of transformation and alterity that are considered to be safe havens and sources of remedies against the urban sicknesses. These shamanic cities are located in the celestial and subterrestrial layers of the cosmos. Two that are frequently invoked are Mapakwa Makakwe (the "great honey place" or "city of the bee spirits"; see Hill 1993) and Kathimakwe (the "place of happiness/joy" or "city of the bird spirits"; see Wright, forthcoming), both of which are sources of powerful antidotes to sorcery. Both cities are *transcendent spaces* in which the lethal effects of alterity can be reversed through shamanic healing powers.

The first holds a prominent place in the incantations to heal a victim of sorcery. The story behind the incantations tells how the younger brother of the Baniwa Creator had been devoured by a predatory water serpent on the Upper Uaupés River, a region of the Eastern Tukano. The younger brother had taken shamanic tools with him to trick the serpent into thinking he was dead, even as, while in the monster's belly (a powerful metaphor for a victim of sorcery), he struggled to stay alive. The serpent was eventually killed around São Gabriel—the place of alterity and transformation—by the Baré, and the young man ripped open its belly and emerged but lay "dead" on the beach. His older brother then initiated with him a shamanic journey of healing by canoeing upriver and returning home, passing through the *transcendent celestial space* called the "great honey place," the "city of the bee spirits," where he received the powerful "sweetness" of the honey of the bee spirits and nectar from fruits, and was gradually healed. Swarming around

this great city—either a single longhouse or a multitude of them—are, shamans say, numerous types of bee spirits, whose honey can reverse a death
(unconsciousness is understood to be a temporary "death") from sorcery. The
younger brother ultimately arrived at Hipana, the Baniwa world center on
the Upper Aiary River and the source of all life. As he approached the center,
the life of the young man was fully restored (*liafetawa*) and he was welcomed
home with a festival (Wright 1998; Hill 1993).

The chanter of the incantations seeks "to revive the soul" in a journey that
passes through the spiritual cities of bees, on the vertical plane above this
world. The story has a strong parallel to the Hohodene clan history, since the
clan ancestors were forcibly taken downriver, lost their children, and "died"
as a social unit but, through their own decision, fled and returned upriver to
their homeland, where they regenerated society.

The second sacred celestial space is called by shamans the "place of hap-
piness/joy" or Kathimakwe, and it is a city of bird spirits (Wright, forthcoming). According to Manuel da Silva, it is "a beautiful place" in a forest of the
otherworld where there is a huge longhouse, "like a city" in which flocks of
bird-people of all kinds live, constantly singing their songs. They greet and
welcome the visiting shamans, who must ascend a long staircase that their
snuff shows them to get there, chanting as they ascend. The "place of happi-
ness/joy" is located at the very tip of the otherworld, where the Creator has
a box of infallible remedies that can cure any sickness and restore health.

Here, the transcendent celestial city space holds multitudes of aesthetically pleasing songbirds that produce joy (*kathima*). The symbolic density
here is that of a multitude of healing agents and powers that overcome the
sadness and bitterness characteristic of grave sicknesses produced by sorcery. Manuel da Silva and other Baniwa shamans have said that contemporary cities may have hospitals with surgery rooms and such, but that the
medicine administered there does not treat the souls (*nakaale*) of the Indigenous sick, unlike the shamans' cures in the cities of the "other world"
(*apakwa hekwapi*), which "revive [peoples'] souls" (*nawafeta nakaale*) from
the lethal impacts of sorcery and sicknesses of the downriver cities.

Cosmogonic Cities

The creation stories of Northern Arawakan-speaking peoples are marked by
multiple "world centers" that some narrators understand to be great cities,

or ancient cities at which major events occurred in primordial times. These world centers are described in minute detail by the spiritual specialists, a select few of whom are capable of explaining every shape and form, inscription, location, and interrelation among elements at these places (see, esp., Gonzalez-Ñáñez 2020; Ortiz and Pradilla 2002).

The world centers can also be considered sanctuaries, the source of the cosmic life force that circulates throughout the universe (Wright, Gonzalez-Ñáñez, and Xavier 2017). Their sacredness involves a deep respect for their intrinsic significance, a strong taboo (enforced by sorcery) against disturbing any aspect or feature in them, and an understanding of their connection with the invisible (except to the specialists) otherworld of the spirits and creator demiurges. Each center is understood to be a unique portal to the sacred. These ancient cities belong to a cosmography of *life-defining transformations*: the first death, the birth of the first animal and the first human ancestors, and the first initiation rites. The landscape of each sacred place is believed to be permeated by the presence of spirits: the pictographs and inscriptions that, it is believed, the primordial people left for their descendants to learn about the cosmos and society and their place in it.

These cities of stone are places where the primordial people, it is said, "transformed into stone": *lipadámaka* (he/it became other) *hipadawa* (stone form). The verb *lipadáma* is used in different contexts related to the ideas of transformation and metamorphosis. The notion of transformation into stone form means that the images into which the subject transformed are not merely signs that point to something else, but rather *are* what they point to, though in a transformed way. Sometimes, it is said, the stones can dangerously affect humans by putting ideas into their heads that lead to moral disobedience, which in turn results in sickness (Oliveira 2015). Thus, we might say that these cities are spaces that can catalyze these transformations. The two discussed here are particularly significant in that they are understood by Baniwa and Kuripako to be the sources of life and death in the cosmos.

The "Ancient City" of Hipana

Cosmogony in the stories and shamans' knowledge define world centers as places where human identity was shaped in primordial times, in stark contrast with alterity or radical difference, the worlds of the dangerous Others. Both Baniwa and Kuripako recognize that there is a "center of the universe"

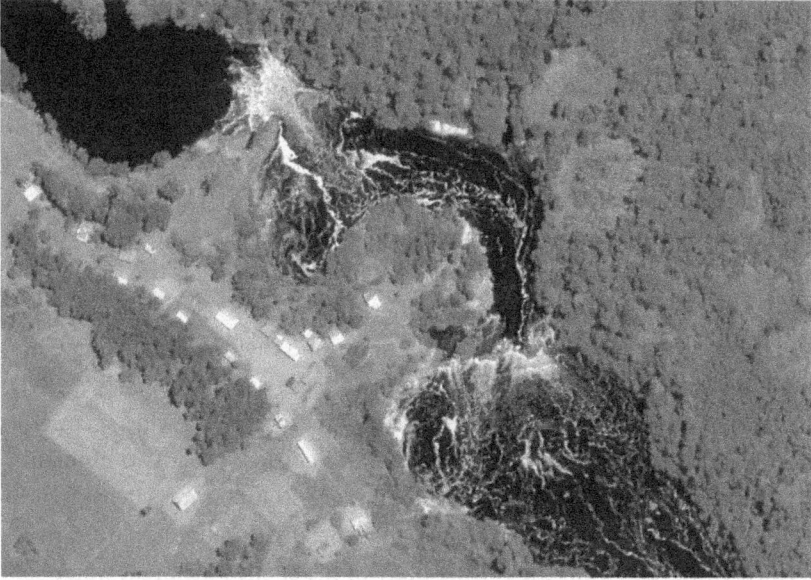

FIGURE 1.2 Aerial view of Hipana rapids and Wapui village. Google Earth.

(*hekwapi pamudzua*), an axis mundi connecting all the layers of the cosmos, where it is believed that the ancestors of all peoples emerged from the holes in the rapids, at the place called Hipana on the Aiary River (figure 1.2).

In a recent filmed interview, former deputy mayor of the city of São Gabriel and important Walipere-dakenai political and spiritual (evangelical) leader André Baniwa said of the significance of Hipana for all Baniwa: "So, the Baniwa were born, other peoples were also born, and the non-Indigenous people in the same place . . . there's a river called the Ayari [*sic*] river. . . . And it has a large waterfall, and the place is like the ancient city of these [ancestral] beings and that's where the birthplace of humanity that exists today is, in the form of stone, that's where humanity appeared for us" (in Prado 2017).

To Manuel da Silva, shaman-caretaker of this sacred place for many decades, Hipana is also called Liwalikwali Eenu, the "belly of the sky," the miniature world of primordial times or the world at its birth. There is a deep hole in the granite at the center of the rapids, which is the place from which were "born" (*medzeniako*) all the first ancestors of humanity, who were not yet even human beings, sort of quasi-animal, quasi-human. Later, the creator demiurge pulled out from the hole the first real human woman, followed by the first man, and sent them to live on their ancestral lands.

Much in the creation stories has its corresponding material feature in the sacred place of Hipana. Situated in the immediate area around the present-day rapids, the primordial world's landscape is dense with meanings directly connecting the stories with the site's signs and petroglyphs (figure 1.3). As the center of the universe, Hipana is believed to connect to all realms of the vertical cosmos and all places in the horizontal cosmos at the same time. Hence the spiritual power of this "city."

Hipana is the source of the clan ancestors and their identifying markers, but it is also a place where various forms of alterity came into being, namely, lethal sickness in the form of poison and sorcery, and the white man. The narratives recount that the white people were born here at two moments: when the ancestors of the white people emerged from the holes in the rapids, along with all other human ancestors; and when the creator demiurge *transformed* two grubs from the rotting body of his enemy, the great water serpent. One of these became the white man, who eventually was given knowledge to produce all merchandise; the other became an Indigenous person, who was given the knowledge and technology for hunting. The white man

FIGURE 1.3 A boulder facing the lake at Hipana, with pictographs related to the cosmogonic narrative, 2019. Photo by Giorgio Palmera.

was sent away to distant lands, while the Baniwa were instructed on how to live well in their territory.

Hipana is a sacred space, where the primordial people *transformed* into their stone images, and where the "animal ancestor" transformed into multiple stone sacred flutes and trumpets. It is understood to be the source of growth in the world as the Baniwa know it. As a city, Hipana is a place that is densely populated with petrified transformations of the primordial beings (see esp. Gonzalez-Ñáñez 2020; Ortiz and Pradilla 2002; Wright 2017; cf. Valle 2012 on the Lower Rio Negro).

The "Great City" of Nhiaperikuli

On a hilltop rising from the Yawiari Creek, tributary of the Upper Içana River, the "Great City," as it is known by the Kuripako, close relatives of the Baniwa, is situated in the traditional territory of the Kuripako people, overlooking a vast area of the headwater region in the Northwest Amazon. This site, called Yakale Makakoe in the Kuripako language, also called Kerhipan (Moon House), is distinctive for its massive scale, as it refers to immense rock formations located on the hilltop. Brazilian anthropologist Carlos Xavier (2008) has authored the only written documentation on this site; his information is based on interviews with the last few knowledgeable elders among the predominantly evangelized Kuripako of this region.

Like Hipana, the Great City is understood to be from another time, an era prior to present-day humanity, a primordial and miniature world, inhabited by the Creator and his brothers, and their enemies, an ancient tribe of arboreal animal-people. The story to which this sacred place is attached is of how these enemies killed the Creator's younger brother by sorcery, and thus how irreversible death entered the world for all future generations: a Kuripako elder declared to Carlos César Leal Xavier, "If [the Creator's] brother had not died, no one would die today" (in Wright, González Ñáñez, and Xavier 2017, 219). It is a story of deception, treachery, thoughtlessness, anger, and ignorance.

A prominent feature in the Great City is a massive boulder perched on the top of a cliff. This "longhouse" of the Creator, Xavier says, "is the central point of the Great City, and the Great City is considered to be the center of the world. The 'domains' of the Great City stretch out from the *maloca* [longhouse] to the mountains, on the horizon, in the four directions—an area that is estimated to cover some 15,000 square meters [3.7 acres]" (in

Wright, González Ñáñez, and Xavier 2017, 219). Xavier (2008, 88) adds his perspective on what he calls a "sign-landscape" following C. S. Peirce's (1985) theory of semiotics:

> We understand the Great City of [the Creator] as a sign-landscape, a landscape invested with meaning, significance, and signification. The transformation of a rocky mountain range filled with stones of various shapes into a real city, with roads, patio, *malocas*, and even a tomb, indicates the presence of, on the one hand, characteristics of this object (the hill and the boulders) that potentially suggest such connections and, on the other, a set of narratives and cognitive operations that actually materially concretize this bond.

The narrative explains, as Manuel da Silva has said (in Wright 1998, pt. 3), that the Great City is where death from sorcery came into the world for all times. Death is seen as the result of the actions of predator enemies exposing the vulnerability of the kin group. Like Hipana, the Great City represents a profound ontological change in the condition of humanity. In contrast with Hipana, which holds the predominant meaning of emergence and continuity, the Great City is a place of eschatological closure, since the primordial world of immortality ended at that moment. Both are understood to be "cities" in the sense of the density of their primordial scapes; they are miniature models of what the world would become for all future generations, with struggles over power between kin and others, and the sickness and misfortune that came into the world, but also, at the same time, the source of growth, ancestry, and important cultural institutions.

Conclusions

The overriding idea in this interpretive excursion is that there are four interconnected levels of the Baniwa and Kuripako urban imaginaries, as well as four notions of cities:

1. The city of São Gabriel da Cachoeira is considered to be a space of alterity and transformation on several levels: (a) the living presence of predatory nonhuman spirit-"peoples" at war with humans (e.g., through sicknesses and social ailments) over sacred spaces and an ideal moral order (the Yoopinai spirits, in particular, are understood to be the agents of transformations, for there is always the threat that their predations may cause someone to

become ill or be abducted and irreversibly "become other"); (b) the material evidence (the fort) of colonial history and domination; and (c) the material representations (e.g., petroglyphs) of primordial transformations.

2. Colonial cities, which are believed to contain pieces of clan identities, are mostly remembered for their virulence, violence, and loss. They are places of historical ethnic transformation from Indigenous to non-Indigenous, of generational loss, and of sicknesses deriving from colonization. Memories of the clan ancestors affirm that Indigenous settlements predated the colonial towns, and that ancestors fled from the downriver colonial cities of the Lower Rio Negro to safe havens in the upriver, homeland territory and source of ethnic regeneration.

3. Shamanic cities are transcendent spaces of healing that are accessed in order to: (a) bring the souls of sorcery victims back to life during a spiritual journey from the downriver cities (São Gabriel da Cachoeira, especially) upriver to the source of life at the center of the Baniwa cosmos; and (b) reveal the sources of infallible remedies against sorcery that will "heal the world" (*pamatchiatsa hekwapi*), restoring collective joy and health.

4. Cosmogonic cities are eternal (*midzakakwa*), sacred places, conceived by many as great cities, believed to be the spaces of the primordial world. These stone cities are the transcendent sources of never-ending and constitutive powers of both life and death, where life-defining transformations that occurred in the primordial past became permanent conditions for all of humanity.

Common to all of these cities, of course, is the problematic relationship to alterity—whether sorcerers in the cosmogonic cities, or the Other in the actual cities, where it can assume the force of demonic figures that prey on humans, as living sorcerers. But this predatory Other can also have the opposite effect, reinforcing the central values defining humanity as, for example, traditionalist and Christian Baniwa understand them today.[5] The transcendent spaces of the shamanic cities in the cosmos afford the possibility that their spirit inhabitants can be enlisted to "revive souls" from the negative alterity of death by sorcery. Evangelical Christian Baniwa appeal to a universal healing power, but they continue to respect the powers of the sacred places such as Hipana and others (see Prado 2017).

All cities are places of transformation, but unlike the primordial places where the stones are the images of the entities to which they refer, or the shamanic cities where shamans transform in order to harness the powers of the "other" spirit world, the historical and present-day cities are places where the constant pull of irreversible transformation threatens the stability of future generations of Baniwa.

As I have stated, today there are many Baniwa living either temporarily or permanently in Brazilian cities seeking jobs and educational opportunities. Likewise, there are more Baniwa attending universities in Brasília, Rio de Janeiro, Campinas, and other cities than at any other time in history. This study has not discussed them, as their experiences are yet unfolding; certainly, a future study should inquire about them. Rather, I have focused here on the representations of cities as expressed by shamans, elders, and political leaders, complemented by studies of an anthropological and historical nature.

Acknowledgments

I wish to thank Fernando Santos-Granero and Emanuele Fabiano for organizing this volume. I dedicate this chapter to my colleague Dr. Omar Gonzalez-Ñáñez, whose work with Northern Arawakan-speaking cultures has been an inspiration for many researchers; and to Manuel da Silva, Hohodene shaman and my principal interlocutor during the various fieldwork periods of my research. Without Manuel da Silva's help and guidance, and the collaboration of Ercilia Lima da Silva, his daughter, none of my publications on Baniwa traditions would have been possible.

Notes

1. In this volume, Natalia Buitron similarly notes that for Shuar people, cities are sources not just of power but also of death, while Pirjo Kristiina Virtanen argues that for Manxineru (Manchineri) people, cities are sources of powers not available in the forest but also dangerously weaken Indigenous people's bodies.
2. The Baniwa idea of transformation is different in degree from that of the neighboring Eastern Tukano, who have the notion of Houses of Transformation, sacred places where the ancestors transformed from one primordial reality to another (Scolfaro 2018).
3. The Federation of Indigenous Organizations of the Rio Negro is the leading Indigenous organization of all the Indigenous peoples of the Rio Negro.
4. Thermonuclear power plants are also understood to be the *fábricas* of the first woman. Emanuele Fabiano's discussion in this volume of the Urarina urban imaginary illustrates in parallel fashion how cities—in this case white people's cities—are represented as places of production of objects and goods (and also of other white people), a process linked to a destructive action associated with diseases.

5. This is discussed, for example, in André Fernando Baniwa's (2019) eloquent book *Bem viver e viver Bem*, especially in the section on "Bem viver e viver bem na pratica," which provides moral guidelines for realizing well-being, an important reflection for Baniwa in the urban context.

References

Baniwa, André Fernando. 2019. *Bem viver e viver bem segundo o povo Baniwa no noroeste amazônico brasileiro.* Curitiba, Brazil: Editora da Universidade Federal do Paraná.

Brandhuber, Gabriele. 1999. "Why Tukanoans Migrate? Some Remarks on Conflict on the Upper Rio Negro (Brazil)." *Journal de la Société des Américanistes* 85: 261–80.

Eloy, Ludivine, François-Michel Le Tourneau, and Théry Hervé. 2005. "Une ville dans la forêt: São Gabriel da Cachoeira, capitale isolée du haut Rio Negro." *Cybergeo: Espace, Société, Territoire*, article 304. https://doi.org/10.4000/cybergeo.3238.

Estorniolo, Milena. 2020. "Manger (avec) l'ennemi: mythe, subsistance et alimentation chez les Baniwa et les Koripako (Amazonie, Brésil)." PhD diss., École doctorale de l'école des hautes études en sciences sociales and Laboratoire d'anthropologie sociale.

Fontes, Fran. 2018. "Hiipana, Eeno Hiepolekoa." MA thesis, Universidade Federal do Rio de Janeiro.

Garnelo, Luiza, and Robin M. Wright. 2001. "Doença, cura e serviços de saúde: Representações, práticas e demandas Baníwa." *Cadernos de Saúde Pública* 17 (2). https://doi.org/10.1590/S0102-311X2001000200003.

Gonzalez-Ñáñez, Omar. 2020. "La lectura de las piedras: arte rupestre y culturas del noroeste amazónico." *Boletín Antropológico* 38 (99): 107–41.

Guzmán, Décio de Alencar. 2021. *Dans le labyrinthe du Kuwai: conquête, colonization et christianisation en Amazonie (xvi–xviiie siècles).* Paris: Editions Lettres Sorbonne Université.

Hill, Jonathan D. 1993. *Keepers of the Sacred Chants.* Tucson: University of Arizona Press.

IBGE (Instituto Brasileiro de Geografía e Estatistica). n.d. "São Gabriel da Cachoeira." Accessed August 7, 2022. https://www.ibge.gov.br/cidades-e-estados/am/sao-gabriel-da-cachoeira.html.

Instituto Socioambiental. n.d. Home page. Accessed July 15, 2022. https://www.socioambiental.org.

Journet, Nicolas. 1995. *La paix des jardins: structures sociales des Indiens Curripaco du haut Rio Negro.* Paris: Mémoires de l'Institut d'Ethnologie.

Lasmar, Cristiane. 2005. *De volta ao Lago de Leite: gênero e tranformação no Alto Rio Negro.* São Paulo: Editora da Universidade Estadual Paulista.

Meira, Márcio. 1993. *Livro das canoas: documentos para a história indígena da Amazônia.* São Paulo: Núcleo de História Indígena e do Indigenismo.

Meira, Márcio. 2018. *A persistência do aviamento: colonialismo e história indígena no noroeste amazônico*. São Carlos, Brazil: Universidade Federal de São Carlos.

Oliveira, Thiago da Costa. 2015. "Os Baniwa, os artefatos e a cultura material no Alto Rio Negro." PhD diss., Universidade Federal do Rio de Janeiro.

Ortiz, Francisco, and Helena Pradilla. 2002. *Rocas y petroglifos del Guainía: escritura de los grupos arawak-maipure*. Tunja, Colombia: Fundación Etnollano.

Peirce, C. S. 1985. "Logic as Semiotic: The Theory of Signs." In *Semiotics: An Introductory Anthology*, edited by Robert E. Innis, 1–23. Bloomington: Indiana University Press.

Prado, Raquel de Almeida, dir. 2017. *Na Cabeça do Cachorro*. Film, 54 min.

Scolfaro, Aline, dir. 2018. *Pelas Águas do Rio de Leite*. Film, 75 min.

Souza, Maximiliano Loiola Ponte de. 2016. "Indigenous Narratives About Suicide in Alto Rio Negro, Brazil: Weaving Meanings." *Saúde e Sociedade* 25 (1): 145–59.

Souza, Maximiliano Loiola Ponte de, and Jesem Douglas Yamall Orellana. 2012. "Suicide Mortality in São Gabriel da Cachoeira, a Predominantly Indigenous Brazilian Municipality." *Revista Brasileira de Psiquiatria* 34:34–37.

Valle, Raoni. 2012. "Mentes graníticas e mentes areníticas: fronteira geo-cognitiva nas gravuras rupestres do Baixo Rio Negro, Amazônia Setentrional." PhD diss., Universidade de São Paulo.

Viana, Natália. 2015. "Reportagem: São Gabriel e seus demônios." *Agência Pública*, May 15, 2015. https://apublica.org/2015/05/sao-gabriel-e-seus-demonios/.

Wright, Robin M. 1998. *Cosmos, Self, and History in Baniwa Religion: For Those Unborn*. Austin: University of Texas Press.

Wright, Robin M. 2005. *Historia indígena e do indigenismo no Alto Rio Negro*. Campinas, Brazil: Mercado de Letras.

Wright, Robin M. 2013. *Mysteries of the Jaguar Shamans*. Omaha: University of Nebraska Press.

Wright, Robin M. 2017. "As tradições sagradas de *Kuwai*." *Mana* 23 (3): 609–52.

Wright, Robin M. Forthcoming. "A Joyful Place." In *Spirit-Based Traditions in the Americas*, edited by Benjamin Hebblethwaite and Silke Jansen. Omaha: University of Nebraska Press.

Wright, Robin M., Omar González Ñáñez, and Carlos César Leal Xavier [as Carlos César Xavier Leal]. 2017. "Multi-Centric Mythscapes: Sanctuaries and Pilgrimages in Northwest Amazonian Arawakan Religious Traditions." In *Pilgrimage and Ambiguity: Sharing the Sacred*, edited by Angela Hobart and Thierry Zarcone, 201–31. Herefordshire, UK: Sean Kingston.

Wright, Robin M., and Jonathan D. Hill. 1986. "History, Ritual, and Myth: Nineteenth Century Millenarian Movements in the Northwest Amazon." *Ethnohistory* 33 (1): 31–54.

Xavier, Carlos César Leal. 2008. "A cidade grande de Ñapirikoli e os petroglifos do Içana: uma etnografia de signos baniwa." MA thesis, Universidade Federal do Rio de Janeiro.

CHAPTER 2

Arboreal City-States, Phyto-Warfare, and Dendritic Societies

An Urarina Metropolitan View of the World

EMANUELE FABIANO

The first time Julián traveled to the big city he was just a young man. The town of Nauta, in Loreto, Peru, had only a few houses and a small port located at the foot of a hill, very close to the confluence of the Marañón and Ucayali Rivers. The road that today connects the town with the city of Iquitos did not exist yet and, at that time, was just a pipe dream in the minds of many local people. In those days, Julián recounts, the Urarina people of the Chambira basin did not have enough money to travel by boat, so they often used rafts to get around. The *patrón* (boss) would charge a trusted group with the timber that he delivered to the sawmills of Iquitos during the wet season, with instructions to take care of the precious cargo day and night. The journeys were long and hard; the tedium and lack of food, together with the sun and rain, put the workers to the test, as they could spend weeks floating on the raft.

When narrating his memories of that time, Julián stops several times, introducing recollections and experiences that evoke a seemingly remote era: a bag of rice belonging to the *patrón* that disappeared, provoking exemplary punishments; an accident when stepping on a raft log; the taste of the farina consumed by the mestizo workers, exchanged during the trip for a pair of Siete Vidas rubber boots. Before, in the times of the *grandes patrones* (big bosses), the white and mestizo landowners who dominated Amazonian society prior to the 1970s land reform, there were not many Urarina who spoke Spanish, and even fewer who knew how to read or write, so it was common to choose the most educated among the young men to tally in the account books the workers' debts and the quantities of products destined for the city. Despite his few years of elementary school, Julián had learned to read and write thanks to having lived with the mestizo workers. These skills allowed him to gain the trust of his employer and even secure boat passage for him and his family to Iquitos. After the initial excitement, Julián soon realized that his stay in the big city and his new job as caretaker of the employer's warehouse were going to last longer than expected.

Julián's narrative, fragmented into a multitude of lived moments and visited places, sometimes becomes confusing and unmoored from time, even though many of these events marked his adult life significantly. His memories and the explanation he gives of them do not provide any element that allows us to evaluate the way in which these spaces, which so amazed him in the past, have changed up to the present, affected by time and the construction of new infrastructure; nor do his descriptions allow us to measure the city's expansion or perceive the temporal differences in terms of its inhabitants and their ways of dressing or communicating. Julián's memories seem to move away from a temporality in which the space of experience exists within a homogeneous medium, developing together with the narration, a "virtual cartography" (Cesarino 2008, 148) that juxtaposes itself to the experience of the urban space and turns it into a physical state of prostration, the consequence of a serious affliction:

> This is the city that I have here [he touches his chest] and that I can tell you about. It's a different city from the one you know, it's a city that doesn't make you feel yourself and that maybe you can't recognize . . . living apart from my family, in the city, can be like a disease: it doesn't let you think well if you find yourself alone. You don't recognize the faces of the people you meet, the food tastes different, you don't sleep like you do at home anymore. In the end, the days go by, and you hardly notice them. It's like being sick.

We cannot assume that an experience as intense and personal as the one narrated by Julián offers an appropriate measure to fully evaluate other similar experiences. Nonetheless, his testimony refers us to a series of elements that are the basic source for understanding the dynamics of Urarina insertion into urban life, while simultaneously offering the possibility of reflecting on the effects caused by the experience of these spaces and their associated imaginaries.

Even though the city is increasingly becoming a strong pole of attraction, Urarina people are convinced that staying there does not offer opportunities for a real improvement in life and that its advantages are inferior to those that could be derived from a more flexible link with their communities of origin. In this sense, bringing the city to the community is, in many cases, an aspiration that translates into changes in the traditional architecture and materials used to build dwellings, into the construction of infrastructure for common use, or into greater access to services that are frequently offered to promote "inclusion" by regional and national institutions (see Buitron in this volume for a similar view among the Shuar of Ecuador).

We should, therefore, not be surprised that for those Urarina who are most critical and reluctant with regard to the presence of mestizo business-men and traders in their lands, the category of "urban" is perceived as tightly linked to the dynamics of assimilation into the non-Indigenous world. All this allows us to reflect on the negative perceptions that several of my inter-locutors associate with the city and the way the latter has been experienced during recent decades. This perception is a clear indicator that this issue is relevant today, but it is also a clear sign of how the city continues to embody the authoritarianism and coercion that Urarina people recognize as a struc-tural component in their past relationships with local *patrones* and, more generally, with those who are not Urarina.

Based on the reconstruction of the power relations that have historically determined the forms and characteristics of Urarina presence in Loreto's most important cities, I analyze how, in this Indigenous people's urban imaginary, the forest is conceived of as occupied by an extensive network of metropolises, each of which has a specific tree at its center. These "den-dritic cities" have strongly normative and oppressive features, inspired by hierarchical and authoritarian models of sociopolitical organization, that structure a dense network of relationships between the nonhuman plant entities that dwell within them, the different tree species, and human be-ings. War, production, technology, and commerce rule the governments of those enormous tree cities: places dedicated to productivity and efficiency, in which intensive cultivation, large-scale cattle raising, and the manufacture of industrial goods feed an expansionist phyto-policy of war.

A description of these densely urbanized places often emerges in shamanic discourse, which classifies them by their harmfulness and makes them
the scene of extraordinary experiences associated with illness and death.
Likewise, there is a certain analogy between these tree metropolises and the
urbanized spaces experienced in ordinary contexts. Such similarities also
suggest the existence of a strong contrast between the practices and behaviors that allow a healthy and productive life, which Urarina people associate
with the safe and familiar space of the community, and practices regarded
as the epitome of a potentially harmful radical otherness, associated with
the city (Andrade, Chiquetto, and Tambucci 2009). This opposition, as we
shall see, arises as a result not only of geographic distance, but also of the
irreducibility of the Urarina and white-mestizo value systems.

The Urarina and the City

The systematic exploitation of rubber during the period known as the rubber
boom (1870–1910) generated a great impulse for all commercial activities
in the region of Loreto. However, in the Chambira basin the exploitation
of this resource did not play a significant role in the local economy. The
characteristics of the basin, an area dominated by enormous extensions of
wetlands and only a scarce presence of rubber trees (not enough to justify
the investment by rubber extractors and merchants), only partly protected
local Urarina groups from the dramatic consequences that characterized this
type of extractive industry elsewhere. Urarina accounts describe the rubber
boom as a period characterized by the forced displacement of a large number
of quasi-slave families, successively sold by local bosses as a slave labor force
to feed the prosperous rubber industry.

Although there is no official record about the Chambira region, the surviving narratives preserve graphic descriptions of the brutality of the foremen and traders, as well as the abductions and violent acts experienced by
Urarina people at the time. Among the oldest Urarina, references abound
to cases of mass deportations whose survivors, after being transferred in
chains to the city of Iquitos, were forced to work as slaves or as servants in
the homes of their *patrones* and other wealthy families. Many stories also
reveal how some Urarina managed to escape and, after spending a period
in hiding, finally settled along the Nanay River, where they founded a new
community, whose inhabitants today continue to preserve a rudimentary

form of the Urarina language, although they have completely forgotten their place of origin. Therefore, although the extractive activities only marginally involved the Urarina people of the Chambira region, there is still a clear perception of the role played by the mestizo *patrones*, undoubtedly contributing to the structuring of the social and economic relations that the numerous Urarina communities established with the mestizo population living along the Marañón River.

During the period of economic depression caused by the fall in the price of rubber (1914–43), Urarina began to maintain more or less continuous relations with the region's mestizo settlements (Kramer 1979, 14). This was due in part to improved transportation services, which increased the possibility of undertaking lucrative productive and commercial activities and attracted new settlers from other regions of the country (Santos-Granero and Barclay 2002). This new phase of the region's economic life coincided with the growing spread of a market economy based on the systematic exploitation of Indigenous labor, a legacy of the quinine and rubber-tapping extractive systems. Thanks to the strategy of forced indebtedness, a labor arrangement known as "debt peonage," family businesses expanded their activities and profitably engaged Urarina in the production and trade in timber, charcoal, and agricultural products to be sold in the Iquitos market. As a result, the city became inexorably closer, marking the beginning of an era that the inhabitants of the Chambira River recall as the time of the *grandes patrones.*

Even though today the figure of the *patrón* seems to have lost the influence and authority it once enjoyed, the logic of the *patrones* persists and continues to reproduce the old forms of labor exploitation of the Urarina population. From the 1990s, the *grandes patrones*, the influential families that had historically exercised economic control of the region, began to be replaced by a growing number of itinerant traders or owners of medium-sized boats (*regatones*), dedicated to the sale of a wide range of products (*aguaje* or fruit of the moriche palm, salted or fresh fish, plantains, etc.), and by the *pequeños patrones* (small bosses) involved in the timber trade, often descendants of mestizo workers (Dean 2004). The greater or lesser presence of these traders is influenced by seasonal price trends in the Iquitos and Yurimaguas markets, as well as by the duration and intensity of rainfall during the wet season, which imposes significant variations in the prices of agricultural products.

Many Urarina families are willing to work in the service of traders and *regatones*, even though the relationship is clearly exploitative. This ambiguity—between the rejection of external interference and the active search for the mediation of non-Indigenous actors to establish economic relations with the urban world—is particularly evident in all activities related to the logging and marketing of timber, an occupation that normally guarantees considerable profits. For many Urarina communities this activity represents the greatest source of cash income. Over the years many loggers and small- and medium-sized enterprises have acquired timber from the Urarina communities at a derisory price, to be sold in the city of Iquitos (Dean 1995, 2009; Walker 2012, 2013).

Although, in the past, reaching the large population centers of the region represented a rare event for the Urarina people of the Chambira basin, today, undertaking a trip on the Marañón River has become a fairly common activity, which, at least in principle, has brought the communities closer to the city, as well as to its economy and institutions. In recent years, the city of Nauta has become the urban center most frequented by Urarina people and the point of reference for the resolution of their administrative affairs, the sale of products destined for local markets, or access to the various services offered by the state. Unlike the surrounding rural communities, perceived by Urarina people as poor and backward places due to their lack of infrastructure and services (Pereira and Torres 2008), the cities closer to the Chambira region, such as Iquitos or Nauta, embody an ideal of modernity like that of Lima and Chiclayo or even the great foreign capitals.

The number of Urarina families that have decided to move to urban areas, or to places close to urban centers, has increased significantly since 2012. Although this trend, while still only involving a minority, can be read as the most eloquent manifestation of an increasingly intense link with the city and its economic and political structures, it cannot be interpreted simply as a movement of Indigenous people toward the white man's world (Alexiades and Peluso 2015; Nunes 2010). Far from representing an ideal solution for mitigating the state of semi-isolation perceived by many Urarina living in the Chambira communities, this phenomenon exacerbates a preexisting condition of economic inequality and vulnerability, and favors the configuration of a normative order in which forms of sociability, work, and residence, as well as the mechanisms of resource use, are being rapidly reconfigured (Horta 2017; Espinosa de Rivero 2009). Even so, through a greater and more intense articulation between urban and rural areas or through hybrid forms of management within this relationship (Peña Márquez 2011; Alexiades 2009), Urarina communities have developed new strategies in the face of the market economy. These allow them to actively participate in the extraction of resources and the production and exchange of goods, resulting in the articulation of the "traditional" economic and productive life with the present-day neoliberal Amazonian landscape (McSweeney and Jokisch 2015).

Despite these new forms of interaction with urban realities, many of my Urarina interlocutors continue to perceive the city as an inhospitable and dangerous place. This negative assessment is evidenced by the extremely small number of Urarina residing in urban areas, many of whom are concentrated near the ports or in a few houses located in peripheral neighborhoods. The vast majority of Urarina people only visit urban areas. For them, a stay in the city does not typically extend beyond the time needed to raise money, offering themselves as day laborers in small, poorly paid jobs or selling modest amounts of agricultural products, only to return to their home communities as soon as they can.

Invisible Cities, Underwater Kingdoms, and Nonhuman Worlds

Several elements that characterize the city in the Urarina urban imaginary coincide with those of other contemporary Indigenous Amazonian peoples. Recurring descriptions in myths and narratives endow the invisible cities of other-than-human worlds with features that are antithetical to those characterizing small Indigenous Amazonian settlements, suggesting an intense identification with Western culture, the non-Indigenous world, and an urban lifestyle (Lagrou 2013, 250; Hugh-Jones 2018, 218–19). Unlike rural Amazonian communities, often defined by their precariousness, scarcity of infrastructure and services, and the absence of planning, these enchanted cities seem to have been built in the image of the white people's great capitals: technologically advanced cities, endowed with a complex urban development, in which access to industrial products, services, knowledge, and wealth is permanently within the reach of their inhabitants.

In these places, nonhuman entities—spirits of the dead or animal spirits— often play the role of rulers or owners, and their activities are carried out in streets and buildings located inside particular landmarks such as hills or

caves, or in underwater kingdoms and chthonic worlds. Amazonianist ethnographies show how these enchanted cities often have the characteristics
of a metropolis, although their spatial locations are not always clearly identified or demarcated. In addition to having an undefined geography, these
cities seem to be the site of a compression or extension of space and time,
often revealing an overlap of elements from a distant past with the latest
technological developments or institutions and governing bodies typical of
the human world (Homan 2018; Lagrou 2013).

In the case of the Urarina, the cities that appear in their myths, even when
they turn out to be dangerous or strange, seem to offer the ideal context to
establish an intense and prolonged relationship between human characters
and the cities' nonhuman inhabitants. Despite being recognized as cities,
these places never acquire the characteristics attributed to the great industrialized cities of white people. Rather, even when their characteristics—
geographic, architectural, and technological—are an amplification of those
of white people's cities, they follow the model of Urarina communities and,
therefore, are familiar to human visitors. Even so, the stories agree in un-
derlining how access to these cities is difficult for human beings, who only
have the power to visit them in dreams, through shamanic experiences, or
as a consequence of being kidnapped by a spirit or marrying a nonhuman
inhabitant.

For this reason, it is not surprising that a stay in these cities is potentially
dangerous. Such a visit can produce bodily changes, which in some cases are
reversible, but in others can even cause death. Conversely, however, the visit
may become a highly formative experience, a source of extraordinary knowledge and better faculties of understanding. A longer stay in these places
is, with rare exceptions, the result of a voluntary choice. Humans may decide to remain in these cities because they are persuaded by the beauty of
their nonhuman wives, who have benevolently consented to marry a foreign
visitor, or because, after some time in captivity, they establish kinship ties
with their nonhuman hosts. In any case, this condition is reversible, and the
abandonment of these places is motivated by a deep desire to return to the
world of humans, a feeling of nostalgia that often surfaces through thoughts/
memories of daily actions or situations of family life and care. The return to
the human world is sudden, and the separation and prolonged distance do
not produce visible consequences (Fabiano 2017; Fabiano, Burnley, and Nuribe Arahuata 2022). As we shall see below, the experiences that characterize

entrance into a tree city, and the encounters with the nonhuman entities that inhabit it, are of a very different nature.

Captive Spirits and Tree Citizenship

The term *ijniaeene* identifies a broad category of entities whose main characteristic is possession of the skills necessary to pursue humans and inflict illness by means of invisible darts, illnesses that result in the kidnapping of the victim's spirit. Within this category, the Urarina employ the term *nünajiaeene* to identify a class of nonhuman entities, feared for their aggressiveness, who inhabit forest areas characterized by the absence of cultivated fields or signs of human presence (*nünakataan*) (figure 2.1).[1] Among the most dangerous of the *nünajiaeene* are the *ijniaeene* of the trees (*enüa*), whose dangerousness is determined by the arboreal species to which they belong. These, in turn, are ordered hierarchically according to the quantity and toxicity of the bitter substances they secrete.

One main characteristic that differentiates tree *ijniaeene* from similar entities is the habit of living within the interior of trees deep in the forest (*nünaana*), a dwelling that they leave only on rare occasions, for the purpose of approaching human settlements (Fabiano, Schulz, and Martín Brañas 2021). When this happens, these entities remain close to the forest areas that surround populated places (*ajainaa*), as the low vegetation protects them from direct contact with humans. Each *ijniaeene* is linked to a specific tree species and has the power to choose an individual tree, to which it will remain linked until the tree is felled or dies naturally, forcing it to look for a younger specimen unoccupied by another *ijniaeene* of the same species. These entities are greatly feared for their vengeful attitude and extreme aggressiveness, which is often unleashed in response to human activity, perceived as an invasion or an act of deliberate aggression. Therefore, the presence of these spirits requires constant prudence; even so, due to the large number of *ijniaeene* inhabiting the forest, it is a frequent occurrence for a person to accidentally incur a vengeful response from an *ijniaeene* by damaging the roots or trunk of a tree.

The attack pattern of a tree *ijniaeene* is not different from that of other *nünajiaeene*, although its level of organization, aggressiveness, and stalking of human victims is much more effective. Due to the territorial behavior of these entities, those most exposed to this type of attack are men and women

FIGURE 2.1 *Nünajiaeene.* Drawn by Esteban Arahuata Ahuite, Chambira River, 2018.

who engage in agricultural or hunting activities in the forest. However, an *ijniaeene* can also reach human settlements, sometimes located at a considerable distance from the arboreal city where it dwells (a city whose territory extends as far as the plant's roots). In addition to remaining in a state of constant vigilance, these entities possess an extremely sensitive sense of smell that grants them the power to perceive odors at a great distance, especially the aroma that Urarina say children leave on their parents' bodies, which presents a powerful attraction for any type of harmful spirit.

Thanks to the odorous trail left by this fragrance (*saiinaa aunaa*), the *ijniaeene* is able to track its human victim and, taking advantage of the darkness of night, quietly encircle human houses to identify its prey. Only then will the *ijniaeene* send its emissary, a "hunting companion" (*kurianera*) who is in charge of sneaking into the house and attacking the designated victim to make him or her sick (Fabiano 2019). When a person is affected by a tree disease, his or her spirit is captured by the *ijniaeene* causing the attack, an act that can cause the person's death within a short time unless the correct treatment is provided. It is not surprising, therefore, that the efficiency and the intensity of an *ijniaeene* attack demand the intervention of an *ayahuasquero*, a shaman who cures his patients under the influence of ayahuasca, a psychoactive brew extracted from *Banisteriopsis caapi*. Such specialists are summoned to interpret the symptoms and heal the sick person, as well as to carry out an intense search for the captive spirit and its assailant.

The process of assimilation that turns human spirits into citizens of a tree city begins days, and even weeks, before the victim's spirit finds itself inside the tree city, that is, "inside the house" (*lureri asaae enuaa*) of the stalking *ijniaeene*. It begins with the abduction of the victim's spirit on the outskirts of the urban tree space, in what could be considered as the tree's extended periphery, that is, the lands occupied by humans.

Although any kind of *ijniaeene* can launch a pathogenic attack on humans, the most dangerous of these afflictions, known as *janai siinenia* (lit. "real illness"), is that inflicted by trees (*elünai*). Often, the target of such an attack is not the person responsible for having injured the *ijniaeene*'s tree, but one of their family members, preferably a newborn or younger child, whose permeable body is more susceptible to disease (Fabiano 2015, 156–57). When an attack is successful, the first symptoms manifest themselves in the victim through frightful nightmares (*lüaa*) and painful migraines (*kuütüri küna*), which, in some cases, can last several consecutive days. The generality of these symptoms makes this type of condition difficult to identify, allowing the spirit attacker to achieve its objective, namely, to weaken the victim until it is possible to kidnap the human's spirit (*kurii*) and take it to the interior of the tree city. The tree spirits in charge of carrying out this task are the *kumakuri*, entities organized according to a military model, like a platoon of soldiers. According to Medardo, an old Urarina *kuitüküera* (shaman), they are "the army at the service of the tree city, under the command of the *ijni-aeene*, the spirit president."

The actions that lead to the abduction of the human spirit follow a precise pattern. First, after the *ijniaeene* identifies its prey (*pekaa*), one of the *kumak-uri* living in its tree city takes on the task of poisoning the victim's body with a bitter substance (*kuura*), endowed with a characteristic stench (*sainati*). Next, the poisoning makes the human spirit fall into a state of prostration, during which, despite the spirit's remaining in its corporeal seat, the human begins to experience feelings of longing and sadness that quickly lead to apathy and a further weakening of the body. My interlocutors assert that during this phase the victim is constantly pursued by the *kumakuri*, who, moving between dreams and the ordinary world, attack the victim with special darts (*kurichana*), whose poison has an odor that marks the victim as prey. This poison acts quickly and contaminates the blood until it reaches the heart.

It is well known that through the exercise of shamanic functions and dreams (*sinia*), as well as through the consumption of psychotropic preparations, it is possible to separate the spirit from the body in a temporary and reversible way. The disease inflicted by tree spirits produces, in contrast, an extremely harmful separation, as detailed by Medardo:

> When a child gets sick because of a tree *ijniaeene* sometimes it is not easy to understand. In reality, parents become suspicious because the child does not sleep and cries a lot. They say that he cries, but not because he is hungry or cold, but he cries as if scared of something, as if something is chasing you and scaring you, not letting you sleep. Also, adults can see the same thing in their dreams; it is like a jaguar or several jaguars that chase you to devour you. When the child sees this in his nightmares, he cries a lot, because it is the *ijniaeene* that sends him these nightmares, because it wants to kill him. The illness begins like this until it weakens them so much that their [the sick child's] bodies can no longer stand it and their spirit separates until the moment comes when they are stolen and placed in the center of the *ijniaeene's* house.

Despite the violence of the attack, a permanent separation does not occur often. The link between the *kurii* and the body—the physical seat of thoughts, memory, and affect—is strong and is preserved throughout a person's existence and even partly after his death. Indeed, it is this very link that ensures the reversibility of the process of separation and the possibility of avoiding death. This is achieved by rescuing the spirit from its captors and reintroducing it into the victim's body. In any case, the process can be long and painful, and as days go by the bond between the *ijniaeene* and the captive human spirit becomes more and more intense, until the nonhuman entity becomes its *nerüra*, that is, its owner or proprietor.

Phyto-Politics of War and Architecture of Domination

Descriptions of the journey that the abducted spirits must face indicate that the abduction marks the beginning of a well-planned process of assimilation of the human spirit into the urban space governed by the *ijniaeene*. Juan, a man originally from the Tigrillo River, a tributary of the Chambira, uses effective words to highlight the main characteristics of these arboreal cities:

> Each tree has within it people with different functions, this is well known. It is known that all [the trees] are like that, but they don't speak the same languages. The *ijniaeene* know what the others are doing, but they don't communicate. It's like a country where people speak the same language. And each one [of the spirits inside the tree] has its function. Of course, they know that there are other *ijniaeene* [in other trees]. Trees that are ruled by a less strong *ijniaeene* do not seek war with a stronger one. They know each other. That's why [the *ijniaeene*] has several spirits at their command and they understand each other, because each one has its own function, a job in the factories and the crops. It's like it is with the [national] government.

According to my interlocutors, tree cities are the perfect expression of a society of spirits that is governed according to a hierarchical order, whose structure allows subordination or alliance with other tree cities. Above all, it allows the exploitation of captive labor, that is, the labor of the kidnapped human spirits (*rai kacha*). At the top of this organization is the *ijniaeene*, "owner" of the tree and "president" of the city; then come the *letunu*, "foremen" in charge of supervising all productive activities; at a lower level are the *kumakuri*, soldiers who control the city; and last there are the captive human spirits. The ranks are differentiated by function and by the control they can exert over other spirits; together the various spirits make the tree city prosper and grow (figure 2.2).

The oppressive aspect of these cities is expressed through two main traits: the expansionist and predatory logic that governs them, and the specialization of the tiers of spirits in the tree city. As for the first characteristic, the productive system of each city facilitates the unlimited production of goods destined to circulate within and between tree cities, within a strict war logic. The phyto-policy of war, in this sense, aims not at the destruction of other enemy cities, but at the subtraction of their labor force and, therefore, at the expansion of their own productive apparatus.

It is difficult not to find echoes here of Lewis Mumford's ([1961] 2014, 78, 81–82, 120) description of the personality of cities and their constant search for domination. War, as defined by Mumford, is not only connatural to technological development, but inherent to the very nature of cities and their survival strategy, which is based on competition and the destruction of other cities. The attempt to dominate other cities is a manifestation of the city's own personality. It is the externalization of a reality shared by all its inhabitants, that is, submission to a single sovereign *I*, to an authority directed by itself, governing itself, and claiming everything that once belonged to the now diminished *we*. The single exalted *I* becomes the divine representative of the larger community. Vertical urban organization, which according to Mumford finds its ideal model in some species of social insects, is therefore based on the presence of a dominant entity that symbolizes life (reproduction), protection, and its ultimate goal: a sectorized organization of labor, a strong specialized military caste, subjugation of the environment, and fratricidal confrontation between communities for the domination of the territory and its resources.

In terms of political topography, and therefore also of the spatial logic that organizes the life of tree cities, Urarina testimonies emphasize the fact that their subjugating force is profoundly intertwined with the very characteristics of the city. Their extension, dimensions, and urban model are emphatically indicated in Urarina narratives, providing the setting through which notions of domination and control are objectified. This topography of subjugation is particularly clear in light of the tree city's architecture. Narrators emphasize the buildings, whose architecture is repeated in an identical manner and suggests a strict control over any type of divergent spatiality; the streets, which follow a strict orthogonal plan and reproduce the urban plan-

FIGURE 2.2 The lupuna (*Chorisia integrifolia*) tree city, with the *ijniaeene* president of the arboreal city in the upper section, dressed in a bowler hat and a spotted suit. Below there is a captive human spirit near a table. Farther down there is an armed *letunu*, and at the base of the tree there is an army of *kumakuri*. Drawn by Esteban Arahuata Ahuite, Chambira River, 2017.

ning of the great cities, and which increase captives' sense of disorientation; and the great central plaza, a central point of urban life dominated by the *ijniaeene*'s mansion, which centralizes the life of the tree city and increases the panoptic power of the presiding spirit. Likewise, the narrow spaces seem to encourage a proximity (if not real interaction) between the captive spirits, whereas the convergent movements of the captive spirits symbolically articulate the synchronized temporalities that govern production and life in general. The Urarina people's architectural imaginary—and, more generally, their urban imaginary—seems not only to derive from an extreme process of selection of the characteristics that, according to my interlocutors, fully describe industrial cities, but also to embody established signifiers in the Urarina imaginary. The origin of these signifiers can be clearly traced to the primeval experience of domination and the loss of autonomy in relation to white and mestizo people.

Order and Hierarchy: The Concentric Space of Production

Each element, each encounter, each moment following the entry of a human spirit into the tree city and throughout the whole period that it will spend in this immense urban space seems to be organized to induce acceptance of the captive population's new situation, conditioned by a strict repetition and rationalization of actions. From the beginning, the captive spirit is forced to dedicate itself to production according to a model that very soon—and for the greater benefit of the tree city—becomes a habit.

The first image presented to the eyes of human spirits is a terrifying spectacle that serves the purpose of impressing newcomers. The territory that is revealed upon one's entering the tree is immense, "almost endless." The extension of these enormous cities is overwhelming; the geometric separation of their spaces is precise and functional. Enormous factories that produce all kinds of artifacts stand next to immense corrals in which countless heads of cattle are raised. A constant flow of manufactured products (*leeucha atane kaje ünaa rüküele*, lit. "things that come from somewhere else") leaves the factory gates to be moved to the *ijniaeene*'s mansion: it is the heartbeat of the tree city that drives its inhabitants, forcing them into a constant movement that fills the streets and covers every space.

Despite the verticality that characterizes the biological development of trees, the topography of the large extensions occupied by these megalop- olises reproduces a concentric vegetal model that unfolds in a horizontal plane (Gow 1987, 117), in which each ring corresponds to an extremely spe- cialized function. This model emphasizes the symbolic construction of hu- man space while at the same time introducing some important differences. Unlike human cities, where concentric sociospatiality attributes greater on- tological distance to greater geographic distance, arboreal cities use distance to mark humans' entry into the sphere of the "locals" and their transforma- tion into tree spirits. Captive spirits acquire the faculty to circulate in the outermost rings only when they have acquired complete "citizenship" in the tree city. Until then, they are held at the center of the city.

Tree cities, then, dissociate human captives from familiarity, kinship, and security by imposing a spatiality and temporality that subvert the processes of human communication and exchange. Such an inversion corresponds to a "dendritic model" that generates an ontological cartography in which the captive human spirits (the outsiders, the Others) occupy the center of the metropolis until they are permanently assimilated into the organization of the city. This takes place when the bonds with their human bodies have been dissolved and they have overcome the state of undeath, during which they still preserve the memories and thoughts of their previous life.

Urarina narratives suggest that this condition of subordination (*sürürüraa*) is the result of a normalized temporality and spatiality, obtained thanks to the constant vigilance of the *ijniaeene* and the spirits subordinated to it— *kumakuri* and *letunu*—and to the implementation of a strict protocol. If the captive spirits are not able to escape, this does not mean that, especially at the beginning, they passively accept their condition as slaves (figure 2.3). However, the city has a scheme of assimilation to the life of the tree that ex- cludes any kind of insubordination or attempt to escape. First, captive spirits are accompanied into the tree city by a gregarious spirit and go through a process of registration before they are allowed to enter and mingle with the mass of workers living inside the tree. Each spirit passes through an office and is given a code that resembles what might be found on an identity card. From this moment on, the number given to it will be a sign of recognition visible only to the spirits of the tree and marking unequivocally the conver- sion of the human into property. This system of accounting not only allows

FIGURE 2.3 Two tree spirits, one dressed in a camouflage suit and armed with a shotgun and the other wearing a dark-colored tunic, drag a captive human spirit to the *ijniaeene*'s mansion. Drawn by Esteban Arahuata Ahuite, Chambira River, 2016.

the spirits in charge of security and the operation of the city to recognize the captives; it also enables the *ijniaeene* to trade in human spirits, either in order to negotiate an alliance with a neighboring tree city or in order to acquire some benefit (Fabiano 2021, 2022).

Humans thus become part of the tree city, citizens of the great metropolis owned by the *ijniaeene*, although the memory of their previous life persists. After receiving their identification number, captives are given new clothes. They all receive a uniform: "city clothes," shoes, and a watch. Each object is new, always of the same color and model. My interlocutors commented to me in amazement that this clothing is made of the best fabric, the shoes are sturdy, and the watch is made of shiny metal, as if these objects had just left the factory. "None of the spirits will be left without a gift [*belaiia*]," Julián explained to me, "but none will be given the chance to give up what they received: everything will be needed for the work that awaits them."

Once the registration formalities are completed and entrance to the city is authorized, the captive spirit with its new clothes is accompanied to the chamber of the *ijniaeene*, the spirit with the highest rank in the tree hierarchy. Shamans agree that what happens from this moment on, although not immediately visible in the human world, induces a rapid process of deterioration of the victim's body, which makes rescuing the captive spirit an extremely difficult undertaking.

The main spirit's mansion, located in the center of the tree city, occupies an entire side of the rectangle that delimits the perimeter of the main square. The view of this building is so amazing that no one puts up any resistance, as if, by crossing the gate that separates the residence of the *ijniaeene* from the rest of the city, captives experience a feeling of acceptance and adopt a submissive attitude. The entrances to the house, carved with the same type of river stone used to sharpen machetes and other cutting tools, have the power to "scrape" from captives their rebelliousness, the nostalgia for their villages, and the feeling of sadness that they might experience when hearing words spoken in their native language. The mansion's interior is permanently illuminated by an enormous quantity of lamps and electrical appliances, industrial objects and devices occupy every free space, and enormous rolls of high-quality fabric pile up to the ceiling. Everything in this place is meant to arouse the astonishment of visitors, who are induced to measure the greatness of the presiding *ijniaeene* and the magnificence of its tree city according to the quantity and quality of the stored goods. Then, the captive spirit is guided through several halls, all identical to one another, until it reaches the last door, which, after being crossed, allows direct access to the "office" of the *ijniaeene*. This last room occupies the central part of the building and, therefore, of the tree city itself. In its interior, behind an enormous table of fine wood, the *ijniaeene* is seated on a throne. At its back, shelves full of books cover the wall, while at the ends of the desk, one on each side, two jaguars of enormous size sit peacefully. After the captive spirit has entered the room, the main door closes silently, and through several secondary entrances of lesser size the chiefs of the gregarious *kumakuri* and *letunu* spirits enter and arrange themselves around the desk until they completely fill the place in rows ordered according to their rank.

Only the *letunu*, the higher-ranking spirits, are allowed to approach the *ijniaeene* to share information and receive instructions on the day's tasks. These are then distributed among the lower-ranking spirits and the entire tree city. Exchanges of words are quick and carried out in a language incomprehensible to human spirits, a language unique to the species of the tree city. The information that the *ijniaeene* receives passes from mouth to mouth, from the lowest-ranking spirits of the army, through the generals, up to the *letunu*, the only ones authorized to communicate directly with him.

Once the extensive ceremony is over, the *ijniaeene* opens a large book located in the middle of his desk and writes down the captive's new name, which is a representation of the olfactory mark of the poison used to capture him, written in an alphabet that is incomprehensible to human beings. After writing the new name, the *ijniaeene* offers the captive a piece of raw meat. Finally, the captive is put under the care of the lower-ranking spirits, thus beginning to "live with foreign people" (*leeucha atane ichaua küüa*). At this point there are evident analogies with some elements of Catholic rituals. The ceremony of "baptism," associated with the acquisition of a new name and its officialization through writing, and the ritual ingestion of meat offered directly from the hands of the *ijniaeene*, which recalls the Eucharist, complement the descriptions of the *ijniaeene*, who are represented as European missionaries, with dark cassocks, light complexions, and long beards (figure 2.4). A more thorough explanation of this aspect of the Urarina's "ontohistorical" discourse (Medrano and Tola 2016) exceeds the purpose of this chapter and is the object of research still in progress. However, it is worth mentioning how various elements associated with the tree cities probably derive from the historical memory of the encounter with the first

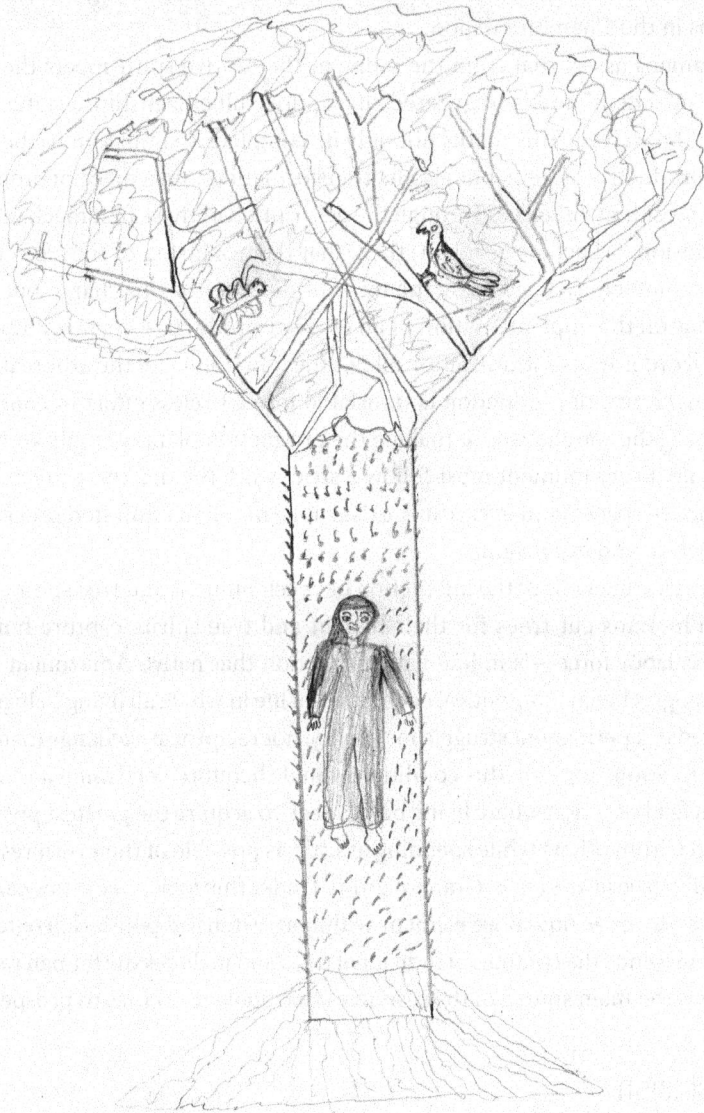

FIGURE 2.4 *Ijniaeene* wearing a dark-colored tunic. Drawn by Esteban Arahuata Ahuite, Chambira River, 2017.

Jesuit missionaries and their earliest attempts at evangelizing the Urarina groups in the Chambira region.

Shamans assert that from the moment the captive spirit meets the tree city's "president" and is "registered," it acquires full citizenship, a status that cannot be waived. This marks not only its complete assimilation to the tree city's productive system, but also its transformation into a piece of property of the presiding *ijniaeene*. Through the description of these first mechanisms of inclusion, it becomes evident, then, that the expansion of the tree city is not guaranteed exclusively by the force of the *ijniaeene* in charge but also depends on the implementation of an efficient productive organization and a social order whose stratification allows the functioning of the arboreal city. The imperative of production is translated into a tireless effort to continue supplying the warehouses or making the production plants comply with the schedule. Every moment must follow a strict work regime, there are no unproductive spaces, and everything exists in terms of an unlimited process of production and expansion.

This Urarina view of the interaction between humans and tree spirits—by which humans cut trees for their benefit and tree spirits capture human souls as labor force—is in line with the notion that native Amazonian eco-cosmologies behave as political economies of life in which all living beings are engaged in a permanent struggle for vitality, not reciprocal exchange (Santos-Granero 2009, 205–7). This condition would therefore determine a cosmological field of action where living beings seek to acquire the greatest possible life force from others while spending as little as possible of their own reserve of vitality (see also Santos-Granero 2019). Under this logic, tree cities cannot survive except as one more element within an extensive political geography that transcends the confines of individual trees and includes the human realm, which is the main source of the resources that allow tree cities to prosper.

Conclusion

The link between the prosperous invisible cities and the wealthy white people is perhaps one of the themes that most characterizes the scarce literature on urban imaginaries in native Amazonian societies. Under this logic, the relationship between the real experience of contemporary or past urban centers and the invisible cities mentioned in shamanic discourses is inscribed within a geography that recognizes the existence of simultaneously present and often connected, though not always perceptible, worlds

(Lagrou 1998, 31), and grants each of them differentiated spatial and temporal regimes.

Despite the differences between the stories, or the emphasis that the narrators place on their own descriptions, there seems to be a general pattern in Urarina imaginaries of the city. Undoubtedly, ethnographic data collected in other contemporary Indigenous societies insists on evidencing a stereotyped association between cities and white people, capitalist consumer culture, and political and social domination. One possible interpretation is that these places have become spaces through which Indigenous societies seek to reappropriate, albeit in an extraordinary dimension, the material wealth that was denied to them. However, the Urarina case demonstrates the limits of unequivocally interpreting these places as "Indigenous utopias" or alternative realities to the non-Indigenous world (Pitarch 2012, 79).

It is clear that the description of the enormous tree cities offered by my interlocutors is associated with their memories of white people's cities. I suggest, however, that in the Urarina case these places are not simply more or less faithful copies of a non-Indigenous reality filtered through the alienation or spatial and temporal distortion described in Julián's narrative. The data makes me think that the Urarina characterization of tree cities fulfills the purpose of translating an asymmetrical social morphology, by means of both a precise urban structure and its logic of operation. Indeed, these cities offer a concrete urban imaginary, ostensibly representing an uncritical understanding of the ordinary world, while on a deeper level confronting the model of modernity based on a productivist rationality.

As indicated by Pedro Pitarch (2012, 83–84), Indigenous virtual worlds are saturated with merchandise and adopt a more Western physiognomy as a function of greater and more intense European presence. According to Pitarch, mediation with the Euro-American world occurs mainly in the field of Indigenous virtual worlds rather than in the area of ordinary social relations and is closely related to the Indigenous valuation of industrial products. Thus, in proportion to European pressure, the mediating function of goods is also intensified through the moral language of Indigenous social relations. This is why the Indigenous souls that inhabit these virtual worlds have access to European goods and body styles, but not to what we would call Western ideologies and institutions.

While useful in explaining Indigenous theories in relation to the notion of modernity, Pitarch's proposal does not, in my view, allow for an in-depth analysis of the specificities of the Urarina case. Despite the existence of a model that points toward an unlimited increase in production, the characteristics of the Urarina people's dendritic cities suggest a different meaning for the overabundance of merchandise, insofar as these captive spirits have access not to the products they produce but precisely to the exacerbated experience of Western ideologies and institutions. The knowledge of and contact with these places would thus become a form of learning that offers the possibility of accessing the concrete experience of a virtuality in which a non-Indigenous normative order is brought to a paroxysm. This is an experience that is both extreme and dangerous, one that strengthens the definition of a political behavior whose objective is the denaturalization of models of social control through the construction and experience of divergent worlds.

We could, therefore, analyze these urban imaginaries not as if they were just an epiphenomenon of the history of contact with white people or of the recent processes of urbanization of Amazonian territories, but rather as an attempt by Indigenous Amazonian societies to reflect on and reconstruct on their own terms the meanings of their experiences of subordination and domination on which current relations of power and dependence are based. In this sense, the historical memory of the events that have had a profound impact on Indigenous life survives—and is constantly being updated—through access to an urban imaginary in which these events are still present in an exacerbated manner.

Acknowledgments

The author thanks Graeme Burnley, Joshua Homan, and Manolo Martín Brañas for their valuable help in the revision, correction, and translation phases of this text. This work was supported by the project "ECO—Animals and Plants in Cultural Productions About the Amazon River Basin," managed by the Centro de Estudos Sociais, Universidade de Coimbra, and financed by the European Research Council (Program H2020, grant agreement number 101002359).

Note

1.   For a more detailed analysis of the complex Urarina classifications of the different types of ecosystems in the Chambira region, see Schulz et al. 2019a and 2019b.

References

Alexiades, Miguel. 2009. Introduction to *Mobility and Migration in Indigenous Amazonia: Contemporary Ethnoecological Perspectives*, edited by Miguel Alexiades, 1–43. Oxford: Berghahn Press.

Alexiades, Miguel, and Daniela Peluso. 2015. "Introduction: Indigenous Urbanization in Lowland South America." In Peluso 2015, 1–12.

Andrade, Jose Agnello, Rodrigo Chiquetto, and Yuri Bassichetto Tambucci. 2009. "Paisagens ameríndias urbanas de Manaus, no Amazonas: primeiros olhares." *Ponto Urbe: Revista do Núcleo de Antropologia Urbana da USP* 4. https://doi.org/10.4000/pontourbe.1988.

Cesarino, Pedro de Niemeyer. 2008. "Babel da floresta, cidades dos brancos? Os Marubo no trânsito entre dois mundos." *Novos estudos* 82:133–48.

Dean, Bartholomew. 1995. "Múltiples regímenes de valor: intercambio desigual y la circulación de bienes intercambiables de fibra de palmera entre los Urarina." *Amazonia Peruana* 25:25–118.

Dean, Bartholomew. 2004. "Ambivalent Exchanges: The Violence of Patronazgo in the Upper Amazon." In *Cultural Construction of Violence: Victimization, Escalation, Response*, edited by Myrdene Anderson, 214–26. West Lafayette, Ind.: Purdue University.

Dean, Bartholomew. 2009. *Urarina Society, Cosmology, and History in Peruvian Amazonia*. Gainesville: University Press of Florida.

Espinosa de Rivero, Oscar. 2009. "Ciudad e identidad cultural: ¿Cómo se relacionan con lo urbano los indígenas amazónicos peruanos en el siglo XXI?" *Bulletin de l'Institut Français d'Études Andines* 38 (1): 47–59.

Fabiano, Emanuele. 2015. "Le corps mange, tout comme ma pensée soigne: construction des corps et techniques de contamination dans la pratique chamanique Urarina." PhD diss., École des Hautes Études en Sciences Sociales.

Fabiano, Emanuele. 2017. "Dos corazones: etnofisiología y procesos de pensamiento/memoria entre los Urarina de la Amazonía peruana." In *El corazón es centro: narraciones, representaciones y metáforas del corazón en el mundo hispánico*, edited by Antonella Cancellier, Alessia Cassani, and Elena Dal Maso, 223–40. Padua, Italy: Cooperativa Libraria Editrice Università di Padova.

Fabiano, Emanuele. 2019. "Lo sciamanismo e le arti della contaminazione: Processi di apprendistato e tecniche di cura tra gli Urarina dell'Amazzonia peruviana." In *Il Cosmo Sciamnico: Ontologie indigene fra Asia e Americhe*, edited by Stefano Beggiora, 285–308. Milan: FrancoAngeli.

Fabiano, Emanuele. 2021. "The Spirits of Extractivism: Non-Human Meddling, Shamanic Diplomacy, and Cosmo-Political Strategy Among the Urarina (Peruvian Amazon)." In *Dealing with Disasters: Palgrave Studies in Disaster Anthropology*, edited by Diana Riboli, Pamela Stewart, Andrew Strathern, and Davide Torri, 43–74. Cham: Palgrave Macmillan.

Fabiano, Emanuele. 2022. "Las enfermedades son espíritus modernos que aprenden en la ciudad: representación urarina de la enfermedad infecciosa del sarampión." In *Las enfermedades que llegan de lejos: los pueblos amazónicos del Perú frente las epidemias de ayer y a la COVID-19*, edited by Oscar Espinosa de Rivero and Emanuele Fabiano, 195–206. Lima: Fondo Editorial de la Pontificia Universidad Católica del Perú.

Fabiano, Emanuele, Graeme Burnley, and Samuel Nuribe Arahuata. 2022. *Inuaelü nenakaaürüte karitiin nereretaaüre. Ninichu kuruuaje nenakaaürü Urarinaaürü nereretaau / The Ancestors Told Me: Urarina Myths and Stories from the Lower Chambira.* Lima: Centro Amazónico de Antropología y Aplicación Práctica.

Fabiano, Emanuele, Christopher Schulz, and Manuel Martín Brañas. 2021. "Wetland Spirits and Indigenous Knowledge: Implications for the Conservation of Wetlands in the Peruvian Amazon." *Current Research in Environmental Sustainability* 3:100–107.

Gow, Peter. 1987. "La vida monstruosa de las plantas." *Amazonia Peruana* 8 (14): 115–21.

Homan, Joshua. 2018. "Inga Rimakkuna: Indigenous Frontiers in the Pastaza Basin, Peru." PhD diss., University of Kansas.

Horta, Amanda. 2017. "Indígenas em Canarana: notas citadinas sobre a criatividade parque-xinguana." *Revista de Antropologia* 60 (1): 216–41.

Hugh-Jones, Stephen. 2018. "Su riqueza es nuestra riqueza: perspectivas interculturales de objetos o gaheuni." In *Objetos como testigos del contacto cultural: perspectivas interculturales de la historia y del presente de las poblaciones indígenas del Alto Río Negro (Brasil/Colombia)*, edited by Michael Kraus, Ernst Halbmayer, and Ingrid Kummels, 197–226. Berlin: Ibero-American Institute.

Kramer, Betty Jo. 1979. "Urarina Economy and Society: Tradition and Change." PhD diss., Columbia University.

Lagrou, Els. 1998. "Caminhos, duplos e corpos: uma abordagem perspectivista da identidade e alteridade entre os Kaxinawá." PhD diss., Universidade de São Paulo.

Lagrou, Els. 2013. "Chaquira, el inka y los blancos: las cuentas de vidrio en los mitos y en el ritual kaxinawa y amerindio." *Revista Española de Antropología Americana* 43 (1): 245–65.

McSweeney, Kendra, and Brad Jokisch. 2015. "Native Amazonians' Strategic Urbanization: Shaping Territorial Possibilities Through Cities." In Peluso 2015, 13–33.

Medrano, María Celeste, and Florencia Carmen Tola. 2016. "Cuando humanos y no-humanos componen el pasado: ontohistoria en el Chaco." *Avá* 29:99–129.

Mumford, Lewis. (1961) 2014. *La ciudad en la historia: sus orígenes, transformaciones y perspectivas.* Logroño, Spain: Pepitas de Calabaza Editores.

Nunes, Eduardo Soares. 2010. "Aldeias urbanas ou cidades indígenas? Reflexões sobre índios e ciudades." *Espaço Ameríndio* 4 (1): 9–30.

Peluso, Daniela, ed. 2015. "Indigenous Urbanization: The Circulation of Peoples Between Rural and Urban Amazonian Spaces." Special issue, *Journal of Latin American and Caribbean Anthropology* 20 (1).

Peña Márquez, Juan Carlos. 2011. *Mitú: ciudad amazónica, territorialidad indígena.* Leticia: Universidad Nacional de Colombia.

Pereira, Hamida, and Iraildes Caldas Torres. 2008. "A imagem da cidade: cotidiano, sonhos e utopias dos moradores do Cacau Pirêra-Iranduba (AM)." *Somanlu: Revista de Estudos Amazônicos* 8 (1): 25–42.

Pitarch, Pedro. 2012. "La ciudad de los espíritus europeos: notas sobre la modernidad de los mundos virtuales indígenas." In *Modernidades indígenas*, edited by Pedro Pitarch and Gemma Orobitg, 61–87. Madrid: Iberoamericana Editorial Vervuert.

Santos-Granero, Fernando. 2009. *Vital Enemies: Slavery, Predation, and the Amerindian Political Economy of Life.* Austin: University of Texas Press.

Santos-Granero, Fernando. 2019. "Amerindian Political Economies of Life." *HAU: Journal of Ethnographic Theory* 9 (2): 461–82.

Santos-Granero, Fernando, and Frederica Barclay. 2002. *La frontera domesticada: historia económica y social de Loreto, 1850–2000.* Lima: Fondo Editorial Pontificia Universidad Católica del Perú.

Schulz, Christopher, Manuel Martín Brañas, Cecilia Nuñez Pérez, Margarita del Aguila Villacorta, Nina Laurie, Ian Lawson, and Katherine Roucoux. 2019a. "Peatland and Wetland Ecosystems in Peruvian Amazonia." *Ecology and Society* 24 (2). https://doi.org/10.5751/ES-10886-240212.

Schulz, Christopher, Manuel Martín Brañas, Cecilia Nuñez Pérez, Margarita Del Aguila Villacorta, Nina Laurie, Ian Lawson, and Katherine Roucoux. 2019b. "Uses, Cultural Significance, and Management of Peatlands in the Peruvian Amazon: Implications for Conservation." *Biological Conservation* 235:189–98.

Walker, Harry. 2012. "Demonic Trade: Debt, Materiality, and Agency in Amazonia." *Journal of the Royal Anthropological Institute* 18:140–59.

Walker, Harry. 2013. "Wild Things: Manufacturing Desire in the Urarina Moral Economy." *Journal of Latin American and Caribbean Anthropology* 18 (1): 51–66.

CHAPTER 3

A Tale of Three Cities

Power Relations amid Ese Eja Urban Imaginaries

DANIELA PELUSO

In a recent work, Miguel Alexiades and I (2015, 7) examined Indigenous urbanization in Amazonia as sets of multidirectional processes that are "often
highly contingent and situational not as a simple or permanent migration to
a city, but rather as part of an ongoing circulation of people that connects
different communities, towns, and multiple-sited dwellings" (see also Alexiades and Peluso 2016; Peluso 2015a; Peluso and Alexiades 2005). Urbanization
is often opportunistic and inspired by an ever-increasing range of drivers,
the most common being labor opportunities, schooling, political work, and
an escape from village conflicts. I have described how urban areas become
villages and how villages become urban, but most importantly how these
processes ultimately begin in people's minds long before they physically
take place, and hence the idea that "urbanization begins at home" (Peluso
2004a, 1). The political stake in such analyses has been to denounce forms
of representation, outreach, and development that trap Indigenous lowland
South American peoples into strictly rural images that uphold unsustainable
stereotypes that are then turned against them. For instance, encroaching
extractive economies leverage images of urbanity to legitimize their expansion of activities to Indigenous lands and processes of deterritorialization
(McSweeney and Jokisch 2015; Peluso, forthcoming). Here, I expand on this
body of work by discussing a nonvisible place as a tacit meeting point between cross realities and different kinds of urbanity—cities of humans, nonhumans, and living and nonliving Others—with the caveat that humanity

is a shared sense of being and that living continues beyond what we might refer to as life.

Amazonian cities are not always visible to the eye of the external observer. Particular types of cities are part of the nonvisible world of human Others; these shape and are shaped by Amazonian rural-urban and creation narrative imagery, as well as the sociospatial knowledge of earthly and cross realities. Numerous scholars document Amazonians' knowledge of villages or cities that exist underwater (Slater 1994), underground (Gow 1994, 2011), or in the overworld (Gow 2001; Kopenawa and Albert 2013; Politis and Saunders 2002). As Peter Gow (2011) has speculated, it is even possible to imagine how Amazonian Piro (Yine) stories about places such as the underworld cities of the white-lipped peccaries might be linked to the former urban centers of the Upper Xingu (see also Heckenberger 2004). Such an analysis potentially identifies the kinds of cities described by Amazonians in their creation stories as residues of a historical but largely forgotten past. These lines of thought build on scholarship that increasingly verifies how several pre-Columbian Amazonian settlements were large scale, urban, centralized, densely populated, and stratified (Denevan 1992; Erickson 2006; Heckenberger et al. 2008), an image that challenges deeply rooted misconceptions of pre-Columbian Amazonia as an area of pristine wilderness with minimal human impact on the environment and settlements that were nondynamic (Fausto and Heckenberger 2007; Alexiades 2009). As Michael J. Heckenberger (2004, 39–41) has argued,

The great shock comes not so much upon realization of the massive physical scale of earthworks, almost ubiquitous in terminal prehistoric settlements, although that is indeed surprising. The real eye-opener is experienced when the ancient and sophisticated architectural plan is revealed in its entirety. The great fortified towns of the remote past, over ten times the size of contemporary villages, and vast deforested agricultural areas associated with them document an unexpectedly dramatic and intentional transformation of the prehistoric landscape. The distribution of settlements, roads, pathways, ports and other sites, demonstrates that in the past, like today, the built environment was integrated across a much broader area, extending well beyond the village areas themselves. Across the region there were many of these villages, undoubtedly home to a large late prehistoric population, numbering in the tens of thousands, densely settled in large, permanent settlements, some likely numbering in the thousands, throughout much of the Upper Xingu basin.

Given such poignant accounts, it is likely that knowledge of great settlements in the past has directly or indirectly played out in Amazonian dwellers' imaginations just as current modern cities likely continue to shape their references to nonvisible cities. Indeed, knowledge and visits to pre-Columbian Andean cities may have also shaped these imaginaries (Santos-Granero, this volume). Amazonian cities or large towns crystallize the social hierarchies in which rural Amazonians are stationed (Peluso 2003). As Rupert Stasch (2017, 449) points out, when people live in multiple places they form part of a larger geographic space where social differences become acute. This means that rural people who live in more than one place "live in hierarchical disparities between those places." Furthermore, locales are not merely produced by groups (Santos-Granero 2005) but accentuated by urbanization, and thus locality is coproduced among collectivities not just in terms of the imagination but through a wide range of ways and forms as people navigate and circulate within such spaces (Peluso 2015b).

Nonvisible cities have featured in the Western imaginary of Amazonia for centuries, reaching mythic status. Such imaginaries serve as extensions of ongoing settler-colonialist power structures that subjugate Indigenous peoples. The most famous such cities are El Dorado and the Lost City of Z. Although these allegedly spectacular and resource-rich cities have never been located despite numerous expeditions, the desire to know them has historically resulted in the surveying, mapping, and conversion of "terra incognita into bounded colonial territories" (Burnett 2001, xii). Indeed, the pursuit for the "discovery" of such places continues today as evidenced by Jamin Thierry's (2006) ongoing relentless search for Paititi. There are also the nonvisible cities of creation narratives as well as those that exist contemporarily alongside the human world. Some of these cities belong to nonvisible beings. For Runa peoples these can be found within landmarks such as volcanoes (Guzmán-Gallegos 2015). Many such cities are in the underworld or sky and can belong exclusively to particular nonhuman animal groups such as jaguars and peccaries or, as for Ese Eja peoples, the underwater anaconda (Peluso 2004b).

Shamans can access crossroads between humans and nonvisible beings and their villages or cities. Such portals can also be accessed by nonspecialists through the use of psychoactive plants (Prance 1970; Arévalo Varela 1986) and through activities and processes that entail or evoke altered states of consciousness such as dreaming, hunting, being ill, being solitary, and participating in rituals (Peluso 2003, 2004b; Opas 2005; Santos-Granero 2012; Mezzenzana 2018). Indeed, it is in these states of increased vulnerability that cross realities can potentially be bridged. There are numerous accounts of nonhuman Others approaching humans to come and live with them in their village, city, or world, usually through temptation, seduction, or abduction. For instance, for Ese Eja, the anaconda can tempt children and adults toward a new place of habitation with the lures of technology and sex, as well as promises of pleasure and abundance (Peluso 2003, 2004b). Michael A. Uzendoski (2004, 888) has recorded accounts among the Runa where beautiful and exotic spirit women have taken men away "to 'serve' as mayors or other administrators in cities in the underworld," instances that Francesca Mezzenzana (2018) refers to in terms of seduction (see also Larochelle 2012). In many cases such narratives explicitly describe thriving nonvisible cities that are also the sources of technology on which modern cities are founded, a point I will return to later (Civrieux [1970] 1997; Kohn 2009; Guzmán-Gallegos 2015). The knowledge of these metropoles is widespread and for the most part remains in the background of daily life unless for particular reasons it becomes important.

In this chapter, I discuss another kind of nonvisible city, the land of the dead. I suggest that the terra incognita of all invisible cities ontologically encompasses vestiges and reserves for nonvisible beings and living mortals who are still able to understand the world as one that is multiple, regenerative, and potentially transformative. While often interpreted as mythical or imaginary, invisible cities comprise cross realities that not only affect everyday life to varying degrees at particular moments in time, but also are perceived to be awaiting us in the future.

The following story takes place in Puerto Maldonado, the regional capital of Madre de Dios, Peru, in 1995. It is here that the Ese Eja from Sonene encountered a mysterious girl. Ese Eja people are part of a lowland Amazonian ethnic group comprising about 2,500 individuals living in eight communities along the Beni, Madre de Dios, Heath, Orton, and Tambopata Rivers along the border regions of Pando, Bolivia, and Madre de Dios, Peru (map 3.1).[1] Most Ese Eja are swidden horticulturalists who also hunt, fish, and gather, as well as extract and process forest resources for their own consumption and

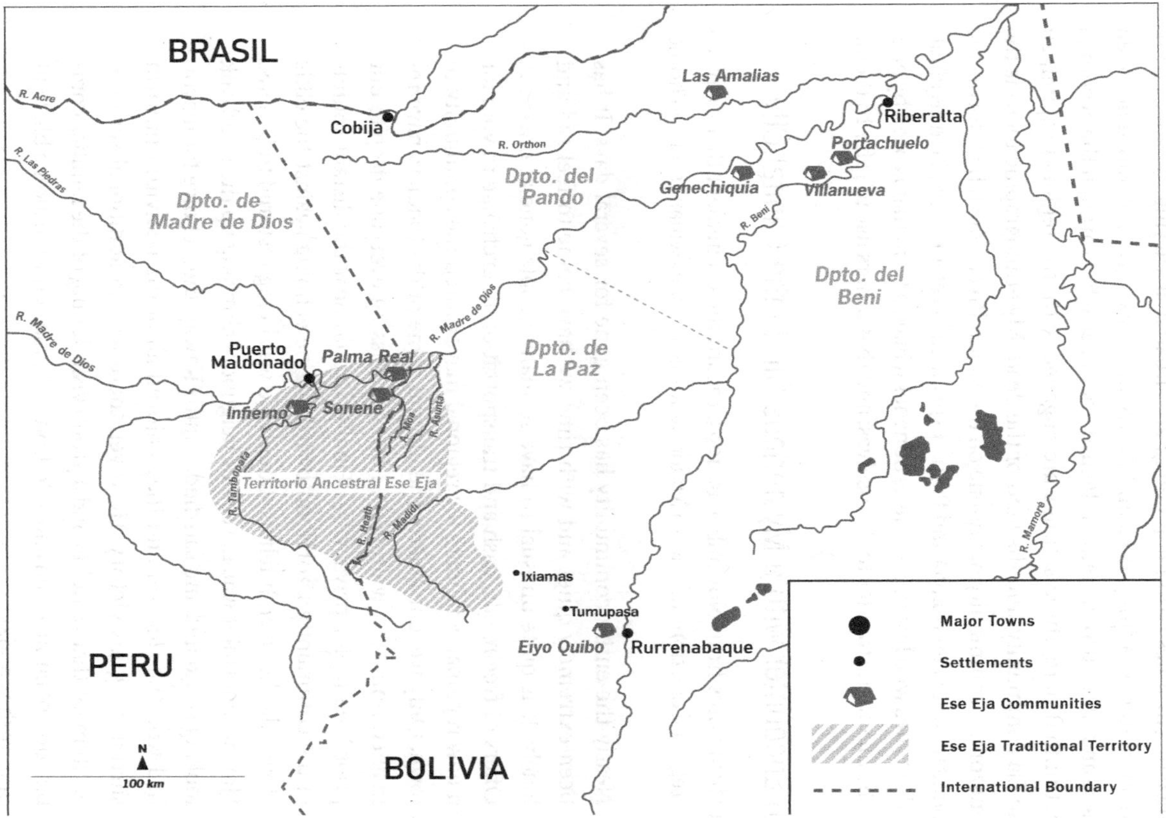

MAP 3.1 Map of Ese Eja communities. Crafted by Miguel Alexiades.

for commercial trade; they also periodically and variably engage in forms of labor with townsfolk. Ese Eja, who live in communities spread over a distance of 310 miles (500 kilometers), are situated at varying distances from urban centers spanning Peru and Bolivia; increasingly, they move between these and other urban centers (Peluso 2004a, 2015b). Through the accounts that unfold here, three settings are engaged with: the regional capital, an Ese Eja community, and the land of the dead. My ethnographic focus is the Amazonian community of Sonene on the Heath River, which here forms the boundary between Bolivia and Peru.[2] I specifically refer to Ese Eja individuals and families who live in Sonene as Sonenekwiñaji, a term that is used by people from Sonene to refer to themselves, and that others use to refer to them.[3]

An Encounter with a Mysterious Girl in the Capital City

My field notes from November 15, 1995, record the excitement that followed the regional elections in Puerto Maldonado, as Sonenekwiñaji returned home:

> Nearly the entire community has been gone for several days. It has been extremely quiet and with time we have come to feel sad and lonely. It is quite unusual to have so many people gone at once. . . . Offers of free meals, cash and transportation in exchange to vote for a new regional candidate for regional mayor lured the community to town. Only we, our elderly friends and some of the toddlers have remained home . . . waiting. . . . We are missing everyone despite our prior longing for privacy. . . . Finally, I could hear the distant sounds of the community's 20HP outboard engine echoing against the cliffs alongside the river. It felt as though life was being restored to Sonene. How wonderful it was to see our neighbors climbing up the riverbank looking so excited and satisfied. Santos Kaway, their choice for mayor, had won the election and they enjoyed all of the festivities in town surrounding his victory. However, there was an additional sense of excitement that went beyond a group visit. It rang of the familiar combination of enthusiasm and agitation that is so common after a big fight or a fresh scandal.

For days after their return from the regional elections, Sonenekwiñaji excitedly spoke about their encounter in Puerto Maldonado with an unusual *deja* (outsider) girl.[4] Individuals—no matter what age—seemed distressed to have met her. Over and over again they recalled their experiences surrounding meeting her and the details that followed as if each time they repeated the story there lay a new possibility that could lead them to uncover a forgotten detail or clue that would eventually unravel the mystery of this encounter. It is from conversations in front of Shasha's house that I thread together snippets of one of these numerous conversations.

The account unfolds as follows: The morning after everyone arrived in town, Shasha's husband, Iba', encountered a young girl of approximately eight years of age begging for bread in the town market (figure 3.1). Shasha explained: "Iba' was watching this girl pleading with people to buy her bread—and he couldn't believe that she was a *deja*! Iba' kept looking to see if someone was with her but she was alone. She was very thin!" Someone else added, "He gave her some bread and she stuffed it in her mouth with both hands as though she hadn't eaten in days! We felt so sorry for her—that is why we fed her. We pitied her!" During the three days that Sonenekwiñaji stayed in

FIGURE 3.1 Ese Eja notice the *deja* girl in the marketplace. Drawn by Sydney Acosta Solizonquehua.

town they continuously shared food with this girl and let her stay with them. Shasha enthusiastically continued, "From that moment on she tagged behind Iba' and the children and followed them all back to the communal house [the shabby empty rooms on top of the native federation's communal house, where, in the early 1990s, Ese Eja usually slept when in Puerto Maldonado, when they were not sleeping in their canoes]. We fed her again. She kept asking us for food." My neighbor added, "We felt very, very sorry for her." Shasha's daughter added, "When we brought her food and drink she would grab it from us." More neighbors explained: "She followed us everywhere we went," "She wanted to be with us adults," "She wasn't interested in playing with the children." And a young girl added, "I was afraid of her!"

What seemed especially eerie and intriguing to them was that this girl insisted that she did not have parents and did not have a name. Shasha explained: "Everyone has a name, a mother and father. Yet, when we asked her for her name she said, 'I have no name.' When we asked her who her parents are she told us, 'I do not have a mother or father!' But someone must be watching over her!" An elderly woman who had not gone to Puerto Maldonado added, "It cannot be that someone does not have a name. Maybe she just doesn't know her name. And even if she was thrown away, someone must have raised her!" Cobishawa agreed: "Even savages like the Iñapaere don't leave their children to die!"[5]

Overall, there was a general feeling that the girl had something inexplicable and strange about her. As Ese Eja navigated the town along the routes that they tend to take, they questioned and requestioned her and looked for signs to see whether she was familiar with the town, but they could not find any.[6] Also worrisome were incidents when she seemed to understand the Ese Eja language. Ese Eja are not accustomed to *deja* understanding their language. This unfamiliarity allows them to talk about things that they might not want *deja* to understand while in their presence. Sixteen-year-old Hiasa explained, "When I told Shasha that I thought the girl was *niñé* [crazy], the girl looked at me and laughed as though she understood. This girl knew how to listen to 'the words we speak.' How can this be?"[7]

Toward the end of the Sonenekwiñaji's stay in Puerto Maldonado, the girl announced that she wanted to return and live with them in Sonene. Ese Eja discussed it and decided against it. There were too many things about her that deeply disturbed them. As Shasha put it, "When she told us that she was coming to live with us here in Sonene, we didn't want that. Some were afraid of the *guardia* [police] because this girl is *deja*. They might say to us, 'What are you doing with a *deja* girl? Where are you taking her?'" Just as the Ese Eja were about to leave Puerto Maldonado, Pasoso and Tewi took the girl to the *guardia* and left her with them. Once the girl was under police care, Sonenekwiñaji immediately embarked on the daylong trip back to their community.

The Community Ponders the Mystery

Sonenekwiñaji were especially disturbed by the girl's familiarity with and contradiction of Ese Eja and *deja* worlds. In overtly hybrid cities such as Puerto Maldonado there are constant engagements with both the familiar and the unfamiliar, meaning that people often encounter things that they do not consider ordinary. For Ese Eja, these encounters are generally quite casually accepted within their open worldviews. But in the case of this *deja* girl, Sonenekwiñaji were troubled by their encounter, which inverted their expectations of what reality normally looks like, particularly in an urban setting where notions of cosmopolitanism and Indigenous cosmopolitanism take hold.[8] The details of their encounter firmly reversed Ese Eja perceptions of power relations between Ese Eja and *deja*, most clearly represented by the girl's desire to return with them to Sonene and live with them—in effect choosing Ese Eja lifestyles over *deja* ones.

This *deja* girl was at once both like and unlike other *deja*, as well as Ese Eja children. As a *deja* child, "white child," and fluent Spanish speaker who de-sired their presence, she presented a disquieting enigma, an anomaly without parallel.[9] In addition, the sight of a "starving" *deja* girl in a *deja* marketplace full of food was also unthinkable—not only her lack of access to food but also the absence of the commensality so fundamentally associated with being a proper human. Indeed, in the absence of the food sharing that constitutes the social person (Fausto 2007), Ese Eja were feeding the girl, and through happenstance they were making her family. Although Sonenekwiñaji can sometimes have the upper hand in social and economic relations, they are accustomed to being the food seekers in an urban marketplace and have sometimes played on people's pity in this regard. Yet they, rather than *deja* people, were the ones who supplied the girl with food and shelter. So although they could relate to the girl's marginality, its context was troubling. The distorted social and economic patterns of urban power relations that she mirrored heightened feelings of suspicion and even fear toward her. Some felt that she had a hidden agenda, although it remained unclear what this might be. Shasha stated, "she wanted to fool us and trick us by getting us to bring her to Sonene." And when thirteen-year-old Estela had asked the girl a question, the child had allegedly grabbed Estela's neck and in a terrifyingly high pitch screeched out, "I am telling you yeeeeeessssss!" Although this can be acceptable behavior for a child, the girl lacked the necessary familiarity to act so unusually, and so her gesture left Estela and others with an eerie feeling.

While the girl herself made Sonenekwiñaji feel anxious, the fact that they had delivered her to the local police struck me as especially unusual. This act further inscribed the reversal of social expectations since generally Ese Eja fear the police, skillfully staying far from their gaze. Yet in this case, an Ese Eja couple approached a policeman and told him that this girl was actively trying to follow them to their community and that she was incessantly clinging to them. Ese Eja turned this *deja* over to the police just as they have been turned in by *deja* themselves on many occasions. This unusual act also left them feeling unsettled, wondering whether they had made a wise choice between leaving her there, reporting her unusual behavior, or bringing her home with them. Sonenekwiñaji were careful about which aspects of and degrees of urbanity they fostered or resisted in their village (see also Buitron, this volume); certainly the raising of a *deja* child and the complications of unknown links to the city threatened the balance of their pick-and-choose approach to urbanity.

Kweijana: The Land of the Dead

Eventually, knowledge about the *deja* girl's identity and the reasons underlying her most enigmatic characteristics—her strange behavior, the absence of family, and her lack of name—emerged in an impromptu *emanokwana* session. In these sessions, Sonenekwiñaji interact with the *emanokwana*, the spirits of the dead who visit (*anikwa'ani*) from Kweijana, the "river" and land of the dead, through the medium of the *eyamikekwa* (shaman). *Emanokwana*, like *deja*, represent a type of otherness that is spatially and temporally distant: whereas *deja* live in the capital city, *emanokwana* live in Kweijana, the place where most dead relatives live and thrive in a variety of increasingly large towns and villages. Sonenekwiñaji view Kweijana as similar to a neighboring community except that this city and its peoples are located and dwell within a cross reality. Like Sonenekwiñaji, *emanokwana* also craft their urbanity as desired. While in theory they can choose to wield extensive control over all forms of technology, their true mastery is over all social and environmental relationships between humans and nonhumans across land, sky, and water. Kweijana is a city because of its population density and Indigenous infrastructure, and while it has the power to incorporate Western goods, *emanokwana* choose to keep their city *Ese Eja nee nee* (truly Ese Eja). Unlike Achuar (Taylor 1993), Piaroa (Overing 1993), and Araweté (Viveiros de Castro 1992), whose "dead" have patterns of social organization that differ from those of the living, the social organization and lives of Ese Eja *emanokwana* mirror those of living Ese Eja. *Emanokwana* continue to have children, plant swiddens, cultivate plantains, hunt and fish, form new connections, and introduce new characters, heroes, and adversaries into their afterlives.[10] They mirror Ese Eja even in their antagonistic relationships toward neighboring and distant communities of *deja emanokwana*. These *deja*, referred to with Ese Eja nicknames, are said to pose a risk at *emanokwana* ceremonies, where they sometimes try to trap the *eyamikekwa* inside the portal between the living and the dead. Similarly, *deja* who are visiting the community can make *emanokwana* ceremonies unviable through their use of light and the excessive noise that they make, which frighten off *emanokwana* (Peluso 2003, 2021).

Emanokwana continually and indirectly affect everyday life through their nonvisible actions. When individuals die, their *eshawa* (personhood, power) makes its way to Kweijana via a road laden with many obstacles.[11] Through *emanokwana* ceremonies, it has been revealed that once the *eshawa* makes a safe crossing it maintains a life similar to that of the living except that it has regained its capacities for transformation, unlike Ese Eja mortals, who can mostly only reside in one place at one time. In Kweijana, one's *eshawa* is now an *emanokwana*, and as *emanokwana*, individuals continue to live, reproduce, and die, but at an accelerated rate (*japanakiani*).[12] Throughout these transformations, personhood never ceases as a state of being, although the type of being a person is does change as they become an *emanokwana*. Despite potentially having multiple future deaths, *emanokwana* retain the identities they acquired in mortal life, including their maleness or femaleness.

The evening that we gathered to inquire about the *deja* girl, the *eyamikekwa* Shaijaimé arrived for this impromptu *emanokwana* ceremony. The ceremony was also being held to cure several small children who had become ill with diarrhea and fever during their trip to the city. We sat on the ground by Shaijaimé's house waiting as the old and frail shaman put on his worn-out bark cloth dress (*daki'nei*) and his battered feather headband/crown (*bopa*) and walked down the embankment toward the forested floodplain amid the moonless night. There, we were told, he enters a hole in the ground, a portal to both the underworld and the overworld, where the *emanokwana* are waiting to visit the community. Shaijaimé's wife, Hewa, had prepared a pot of fermented sour-plantain beer (*epoi'sese*) to offer to the *emanokwana* when they arrived.[13] We waited for the emergence of the first *emanokwana* into our world. Shaijaimé had been gone for about fifteen minutes, and the children were restless. Finally, the first *emanokwana* approached, having emerged from the portal in the ground using the *eyamikekwa*'s body as his avatar.[14] We could hear him as he rustled through the surrounding forest making his presence known. Tewi, Shaijaimé's son, signaled to the *emanokwana* where we were sitting so that he could come toward us. Tewi asked the *emanokwana* to reveal his identity. However, *emanokwana* do not say their names up front. After a series of clues, someone guessed who it was.

After several different *emanokwana* had visited and finished curing the children, one of our neighbors, Bewa, directly addressed the matter of the mysterious girl with Kwashi, an *emanokwana* and the spirit sibling (*ekwe'doe*) of her husband (also named Kwashi).[15] Waiting until after the *emanokwana* Kwashi had finished telling us the good places to go hunting and cured two of Kwashi and Bewa's sick grandchildren, Bewa began to question him:

BEWA: Who was this girl that we met in Maldonado?

KWASHI: This girl was the daughter of Dabicho.

BEWA: So then, the girl was the daughter of *deja* people?

KWASHI: No, she was not the *deja*'s. Instead, she was of theirs! [meaning the *emanokwana*]. This girl's name is Kwi'ao'coja'ta'ee.

BEWA: Oh! For this reason, then, when they asked her if she had or didn't have a mother, this is why she answered that she had neither a mother nor a father!

KWASHI: She was Dabicho's *ebacuase* [adopted daughter].

SHASHA: This girl was very charismatic!

TOBOCO: This girl had [skin] fungus. She was uncared for!

KWASHI: So that Dabicho could become good with you, you had to raise this girl. And because you did not raise/adopt her, he is going

to continue to mess with your lives! (*With these last words the* emanokwana *began to leave.*)
BEWA (*calling out after him*): Take good care of yourself, and if you
care to, do kill some illnesses for our children!

What the *emanokwana* Kwashi revealed was surprising to everyone. This
mysterious girl from the regional capital turned out to be an *emanokwana*
herself—a daughter of the dead! She was also related to Sonenekwiñaji, being the daughter of their deceased relative Dabicho. And like all Ese Eja, of
course, she had a name: Kwi'ao'coja'ta'ee (Black-Eyed River Turtle). Yet despite her request to return with them to Sonene, Sonenekwiñaji had failed
to take her home to live among kin.

A Bridge Between Cities

Kwi'ao'coja'ta'ee was a living portal between the visible and invisible cities of
cross realities, an ultimate hybrid of beings, bodies, and places. She was Ese
Eja, *deja*, mortal, and *emanokwana*. She had claims to all three settlements—
Puerto Maldonado, Sonene, and Kweijana—and as an *emanokwana* she was
"other" to Ese Eja and to *deja*. Kwi'ao'coja'ta'ee embodies several reversals
that characterize Ese Eja social alterity, as well as the power relations characteristic of particular places, and yet as an *emanokwana* she was simultaneously detached from *deja* and Ese Eja worlds. The inconsistencies of her
position crowned her with a magical aura while simultaneously signaling
that something was not quite right. Sapahewa, in retrospect, knowingly told
me, "I took a very good look at her—her eyes were red!!!"

Kwi'ao'coja'ta'ee was the daughter of the infamous Dabicho, a legendary
troublemaker in both the mortal and the nonvisible worlds. Kwashi explained
that if Sonenekwiñaji had agreed to "adopt and raise" Kwi'ao'coja'ta'ee by
respecting her desire to return to the community to live with them, then
Dabicho would have shown his appreciation toward his mortal relatives by
quelling all the misery and suffering that he consistently inflicts on them.
Sonenekwiñaji were quite excited that Dabicho, the "modern" *emanokwana*,
was discovered to be behind this puzzling encounter. Their relationships
with Dabicho have long been ambiguous and complex. Dabicho is the deceased son of Kwashi and Bewa. Although he appeared normal at birth, his
head allegedly became enlarged soon after, and he died of "a swollen head"

as a newborn. Bewa once mentioned that she thought Dabicho might have suffered a head injury when her daughter Shaka accidentally stepped on him.[16] Upon his death, Dabicho grew rapidly in Kweijana, and, as is known through contact with the *emanokwana*, he now has a large family with several children, and they have formed a powerful group in the densely populated Kweijana.

Dabicho is considered to be particularly bad (Sp. *malo*) and mischievous, yet he is also seen as heroic as his deeds are far reaching, and he impressively wreaks havoc in non–Ese Eja worlds. *Emanokwana* also complain about their ongoing struggles with Dabicho as they strive to protect their living relatives. Indeed, individuals often ask *emanokwana* about Dabicho's whereabouts as a way of gauging or anticipating difficulties. Being that Dabicho is Ese Eja and *emanokwana*, his desires expand beyond his home, town, and region, and indeed into more distant urban parts of the world, to which some Ese Eja may sporadically escape for safety from the sometimes overwhelming intimacy and lack of anonymity that is a phenomenon of life within villages (Peluso 2015b). Allegedly, no city is off limits for Dabicho. For instance, he is blamed for many illnesses and misfortunes that occur not just in Sonene but in the rest of the country, affecting Ese Eja and *deja* all over Peru. Yet like other powerful characters, Dabicho is also heroic. He is blamed, for instance, for natural and unnatural disasters, including crimes, airplane crashes, and fires as far away as Lima, the national capital.

Similar to Watunna creation narratives, Ese Eja stories about how nonvisible Ese Eja affect modern and urban landscapes reveal an ambivalent control over the surrounding world. The wielding of Western technology forms part of a widely spread practice whereby Indigenous origin stories and creation narratives (Civrieux [1970] 1997), discussions of heroic exemplars (Peluso 2014), hallucinatory visions (Arévalo Varela 1986), and nonhallucinogenic visions of healing or diagnosis and dreams (Peluso 2003, 2004b, 2021) meaningfully incorporate and reinterpret technology into local geographies (Guss 1989). Indigenous recastings of technology speak to power through Indigenous agency, whereby they narrate their own histories and realities toward their own self-determination. I will return to this point when I discuss the manner in which power relations are also removed from their expected zones in the story about Kwi'ao'coja'ta'ee.

Tales of Dabicho also allude to Ese Eja ancestral "wildness," a time in which people were more fluidly interchangeable between animals and spirits than they are today, and social conduct was unruly. Yet these tales also intimate present ongoing village and rural-urban struggles. It does not slip my notice that Dabicho is the child gone wrong of an extremely conflictual household. Dabicho is from a family that represents a history of conflict but also one of resistance. As an *emanokwana*, he is part of the extended Washapa family, one of the largest households in Sonene, headed by Kwashi and Bewa. The Washapas moved to Sonene from a rival Ese Eja community, and they are often blamed for much of the discord in Sonene. They are Na'tewekwiñaje (people from Na'tewe), an Ese Eja group from the Madidi River and one of the last in Peru to have been drawn into a sedentary lifestyle. Even though the *emanokwana* Kwashi reveals that Dabicho is the manipulator behind the strange encounter in Puerto Maldonado, ultimately it is the *eyamikekwa* (who is not a Washapa) as the medium for Kwashi (who is a Washapa) that places Dabicho at center stage of this drama. The *eyamikekwa* consistently reinforces the idea that Dabicho reflects not only what is wrong with the world at large but also what is wrong in the community. Everyone, including the Washapa family, seems to embrace this representation of Dabicho. Interestingly, as strict attendants and participants of all *emanokwana* ceremonies, the Washapas are the first to claim how "bad" Dabicho is; they often ponder over why he is so awful, his accidental premature death being cited as the only possible cause. Yet according to many elders, Kwashi and Bewa cannot control their own children. Dabicho personifies their own domestic anarchy. So, then, why do the Washapas accept the *eyamikekwa*'s claim that a Washapa is the source of much adversity?

On the one hand, images of insubordination and hostility attributed to the Washapas are highly valued, especially when they can be claimed and reframed in the guise of an Ese Eja cultural hero such as Dabicho, thus ensuring that he belongs to all Ese Eja. Indeed, there are moments when Dabicho is metaphorically at the forefront of struggles between Ese Eja and *deja*, and he represents a source of pride for many individuals, such as when he released the fastened boats of encroaching *deja* when the river rose. On the other hand, Washapas feel a strong sense of pride in the idea that Dabicho is one of "theirs," not just an Ese Eja but a Washapa. Just as one may speculate that part of the shaman's message is, "You Washapas are at the root of so many problems!" one can also speculate that their response might be, "That's right. That's what happens when you mess with us!" As awful a reputation as Dabicho has, in the end, he is an Ese Eja creation. Yes, he can create problems at home, but ultimately he is an Ese Eja person with a powerful ability to reach out into the larger world.

Dabicho may also in some ways express the family's feelings of guilt toward the death of their child through negligence. Kwi'ao'coja'ta'ee's appearance represented the opportunity to do it right, to raise a child properly, unlike what happened with Dabicho. It did not go unnoticed, retrospectively, that in the regional capital, Kwi'ao'coja'ta'ee first approached her own family. Iba', the man who first spotted Kwi'ao'coja'ta'ee in the marketplace, is Dabicho's *ewape* (brother-in-law, his sister's husband). Following the ceremony, Bewa noticed in hindsight that Kwi'ao'coja'ta'ee clung to Kwashi (Kwi'ao'coja'ta'ee's father's father), and she remarked: "This girl only liked Kwashi, she liked only him! She wanted to stay with him all the time because she is his granddaughter! And afterward in the night she would go crawling to Shaka's mosquito net!" Shaka is the girl's aunt (her father's sister), the sister who allegedly squashed her father's, Dabicho's, head.

In sum, the *emanokwana* had elucidated that when Dabicho, neglected as a newborn and now troublesome as an *emanokwana*, sent Kwi'ao'coja'ta'ee, he was sending his most precious gift, his child. There is nothing more important to Ese Eja than their children (Peluso 2015a). Some say that an adopted child is even more loved than a birth child because it was sought after. When Ese Eja individuals give their child to their parents to raise, it is, in part, a reciprocal gesture of recognition and appreciation for their own upbringing (Peluso 2003). The generosity inherent in such an offer is highly praised, and its rejection is socially frowned on. The girl uniting the three cities—the urban, the rural, the dead—was denounced for her uncanny desire to connect these spaces, showing reality for what it actually is and solidifying relatedness through the sharing of spaces. Somehow Ese Eja ignored the possibility of challenging the familiar spatialization of social relationships and hierarchies while still upholding their unique claims to be able to do so.

Unified Cityscapes

The choice of Sonenekwiñaji to ignore the mysterious girl's wishes is a powerful metaphor for the dangers of transgression that life across multiple kinds of dwelling spaces entails; even the *emanokwana* avoid such trespasses, since in Kweijana they keep their cities separate from those of *deja*.[17] Although taking the child to the *guardia* may have played out an inversion of their social position within the locale of the regional city, this action did not correspond to Sonenekwiñaji's overarching awareness that something was exceptionally strange and peculiar about the *deja* girl. Ese Eja actions made sense according to the details, but the larger framework remained problematic for them. These unsettling feelings ultimately led them to consult the *emanokwana* as they are seen as knowledgeable about, and sometimes responsible for, any unusual events. By consulting the *emanokwana*, Sonenekwiñaji probed their own hasty decision to turn the child over to the police. They understood that local police, like their uninformed selves, were not in a position to see the situation for what it really was. This is not to say that the state system is inefficient, just that it is not *sufficient*. Had delivering this girl to the police adequately addressed the odd urban social reversals that made Sonenekwiñaji so apprehensive, then the *emanokwana* might not have been consulted.

Yet the decision to take the girl to the police affirmed the *guardia*'s position as local state authorities and agents of power and surveillance. It is the state's obscure presence that brings Ese Eja to Puerto Maldonado for the municipal elections in the first place, outfitting them with cash and the incentives of festivities. It is precisely during this anomalous period of grace—in which their presence in the regional capital was sanctioned by the invitation they received from the victorious mayor of the city—that the girl was handed over to state representatives. In retrospect, this resonates with Michel Foucault's (1977) observation that the gatekeeper of the panopticon does not actually have to be *present* in the tower for the prisoners to remain inside. The *guardia* did not actually have to regulate Ese Eja behavior and free will across geographic spaces. Their choice unknowingly favored the state's visible control over that of the *emanokwana*.

While the actions of Sonenekwiñaji reflected city methods, when they sought an explanation for the appearance of the girl, they approached the *emanokwana*. This is because in the larger picture *emanokwana* must always be reckoned with, as it is the cross reality of the nonvisible world that animates what is visible in daily life. In other words, these spaces of varying urbanity are part of a larger whole, a fact that, as far as Ese Eja are concerned, *deja* simply do not understand. The *emanokwana* Kwashi confirmed the women's suspicion that there was more to the *deja* child than met the eye. The *emanokwana* did not judge people's decision not to raise Kwi'ao'coja'ta'ee; they simply added a new dimension to the dynamics of Ese Eja social relations, which inevitably include these connected cross realities. It was

Sonenekwiñaji themselves who interpreted the *emanokwana*'s words and critiqued their own choices and behavior. After the identity of Kwi'ao'coja'ta'ee became known to them, their conversations and curiosity continued for weeks. Yet while there was still excitement in their exchanges, they now also expressed sadness about their lost opportunity.

Kwi'ao'coja'ta'ee's appearance in Puerto Maldonado was an unprecedented way of linking the cities of Ese Eja, *deja*, and *emanokwana*, as well as of the living and the dead. Although the worlds of the dead and the living are also linked by a system of relatedness that extends into both realities, it is rare—apart from the appearance of *emanokwana* via the medium of the *eyamike-kwa* during *epoi'sese* and *shashapoi'* ceremonies—for *emanokwana* to appear in visible human form. An exception is through the personification of certain animals, particularly large packs of *ño* (white-lipped peccaries), which are hunted communally by Ese Eja. On these occasions, *ño* are believed to be transformed *emanokwana* who will once again return to their *emanokwana* state. Ese Eja eat their dead relatives, personified by *ño*, with gratitude, an act that symbolizes reciprocity and exchange.[18] The intimate acts of conversing, sleeping, and eating with Kwi'ao'coja'ta'ee provided social and spiritual nourishment—and began a process of kin-making (Vilaça 2002) that only in retrospect can be seen as a remaking of kin. Undoubtedly, the possibility of raising an *emanokwana* in the world of the living rather than the more typical scenario—of an Ese Eja going to live in an animal underworld or eventually reaching the destined land of Kweijana—certainly signifies a novel and intimate exchange between the living and the dead across a larger landscape of connected spaces. Just as the coming of *ño* is a voluntary gift on behalf of the *emanokwana* benefactor from Kweijana to the community, so was the appearance of Kwi'ao'coja'ta'ee in the capital city a voluntary precious gift from Dabicho.

Conclusion

Indigenous Amazonian spaces span a rich geographic landscape, with varying degrees of urbanity that connect cross realities: from urban imaginaries that begin in the mind to those that constitute the core canon of creation stories and others that transform villages and cityscapes through exchanges. These deep histories reflect times of undifferentiation between humans and nonhuman Others, as well as their potential for multiplicity and transformation alongside possible imaginaries of pre-Columbian societies (Gow 1994), centuries of Indigenous mobility and migration (Alexiades 2009), and more recent dislocation through colonization, missionization, dispossession, and marginalization. Embedded in these cities are social hierarchies vis-à-vis the larger world that privilege particular people, such as Ese Eja in Sonene, *deja* in Puerto Maldonado, and *emanokwana* in Kweijana. Together, these cities are part of more global geographic spaces to which Ese Eja see themselves as belonging, in particular those of Peru, Bolivia, and Amazonia. Within these broader landscapes social differences become more pronounced, even when *emanokwana* such as Dabicho prove themselves to be powerful forces.

The unusual emergence of Dabicho and Kwi'ao'coja'ta'ee from the invisible city of Kweijana can be seen as a form of ethnogenesis, as Ese Eja mark territories that form part of their histories while creating a more unified ethnic consciousness across such spaces. This suggestion builds on studies of how personhood and the making of the self and the body are forms of ethnogenesis (Santos-Granero 2009), alongside the idea that the refashioning of Amazonian oral narratives is also an ethnogenetic process (Hill 2009). With cities representing spaces in which people can navigate new ways of being—for example, new lifestyles, dressing and eating choices, and kinds of space (Santos-Granero 2009; Peluso 2015b)—then it should follow that moving between cities allows new possibilities for transformation. We are already aware of how lowland South American beings and bodies are processualy made, as well as how proximity and residence create people and their potential for unity. As with sociality, commensality, and consubstantiality, sharing cities is a way of becoming, maintaining, or transforming people and kin. Yet the way that Ese Eja recount stories about encounters with Dabicho and Kwi'ao'coja'ta'ee goes further than rehistoricizing or remaking Ese Eja identity (Hill 2009, 25–26). The ongoing privileging of meeting kin through portals between cross realities is a cumulative and ardent force of ethnogenesis that links urban imaginaries by traversing local and broad ontological and geographic Amazonian spaces.

Here, I have recounted a particular and unusual meeting point between three metropoles with three distinct urban imaginaries: the Indigenous community where urbanity begins and is imagined, the regional capital as the popular urban setting, and the land of the dead where urbanity has long been actualized in Ese Eja fashion. Such meeting points and their potential for conflict and rapprochement between simultaneous Amazonian cross realities can be glimpsed or accessed in many states of being, as mentioned previously, such as through dreams, hunts, illness, solitariness, and rituals. What these states have in common is a sense of vulnerability and the ability to expose people and beings for who they really are. Meeting places between different worlds reflect the collapse of binaries. The encounter with the *deja* girl brought into focus the destabilizing of Ese Eja, *deja*, and *emanokwana* identities and their locales. Questions of self and other, the dead and the living, as embodied in this strange *deja* child challenged Sonenekwiñaji's essentialist assumptions about identities and their roles in the social and economic aspects of everyday life, particularly as played out in Puerto Maldonado, which is quintessentially *deja* territory. The shifting and reversing of conceptual political spaces such as police/victim, abundance/starvation, and margin/center as highlighted by the emergence of the daughter of the dead gives emphasis to transforming vertical and horizontal power relations between Ese Eja, *deja*, and *emanokwana* across different types of spaces. Just as processes and conditions of hybridity can be a threat to colonial and cultural authority (Bhabha 1985), Ese Eja found this hodgepodge of twisted oblique referents to both subvert and uphold their own typical understandings of power relations and identity as they relate to place. My analysis of why they found this encounter so unsettling concerns histories and issues of political economy, postcolonialism, and the view of Amazonia as a site for perennial frontiers between the state and the capital in its various guises.

The appearance of Kwi'ao'coja'ta'ee marked a unique chance for rapprochement between the worlds of the dead and the living and the worlds of *deja* and Ese Eja, but Sonenekwiñaji missed it. Kwapiso, a nonrelative, regretfully remarked, "I was going to raise this girl—but since Tewi took her to the *guardia* then I couldn't. It was too late." Yes, Sonenekwiñaji might have finally resolved their long-standing antagonism with Dabicho and maybe with the cosmos at large, and perhaps they have not submitted to or enacted state power in the capital. But on the other hand, who wants to live with an *emanokwana*, the daughter of the dead, even if she does have a name after all? As I write these last words and wonder how I can convey these experiences while respecting the idea that this girl may have indeed come from the land of the dead as my Ese Eja companions claimed, a large bird suddenly crashes against the window behind the computer screen that I am facing. Yes, every now and then these passages open up between realities, and for better or for worse one is at a loss of what to make of them.

Acknowledgments

I am indebted to Sonenekwiñaji for their ongoing hospitality and kinship. I greatly appreciate the support of the Native Federation of the Madre de Dios River and Tributaries, the British Academy Small Research Grant, the Wenner-Gren Foundation for Anthropological Research, the Social Science Research Council, the Fulbright Institute of International Education, and the Association for Women in Science. Many thanks to Miguel Alexiades for his comments and our many conversations about Kwi'ao'coja'ta'ee.

Notes

1. The Ese Eja language belongs to the Tacana language family, part of the Macro-Panoan group of languages of western Amazonia.

2. My doctoral fieldwork (1993–96) was supported by grants from the Social Science Research Council, the Fulbright Institute of International Education, the Wenner-Gren Foundation for Anthropological Research, and the Association for Women in Science. The research for this article builds on over sixty months of multisited fieldwork among Ese Eja communities, which began before and has continued since my doctoral research.

3. While this account takes place in 1995, its relevance holds as of 2022 as these worlds continue to overlap. Sonene, Puerto Maldonado, and Kweijana have all undergone transformations in the intervening years. The population of Sonene is lower due to deaths among the older population and a move by two large families to another community, but it is currently on the rise. Puerto Maldonado's population has more than doubled, but its territory has also greatly expanded. The transoceanic highway has been completed. The capital's informal economy has grown (Peluso 2018), alongside prostitution and sex trafficking (Goldstein 2014), drug trafficking, gold mining (Wagner 2021), and associated mercury poisoning (Ashe 2012). While these changes have shaped current discussions of Indigenous experiences of urbanization in Puerto Maldonado, Sonene Ese Eja urban residences continue to be temporary (Peluso 2015a). According to Ese Eja, Kweijana has grown exponentially from what was already a densely populated state. This is because the dead regenerate rapidly and continue to have children.

4. *Deja* is an Ese Eja label of social alterity, referring to individuals and groups who are perceived by Ese Eja to have greater contact with, dependence on, and affiliation with markets and external agents. When using Spanish they say *mestizo*, which reflects the general usage of the term *deja*, although *deja* can also imply any type of outsider (Alexiades 1999; Peluso 2003).

5. Iñapaere people live in voluntary isolation; Ese Eja claim to have had some interactions with them. They are also referred to as *los calatos* (the naked ones).

6.   When in Puerto Maldonado, if I want to find an Ese Eja person or group of people, I have learned precisely where to look, in terms of both actual locations and routes.

7.   *Niñé* is a culture-bound illness that causes madness or insanity. Sometimes it can be brought on by drunkenness. It is often used as a diagnosis for odd behavior.

8.   *Indigenous cosmopolitanism* is a term coined by Thomas Biolsi (2005, 249), which he uses to imply "that [American] Indians are at least as at home in cities, universities, the mass media, and so on, as they are on reservations." I discuss Ese Eja Indigenous cosmopolitanism elsewhere (Peluso 2015a).

9.   Ese Eja, like other Indigenous populations in the region, refer to *deja*, non-Indigenous people, as *gente blanca* or mestizos. This reference has nothing to do with skin color, as "white people" can be darker than Ese Eja.

10. Anne Christine Taylor (1993) says that the Achuar do not make heroes of the dead. I think it is remarkable that Ese Eja have not only produced heroes (such as Shajaó) in their histories but also continue to create new ones (such as Dab-icho) in the world of the dead (Peluso 2014). Ese Eja also controvert Taylor's (1993) claim that lowland Amerindians work diligently to forget the dead. This may be true upon the immediate death of an individual, but ties are soon re-established through *emanokwana* ceremonies. Indeed, Beth Conklin (2001) argues that the dead and living can only approach each other once they have become reconciled to their new worlds.

11. Not all individuals go to Kweijana upon death, a topic beyond the scope of this chapter (see Peluso 2003).

12. *Japanakiani* is a state of rapid growth, birth, and regeneration. For instance, an Ese Eja friend in Portachuelo, Bolivia, described how her recently deceased infant sister was now at least my age only months after her death. On another occasion a woman spoke to me about her husband, who had died thirty years earlier: "Oh, he has remarried and died again so many times. He has so many children now and he has had so many other wives. He doesn't think of me anymore."

13. *Epoi'sese* is a casual form of a much more elaborate ceremony (*shashapoi'*) designed to engage more fully with *emanokwana* and nonhuman Others.

14. Bernd Brabec de Mori (2012, 86) refers to acts where the spirits speak through a shaman's body and his voice becomes altered in communicating their voices as "voice masking."

15. An *ekwe'doe* or *ekwedoyase* is one's own mirror-image soul brother or sister in Kweijana. The prefix *ekwe-* is the possessive personal pronoun "my." As one friend clarified, "My *ekwedoyase* is really me, she is like me, it is the same as me, but it is also different."

16. Similar accidents have occurred among siblings and are usually not judged or reprimanded, despite the sadness felt by the family.

17. Unlike Marshall Berman's (1982, 24) proposition that "modernity is either embraced with a blind and uncritical enthusiasm or else condemned with a neo-Olympian remoteness and contempt," Ese Eja are quite ambivalent about it.

18. See Robert A. Brightman (1993) for an excellent discussion on how Cree prefer to—morally, aesthetically, and strategically—view animals as benefactors rather than as opponents.

References

Alexiades, Miguel. 1999. "Ethnobotany of the Ese Eja: Plants, Change, and Health in an Amazonian Society." PhD diss., City University of New York.

Alexiades, Miguel, ed. 2009. *Mobility and Migration in Indigenous Amazonia: Contemporary Ethnoecological Perspectives.* Oxford: Berghahn Books.

Alexiades, Miguel, and Daniela Peluso. 2015. "Introduction: Indigenous Urbanization in Lowland South America." In Peluso 2015c, 1–12.

Alexiades, Miguel, and Daniela Peluso. 2016. "La urbanización indígena en la Amazonia: un nuevo contexto de articulación social y territorial." *Gazeta de Antropologia* 32 (1): 1–22.

Arévalo Varela, Guillermo. 1986. "El ayahuasca y el curandero shipibo-conibo del Ucayali." *América Indígena* 46 (1): 147–61.

Ashe, Katy. 2012. "Elevated Mercury Concentrations in Humans of Madre de Dios, Peru." *PLOS One* 7 (3). https://doi.org/10.1371/journal.pone.0033305.

Berman, Marshall. 1982. *All That Is Solid Melts into Air: The Experience of Modernity.* London: Verso.

Bhabha, Homi K. 1985. "Signs Taken for Wonders: Questions of Ambivalence and Authority Under a Tree Outside Delhi, May 1817." *Critical Inquiry* 12 (1): 144–65.

Biolsi, Thomas. 2005. "Imagined Geographies: Sovereignty, Indigenous Space, and American Indian Struggle." *American Ethnologist* 32 (2): 239–59.

Brabec de Mori, Bernd. 2012. "About Magical Singing, Sonic Perspectives, Ambient Multinatures and the Conscious Experience." *Indiana* 29:73–101.

Brightman, Robert A. 1993. *Grateful Prey: Rock Cree Human-Animal Relationships.* Berkeley: University of California Press.

Burnett, D. Graham. 2001. *Masters of All They Surveyed: Exploration, Geography, and a British El Dorado.* Chicago: University of Chicago Press.

Civrieux, Marc de. (1970) 1997. *Watunna: An Orinoco Creation Cycle.* Austin: University of Texas Press.

Conklin, Beth. 2001. *Consuming Grief: Compassionate Cannibalism in an Amazonian Society.* Austin: University of Texas Press.

Denevan, William M. 1992. "The Pristine Myth: The Landscape of the Americas in 1492." *Annals of the Association of American Geographers* 82:369–85.

Erickson, Clark L. 2006. "The Domesticated Landscapes of the Bolivian Amazon." In *Time and Complexity in Historical Ecology: Studies in the Neotropical Lowlands,* edited by William Balée and Clark Erickson, 235–78. New York: Columbia University Press.

Fausto, Carlos. 2007. "Feasting on People: Cannibalism and Commensality in Amazonia." *Current Anthropology* 48 (4): 497–530.

Fausto, Carlos, and Michael Heckenberger. 2007. *Time and Memory in Indigenous Amazonia: Anthropological Perspectives.* Gainesville: University Press of Florida.

Foucault, Michel. 1977. *Discipline and Punish: The Birth of a Prison.* New York: Pantheon Books.

Goldstein, Ruth, 2014. "Consent and Its Discontents: On the Traffic in Words and Women." *Latin American Policy* 5 (2): 236–50.

Gow, Peter. 1994. "River People: Shamanism and History in Western Amazonia." In *Shamanism, History, and the State,* edited by Nicholas Thomas and Caroline Humphrey, 90–113. Ann Arbor: University of Michigan Press.

Gow, Peter. 2001. *An Amazonian Myth and Its History.* New York: Oxford University Press.

Gow, Peter. 2011. "Rethinking Cities in Peruvian Amazonia: History, Archaeology and Myth." In *The Archaeological Encounter: Anthropological Perspectives,* edited by Paolo Fortis and Istevan Praet, 174–203. St. Andrews: Centre for Amerindian, Latin American and Caribbean Studies.

Guss, David M. 1989. *To Weave and to Sing: Art, Symbol, and Narrative in the South American Rainforest.* Berkeley: University of California Press.

Guzmán-Gallegos, María. 2015. "Amazonian Kichwa Leadership: The Circulation of Wealth and the Ambiguities of Mediation." In *Images of Public Wealth or the Anatomy of Well-Being in Indigenous Amazonia,* edited by Fernando Santos-Granero, 117–38. Tucson: University of Arizona Press.

Heckenberger, Michael J. 2004. *The Ecology of Power: Culture, Place, and Personhood in the Southern Amazon, AD 1000–2000.* New York: Routledge.

Heckenberger, Michael J., J. Christian Russell, Carlos Fausto, Joshua R. Toney, Morgan J. Schmidt, Edithe Pereira, Bruna Franchetto, and Afukaka Kuikuro. 2008. "Pre-Columbian Urbanism, Anthropogenic Landscapes, and the Future of the Amazon." *Science* 321 (5893): 1214–17.

Hill, Jonathan D. 2009. "History, Power, and Identity: Amazonian Perspectives." *Acta Historica Universitatis Klaipedensis* 19:25–47.

Kohn, Eduardo. 2009. "Form's Effortless Efficacy: A Multispecies Amazonian Account." Paper delivered at Agrarian Studies Colloquium Series, Yale University, January 23, 2009.

Kopenawa, Davi, and Bruce Albert. 2013. *The Falling Sky: Words of a Yanomami Shaman.* Cambridge, Mass.: Harvard University Press.

Larochelle, Jeremy. 2012. "Writing Under the Shadow of the Chullachaqui: Amazonian Thought and Ecological Discourse in Recent Amazonian Poetry." *Review: Literature and Arts of the Americas* 45 (2): 198–206.

McSweeney, Kendra, and Brad Jokisch. 2015. "Native Amazonians' Strategic Urbanization: Shaping Territorial Possibilities Through Cities." In Peluso 2015c, 13–33.

Mezzenzana, Francesca. 2018. "Encountering Supai: An Ecology of Spiritual Perception in the Ecuadorian Amazon." *Ethos* 46 (2): 275–95.

Opas, Minna, 2005. "Mutually Exclusive Relationships: Corporeality and Differentiation of Persons in Yine (Piro) Social Cosmos." *Tipití: Journal of the Society for the Anthropology of Lowland South America* 3 (2): 111–30.

Overing, Joanna. 1993. "Death and the Loss of Civilized Predation Among the Piaroa of the Orinoco Basin." *L'Homme* 33 (2–4): 191–211.

Peluso, Daniela. 2003. "Ese Eja Epona: Woman's Social Power in Multiple and Hybrid Worlds." PhD diss., Columbia University.

Peluso, Daniela. 2004a. "Urban Ethnogenesis Begins at Home: The Making of Self and Place Amidst the Environmental Economy in Amazonia." *IASTA Working Paper Series* 177: 1–14.

Peluso, Daniela. 2004b. "That Which I Dream Is True: Dream Narratives in an Amazonian Community." *Dreaming* 14 (2–3): 107–19.

Peluso, Daniela. 2014. "Shajaó: Histories of an Invented Savage." *History and Anthropology* 25 (1): 102–22.

Peluso, Daniela. 2015a. "Children's Instrumentality and Agency in Amazonia." *Tipití: Journal for the Society of Lowland South America* 13 (1): 44–62.

Peluso, Daniela. 2015b. "Circulating Between Rural and Urban Communities: Multi-Sited Dwellings in Amazonian Frontiers." In Peluso 2015c, 57–79.

Peluso, Daniela, ed. 2015c. "Indigenous Urbanization: The Circulation of Peoples Between Rural and Urban Amazonian Spaces." Special issue, *Journal of Latin American and Caribbean Anthropology* 20 (1).

Peluso, Daniela. 2018. "Traversing the Margins of Corruption Amidst Informal Economies in Amazonia." *Culture, Theory and Critique* 59 (4): 400–418.

Peluso, Daniela. 2021. *Ese Eja Epona: el poder social de la mujer en mundos múltiples e híbridos.* Lima: Centro Amazónico de Antropología y Aplicación Práctica.

Peluso, Daniela. Forthcoming. "The Politics of Indigenous Urbanite Images in the Peruvian Amazon." In *Urban Indigeneity from a Global Perspective*, edited by Dana Brablec and Andrew Canessa. Tucson: University of Arizona Press.

Peluso, Daniela, and Miguel N. Alexiades. 2005. "Indigenous Urbanization and Amazonia's Post-Traditional Environmental Economy." *Traditional Settlements and Dwelling Review* 16 (11): 7–16.

Politis, Gustavo, and Nicholas Saunders. 2002. "Archaeological Correlates of Ideological Activity: Food Taboos and Spirit-Animals in an Amazonian Hunter-Gatherer Society." In *Consuming Passions and Patterns of Consumption*, edited by Preston Miracle and Nick Milner, 113–30. Cambridge: Oxbow Books.

Prance, Ghillean T. 1970. "Notes on the Use of Plant Hallucinogens in Amazonian Brazil." *Economic Botany* 24 (1): 62–68.

Santos-Granero, Fernando. 2005. "Arawakan Sacred Landscapes: Emplaced Myths, Place Rituals, and the Production of Locality in Western Amazonia." In *Kultur, Raum, Landschaft: Zur Bedeutung des Raumes in Zeiten der Globalität*, edited by Ernst Halbmayer and Elke Mader, 93–122. Frankfurt: Brandes and Apsel Verlag.

Santos-Granero, Fernando. 2009. "Hybrid Bodyscapes: A Visual History of Yanesha Patterns of Cultural Change." *Current Anthropology* 50 (4): 477–512.

Santos-Granero, Fernando. 2012. "Beinghood and People-Making in Native Amazonia: A Constructional Approach with a Perspectival Coda." *HAU: Journal of Ethnographic Theory* 2 (1): 181–211.

Slater, Candace. 1994. *Dance of the Dolphin: Transformation and Disenchantment in the Amazonian Imagination*. Chicago: University of Chicago Press.

Stasch, Rupert, 2017. "Afterword: Village Space and the Experience of Difference and Hierarchy Between Normative Orders." *Critique of Anthropology* 37 (4): 440–56.

Taylor, Anne Christine. 1993. "Remembering to Forget: Identity, Mourning and Memory Among the Jivaro." *Man*, n.s., 28 (4): 653–78.

Thierry, Jamin. 2006. "Sur les traces de Païtiti, la cité perdue des Incas." *La Géographie* 1522:61–71.

Uzendoski, Michael A. 2004. "Manioc Beer and Meat: Value, Reproduction and Cosmic Substance Among the Napo Runa of the Ecuadorian Amazon." *Journal of the Royal Anthropological Institute* 10 (4): 883–902.

Vilaça, Aparecida. 2002. "Making Kin Out of Others in Amazonia." *Journal of the Royal Anthropological Institute* 8 (2): 347–65.

Viveiros de Castro, Eduardo. 1992. *From the Enemy's Point of View*. Chicago: University of Chicago Press.

Wagner, Livia. 2021. *The Ecosystem of Illegal Gold Mining: Organized Crime Dynamics in the Artisanal and Small-Scale Gold Mining Sector of Peru*. Jack D. Gordon Institute for Public Policy, Florida International University. October 2021.

PART II

Forest-City Tensions and Interactions

CHAPTER 4

Cities of the Forest

Urbanization and Defiance Among the Shuar of Ecuadorian Amazonia

NATALIA BUITRON

One day in March 2012, my friend Marco, his first wife, Marisa, and I had just returned from a trip to Macas, the nearest settler town. The trek home had been demanding. We were caught in a torrential rain while carrying several cardboard boxes of provisions for the family, all the way from the endpoint of the road under construction, still some hours' walk away from the small forest trail that led to Kuamar, the forest village where they lived. The cartons were destroyed by the rain, and we juggled several packs of salt, noodles, and sardine cans. Nonetheless, my hosts were cheerful: at last, we were far from the hustle and bustle of the city! Once we reached home, Marco lay in his hammock and sipped from his bowl of manioc beer as I dried my clothes, listening to the soft crackle of the fire on which Marisa began to cook our meal.[1] Contentedly, he pronounced: "We live so well in the interior!"—a sentence that had become proverbial among my Shuar friends. As if this needed explanation, he added, "You know why we live so well? Because everything is free here; no one is starving or forced to work."

If life is good and free in the interior, it is because there Shuar have their homes and their gardens; they need no money to eat. But it is also free because they can live and work as they please, without having to follow orders, in contrast to those who are forced to work for others in towns. The Shuar today never get tired of comparing the forested interior with the town "out there": that is, the frontier market towns of Macas, Sucúa, and Puyo, where the interior Shuar often become homeless, landless, and weak, where people go hungry and know no one, and where everything has a price.

The negative image of the local market towns does not, however, imply that the Shuar dislike urbanity in general. On the contrary, urban life exerts a strong fascination on my Shuar friends. They often describe the riches and technological wonders of cities, places where people have uninterrupted access to hospitals, electricity, running water, paved streets, TVs—all things that the *apach* (as they call Ecuadorian mestizo nationals) can make, thanks to their entrepreneurial abilities. Many of the Shuar people I know harbor strong desires to harness such foreign abilities and enjoy the goods available in the city, and, thus, they seek ways to connect the forested interior with the life of towns.

Just as they seek to create connections, they also struggle to uphold the symbolic and material boundaries between forest and town. As per Marco's comments, market towns are charged with moral and political qualities that the interior Shuar, and specifically those living in the Makuma area, where I conducted fieldwork, detest.[2] Most importantly, they have a stereotypically negative image of the *apach*, also referred to as *colonos*, that is, the colonists from the Andean highlands who have settled and urbanized the Ecuadorian lowlands. These urban dwellers are stingy, bossy, and disrespectful people with bodies that are fluffy and fat: "bodies mixed like chicken fat," as a friend in Makuma liked to put it.

Images of places and people are intimately interlinked, and therefore attitudes toward urban life are fundamentally ambiguous. Because of this ambiguity, the interior Shuar do not aspire to relocate permanently to market towns; instead, they spend a great deal of time and energy trying to urbanize the forest. In my time there, they were passionate about developing their villages by equipping them with roads, high schools, infirmaries, football fields, markets, electricity, concrete bridges, stadiums, and all the amenities available in big market towns. In what often struck me as a form of competitive antagonism vis-à-vis the *apach*, they also imagined scenarios whereby their villages would become so large, bountiful, and well equipped that the *apach* would have no choice but to visit the interior for holidays or to regularly shop in the Shuar forest market towns.

In this chapter, I trace the connections Shuar people create with the urban exterior and foreign Others through imaginaries such as that of the urbanized forest village. In doing so, I highlight the prominent role of place-making—such as in contemporary village development among the Shuar—in native Amazonians' engagements with wider structures of power. Starting from the opposition of forest and town, I discuss how meaningful places and spatial categories that are crucial to the ongoing transformations of Shuar worlds emerge. I also emphasize the challenges of well-being as they present themselves to Shuar people today, in particular, through the mastery of relations with Others in the face of imminent danger and decadence.

In this, I am inspired by recent anthropological work that highlights how people mobilize moral geographies to articulate the rural and the urban (Chio 2017; Peluso 2015; Peluso and Alexiades 2005; Stasch 2017). This work shows how people living in peripheral areas engage with the contradictions of space-specific social orders, particularly as represented in the metanarratives of economic progress and development, narratives in which "cities are the superior present or future, while forest and rural settlements are the inferior past" (Stasch 2017, 446). This chapter demonstrates that Shuar people disrupt this metanarrative in various ways. They imagine the forest village as a model of Shuar urbanity while locating this village in the future of settler market towns, that is, as a semiautonomous space that could become a site of Shuar-mestizo relations. Through this image, as we shall see, they not only re-create the outside in their own terms, but also strive to take control over relations with urban dwellers to avoid subjection to settlers' conditions in towns.

When Shuar compare the interior and the exterior, they compare different sociopolitical orders, to wit, the spaces of well-being and freedom they value and the spaces of debilitation and oppression that they associate with *apach* ways of life. The colonists of Ecuadorian frontier towns are not the only inhabitants of Shuar urban imaginaries; there is also a colorful squad of spirits and monsters with characteristically urban skills and habitats, suffused with colonial attributes. Relations with both the townsfolk of the exterior and the urban monsters of the interior always remain ambiguous: Shuar simultaneously relate to them and seek to distance themselves from them. In regional scholarship, it is well established that relations with alterity are characterized by a long-standing openness to the Other (see Lévi-Strauss 1995). In ethnographies of contact situations and recent engagements with the state, this scholarship often shows that native Amazonians manifest a sort of ontological proclivity to being open to relations with a growing constellation of Others, whether Indigenous people, mestizos, or white people (Albert and Ramos 2000; Gordon 2006; Vilaça 2010; Kelly 2011). Rather than being captured in a dynamic of ethnic resistance, Indigenous people capture others by making them into kin through practices of consubstantiality or by mimetically appropriating or cannibalizing elements of their power (Fausto 2007; Santos-Granero 2009).

But while most such studies assert that relations with Others are dangerous and often take on explicitly negative qualities, they emphasize relationality over detachment. This tendency in Amazonianist ethnography corresponds to a general bias in anthropology to prioritize connection and attachment over disconnection and separation. As Matei Candea and colleagues (2015, 28) argue, much social theory foregrounds engagement and relationality, thus omitting how people live out and value detachment. Part of the reason may be because detachment has been conflated with cold disinterest or with an ideology of objectivity that eclipses the Other. Yet when seen through a person-centered perspective (that of our informants), detachment may appear less as an ideology and more as the cultivation of a particular stance. In the Shuar case, this stance is antagonism and defiance. For them, conceptions and practices of well-being require the cultivation of material and symbolic separation from otherwise valuable Others. This is evident, for example, in their reluctance to being co-opted or controlled by Others even while they often try to lure, control, and overtake those Others so as to harness their powers. Another way of putting this is that an engaged stance with Others stems from, and is premised on, cultivating defiance toward them.

This chapter thus traces the way in which my Shuar interlocutors engage urban imaginaries by defying the monstrous Others that populate them. In the first section, I describe the urban villages that are being constructed in the forest nowadays. In the second section, I show the ways in which Shuar people strike a balance between the double challenge of (rural) deprivation and (urban) decadence. In their engagement with both the *apach* of the market towns and the (urban) monsters of the forest, the Shuar are characteristically defiant. The third section and conclusion thus describe the landscapes of alterity that are formed in the defiant engagement with urban Others, under the threat of coercion, exploitation, and death.

Urbanizing the Forest

Shuar number more than one hundred thousand people and inhabit a large portion of Ecuadorian Amazonia. My observations about urbanization apply primarily to the Shuar living in the network of forest villages of Makuma, an area of evangelical implantation, in the province of Morona Santiago. In this province, the process of colonization has given rise to a prominent geopolitical and to some extent sociocultural distinction between the Amazonian interior and the market towns of the Andean piedmont. Geography is central in this distinction as the interior is separated from settler towns by the Kutukú, an imposing mountain range rising to 8,200 feet (2,500 meters) above sea level. Although the difference does not exactly map onto a rural/urban dichotomy, the Shuar associate living far away from market towns, "beyond the Kutukú" (Trans-Kutukú), with more traditional ways of living. So, compared to the Shuar living in towns or *muraya shuar* (lit. "people of the mountains"), the Shuar of the interior, of *adentro* (inside), are described as speaking better Shuar and eating more game.[3]

At least since the 1960s, the majority of Shuar have concentrated in villages called *centros* (lit. "centers"), Indigenous sedentary communities. These communities are administrative and juridical entities recognized by the Ecuadorian government. The creation of a *centro*, as its name suggests, involves the clearing of forest to create a center in an otherwise reticular and dispersed landscape. Its open and clear space therefore affords enhanced concentration and proximity of people and dwellings. *Centros* are divided into an urban center (*urbanización*) and more distant fields (*terrenos*). In the urban center there are also plots (*parcelas*) for the households of individual families.[4] The houses are usually built next to one another around a central plaza. The urban center is also the area where all public buildings and urban facilities are built: the central plaza, which comprises the soccer and volleyball fields; the assembly hall called "roofed space" (*espacio cubierta*) for village meetings; the room for the shortwave radio; the nursery; and the school. This area is the heart of the village (figure 4.1). This is not only because villagers emphasize that to live well in the present means to be settled and proximate to one another (Buitron 2016a), but also because access to schooling, urban services, and technology has been crucial in fostering the desire for nucleated living.

Village formation has been the result of a century-long process of state-led colonization pursued through missionization, settler encroachment, and sedentarization. In Makuma, evangelical missionaries encouraged a village-based way of life by promoting a strategy of community development centered on cattle cooperatives with public infrastructure such as

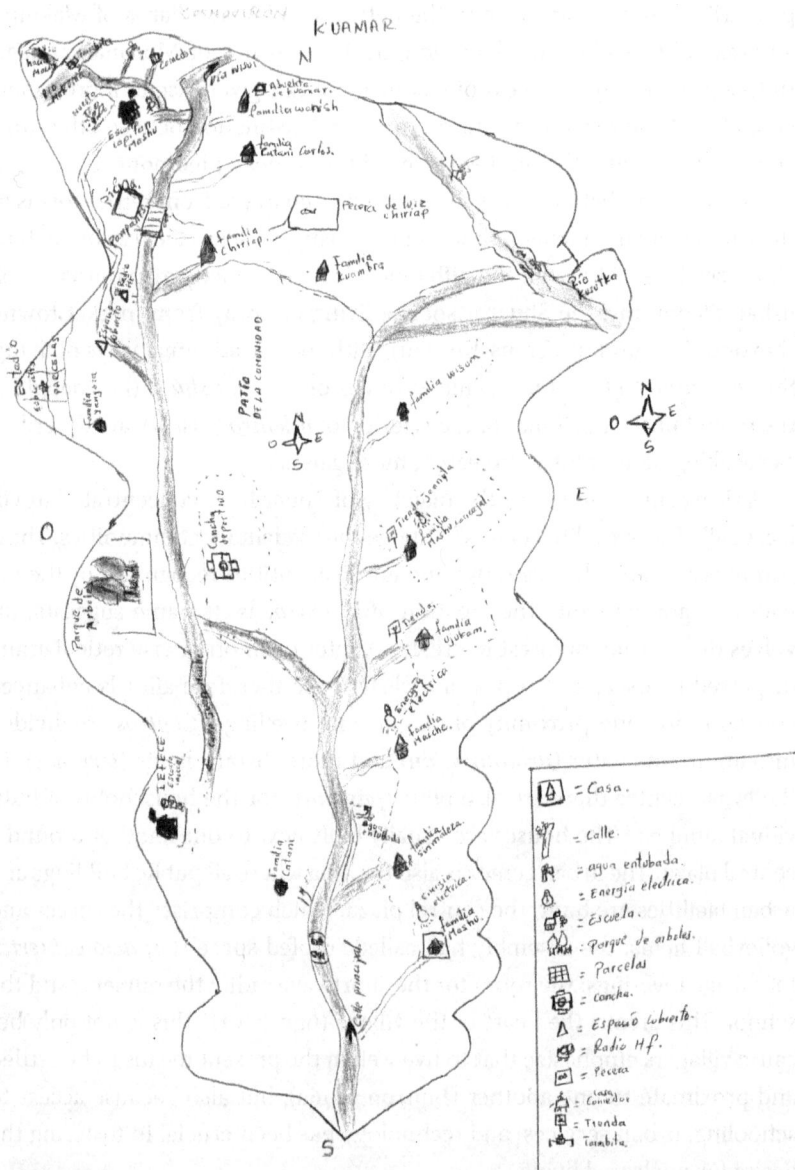

FIGURE 4.1 Child's drawing of Kuamar village's *urbanización*. The key enumerates all desired urban services: house, street, potable water, electricity, school, tree park, plots, field, roofed house, shortwave radio, fishpond, dining hall, shop, cable car basket. Printed with permission of the child's parents.

airstrips, a mission school, radio stations, shops, and a hydroelectric plant. Over the years, the influence of the missions has declined, but the cooperatives promoted by them provided a model for creating an ethnic federation that allowed Shuar people in Makuma to apply for collective land titles and prevent settler encroachment. Rapid state-sanctioned agricultural colonization had posed a clear threat to Indigenous autonomy—both material and political—and this threat has transformed the Shuar village into a space from which to pursue territorial self-determination. Urbanization has been key to this process.

It is hard to overstate the importance that urbanizing the interior holds for villagers. One of my first memories of walking around the muddy trails of Kuamar's *urbanización* was the villagers' insistence on calling the irregular and weedy trails "streets." I realized they were not describing the actual trails as much as the street grid plan that commissioned engineers had drawn up a decade earlier. The streets, a villager assured me, would be like those of Ecuadorian cities: bordered with ditches, paved with cobblestones or concrete, and they would also bear plates with the names of the village founders.

Centro membership often comes with the expectation that residents will work together toward village development. In 2013, the residents of Kuamar got involved in negotiations with *apach* politicians to obtain electricity from Macas. They saw the electrification of the village as a necessary upgrade from the intermittent power provided by the local hydroelectric plant, which missionaries had installed in the 1970s and which still relied on power from the Makuma River flow. When I returned to Kuamar in 2018, the trails still looked muddy and irregular, but most houses had electricity. Every villager had stories about the gargantuan work of carrying lampposts from the endpoint of the road: "We were in permanent *minga* [work party]," they told me.

The question of village expansion and the projects for development are constantly debated among villagers. People have specific visions for how a Shuar village should look, which was confirmed in a meeting Kuamar's schoolteacher summoned in 2013. He asked villagers to describe "how they envisioned the future of the village," so as to include their ideas in "a plan of coexistence" required by the provincial directorate of education. Contrary to my expectations—after all, this was a bureaucratic exercise—forty or so villagers, young and old, spent an hour imagining Kuamar's future. They came up with a list that included the following items:

- I dream that Kuamar becomes a tourist city and that children speak well Shuar and Spanish
- that Kuamar will be visited by people from all over
- that it becomes a tourist city, with swimming pools, cultural houses, parks, etc.
- that Kuamar has a roundabout, a library, and a university
- it should have dams, a lake, animals in the zoo so that visitors come to see them
- ecological roads and streets
- that Kuamar has all basic services: potable water, electricity, telephones, improved houses, and good systems of production
- a model city that other people come to visit to admire its agriculture, tourism, and ecology
- a city with sources of income, where families have their own advanced production systems (husbandry, shops, etc.)
- Kuamar should have its own businesses and markets so that the *apach* come to shop here

It is clear from this list that villagers associate future well-being with the spaces, the aesthetics, the infrastructure, and the goods of contemporary cities. Most people I met truly relished public infrastructure and services: they not only found these entities beautiful but also considered that they have made life considerably less painful. One day when I returned from town and asked a group of women in Kuamar whether there had been electricity in the village (a rare event back in 2013), a middle-aged woman, Juana, replied, "No, we are suffering." I heard similar comments about the lessening of suffering in relation to the advent of running water and the approaching road. People often engage in evaluative comparisons with the serviced world of towns: "They [the *apach*] don't suffer like us, they have everything."

In Indigenous accounts of village formation across the world, a compelling reason for embracing sedentary life is the bodily and material transformation that villages facilitate through improved access to consumer goods and infrastructural development (Killick 2008; Rival 2002, 161–66; Stasch 2013). Rupert Stasch (2016, 259, 263) observes that for the Korowai of West Papua, the city is a figure of foreign people's economic systems, a world of money-mediated consumption that casts a shadow of inferiority on their own lifeways. While the Korowai eagerly develop villages, they also acquire a particular historical consciousness, whereby they, as former forest dwellers, occupy positions of inferiority in wider translocal hierarchies. "To engage with villages is to enter a process of humiliation," amid the recognition that to overcome their state of commodity deprivation they need to appropriate versions of the national and international ideology of civilization (Stasch 2013, 563).

Shuar are certainly aware of similar ideological hierarchies, and their discourses of suffering are based on evaluative comparisons and self-pity. Yet their ways of making sense of this dynamic seek to undo humiliation by defiance; suffering leads people to fight back. Consider, for example, the combative attitude of Maria, an elderly woman, when she lectured Shuar officials in charge of road building: "I am speaking Shuar to you because you are not colonists. You are drinking manioc beer because you are not colonists. Don't deceive us like some do. Leaders, build the road, do it fast! Once we have the road our children will go to school like the children of the colonists, without getting covered in mud. But the road isn't going to get built unless you rush the contractors and drivers, those good-for-nothing [*apach*] beer drinkers." Instead of surrendering to their material subordination, Shuar intend to outdo their *apach* neighbors. In effect, Shuar do not simply aim to replicate the market towns they know best, such as Macas and Puyo, which don't actually have functional universities, zoos, or ecotourist enterprises. Rather, they are keen to innovate on the idea of a market town. Instead of building ordinary towns, they want to create model tourist cities with ecological roads (figure 4.2). They imagine towns that have all the basic facilities of the colonial frontier, but that are so much more beautiful and advanced that not only mestizos but people from all over would come to visit them.[5]

To some extent, the distinction Shuar draw between market towns and their own version of urbanization recalls the contrast between two urbanist models that have sprung up in recent years in Ecuador: the millennial city (*ciudad del milenio*) and the intercultural city. The first was the urbanist brainchild of President Rafael Correa's Citizens' Revolution (2007–17). Built in concrete as a block of standardized houses and public buildings, these cities promised a first-rate connection to modern infrastructure and services to populations directly affected by extractive industries in the northern Ecuadorian Amazonia (Wilson and Bayón 2017, 86; Vallejo et al. 2016). The intercultural city, by contrast, is an emerging countermodel of rural urbanism

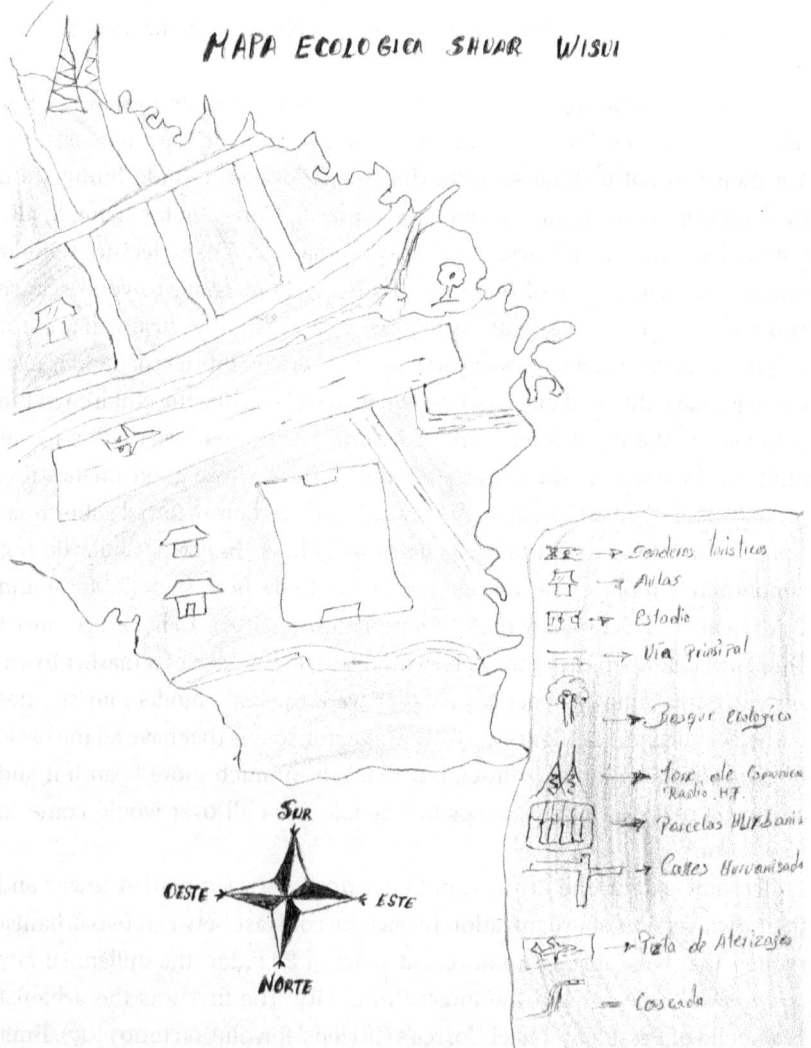

FIGURE 4.2 Child's map of the ecological urbanized village Wisui. The key shows tourist trails, the stadium, urbanized plots, the airstrip, and a waterfall. Printed with permission of the child's parents.

that blends Amazonian architectural design with ecological entrepreneurship to incentivize Indigenous development. The Shuar of Makuma view the former as externally imposed sterile settlements that lack attachment to territory, and the latter as an urbanist model of Indigenous self-determination. The urbanized villages Shuar dream of are places where Shuar people can enjoy the opportunities of the city without putting up with the expenses and abuses of living among mestizos. In practical, forward-facing terms, this means for example managing an ecotourist enterprise in the interior where one can go on eating one's foodstuffs, working at one's own pace, speaking Shuar, and living with kin, all while making money from foreign tourists. Ultimately, the production of urbanized villages is tied to the desire to guarantee self-sufficiency, even if this means articulating the interior with markets and infrastructural development.[6]

The foregoing shows that Shuar invest materially and emotionally in connecting themselves to urban Others yet at the same time cultivate detachment from those Others. The opposition between interior and exterior never disappears in emulation but is surpassed in excess. Just as they engage with Others and their ways of living, they express a desire for separation motivated by their suspicion and dismissal of the *apach* and their lifeways. These feelings emerge in part from their experiences in frontier market towns.

Attraction and Weakness in Towns

Despite living permanently in *centros*, the Shuar of Makuma are extremely mobile and occasionally visit market towns, taking advantage of the fact that some of their relatives might be temporarily settled there for work. At times, these relatives may be Kichwa and Achuar affines, and even mestizos from the Andean highlands. But while interethnic marriages do occur, cohabitation and kinship (whether in the exterior or the interior) do not weaken the distinctions that the Shuar of Makuma draw between cities of the forest and decadent market towns.[7]

Most adults and elderly people who visit market towns do so to seek cures for grave illnesses, since both hospitals and the most powerful shamans can be found in frontier towns (see Deshoulliere 2017; Taylor 2007).[8] For young people, on the contrary, the primary motivations tend to be work, formal education, and short stints in the army.[9] Given how the older generation now praises the good life of the interior (as in Marco's proverbial sentence), one might suspect that sojourning in mestizo towns is a recent trend. But in fact, most senior people in Kuamar (that is, individuals over forty years of age) also experienced city life in their teens, a fact that is brought home in a series of stories written in Shuar in the 1980s and collected by the Protestant missionaries of Makuma. The stories, which describe ordinary impressions of cities, were written by the first generation of teachers from Makuma to be trained, in the 1970s, in the bilingual institute of Limoncocha.[10]

One of these teachers described Puyo thus: "Beautiful, there is a bit of everything, cars, big built houses with rooms for selling stuff. In those lands, live many, many *apach*, who eat different foodstuffs." Another teacher wrote the following about Ambato, a city in the highlands: "There are many *apach* in that town, many cars and military men, and many clothes, whatever you want, ice cream and beautiful houses, but there are also many thieves. If you get robbed, there is no way to catch the thief among so many *apach*. The *apach* are well educated [they have studied much] but they have also studied to steal. And because there are so many things [and people], Ambato is dangerous." In these stories, commercial activity and the *apach*'s food habits take center stage, while the sheer technological might, anonymity, and scale of the city never fails to make an impression: a conglomeration of so many unknown *apach* and so many things. An unmissable reference is also military power, which, as we shall see, Shuar unfailingly associate with the coercive power of urban dwellers. The stories also reveal the ambivalence of their authors to the defects of the *apach*. If theft appeared problematic to occasional Shuar travelers in the 1970s, more recent oral stories focus on the feelings of unbearable debilitation experienced in the city and people's gradual return to a good life in the forest.

Take for instance the case of Miriam, a middle-aged woman from Gualaquiza who is now married and lives in Kuamar. She left her parental home when she was twelve, upon the death of her mother, becoming a domestic servant in Quito, the capital. As Miriam put it, in Quito she was often scared and ill: "I did nothing else but work, without any family. I just suffered." Adding to the horror of aimless, lonely work, Miriam fell suddenly ill, and so her bosses took her to the hospital, where she was told she needed surgery. With fear still reflected in her eyes, she told me that if her dad had not picked her up from the hospital and taken her back home, she "would have died in the operating theater," by which she meant that the doctors would have probably killed her. To be sure, nothing scares Shuar women more than the prospect of being forced into immobility on a stretcher by a group of white-gowned faceless doctors who would proceed to cut open their bodies or pull babies from their wombs. Men, for their part, have parallel experiences of suffering in the army, where they are subjected to unspeakable ordeals—unspeakable because the abuse and the violence meted out by bewilderingly ranked men in uniform is perceived as absolutely gratuitous. Indeed, much of the horror that doctors and colonels inspire stems from the faceless and inexplicable nature of the violence they can exercise on Shuar bodies.

Shuar and other peoples of the Aénts Chicham language family—previously known as Jivaro—are among the few fortunate native Amazonians to have largely escaped the abuses of the rubber boom that affected the Upper Amazon region in the late nineteenth century.[11] But while few people experienced permanent or complete peonage, most Shuar men and women I came to know closely had at some point in their lives experienced painful subjection to mestizo bosses and institutions. For men this often occurs when they become seasonal laborers in factories, farms, or the army, while women experience similar forms of subjection as domestic servants in middle-class households or as sex workers in the brothels at the outskirts of mestizo towns.

The suffering experienced in urban settings is seen as weakening their bodies, precisely because it negates the personalized and contentious ways in which Shuar typically understand and deal with conflict. In her analysis of traditional warrior autobiographies, Anne-Christine Taylor (2014, 108) observes that Aénts Chicham people "typically stress individual agency and the consequences of intentional acts," whereas colonists are perceived as wreaking havoc "in an indeterminate, impersonal, and continuous way." In the city, Shuar experience a form of vulnerability stemming from impersonal yet threatening situations at the behest of strangers, rendering them incapable of responding appropriately to conflict. This happens, for example, when they must obey the senseless commands of a drill sergeant, or when they must lie down in front of a gowned doctor.

My interlocutors often told me that if they lived too long in the city, they would become ill and die (see Virtanen, this volume, for similar Manxineru perceptions about how life in the city weakens their bodies). While it was not always clear what exactly would cause such a fatal outcome, villagers highlighted a combination of factors: the mixed food of the colonists, their rude manners, and the irrepressible sadness for the relatives and pets left behind. In this sense, the forested interior becomes a permanent shelter zone of convalescence and liberation, in the intimacy of close-knit relations with kin and nonhumans.

This raises a question, however: why would Shuar want to urbanize their own environs in the forest, thus re-creating the morbidity of the town in the forested interior? The most common answers my interlocutors gave to this question play once more on the manifold meanings of suffering—in this case, they urbanize to overcome the suffering of deficit and absence. As per the visions for Kuamar's future recounted above, Shuar people want to re-purpose urban development to achieve well-being in the interior while over-coming a sense of having been deprived of essential services and opportuni-ties. Infrastructure and services help Shuar turn the tables of the comparison with the *apach*, thus diminishing their feelings of inferiority and domination. By funneling urban resources, Shuar people can not only live better—that is, autonomously, shaping their own livelihoods and existences—but also lay claim to wealth historically controlled by the *apach*. This strategy aims at inverting the forms of existential suffering and disempowerment Shuar associate with subordination to urban dwellers in big cities. As we shall see, however, disempowerment is not simply a function of living in mestizo cit-ies. Some of these feelings extend to the forest, which is replete with ambig-uous urban-like creatures.

Landscapes of Alterity: Coercion, Death, and Cunning

How should anthropologists study the relationship between people's spa-tial imaginaries and their practical engagement with place and people? An answer in this direction is provided by Eric Hirsch and Michael O'Hanlon (1995, 3), who argue that engagement with landscapes entails a relationship between the foreground and background of social life. The foreground re-flects the "concrete actuality of everyday social life ('the way we now are')," whereas the background is "the perceived potentiality thrown into relief by our foregrounded existence ('the way we might be')."

Peter Gow (1995, 51–55) offers an interesting application of the relation-ship between background (imaginary) and foreground (everyday practice). He shows how land and kinship are co-implicated as the Amazonian Piro (Yine) produce themselves as people (and kin) through home building and garden-making. This is their foregrounded actuality. But the here and now–ness of place expands to a more distant horizon, constituted by past and ongoing relationships with Others. This horizon includes the spaces of the wandering dead souls that Piro people leave behind when they abandon the houses of their relatives to be recolonized by the forest. And beyond the landscapes of living and dead humans are the worlds inhabited by the owners and mothers of the forests and rivers, worlds inhabited by giant anacondas and white foreigners who are indifferent to human beings. Though these autonomous spaces of superhuman power lie in the background of experience, they occasionally come to life through narratives of sickness, since humans are forced to invade their spaces through hunting, fishing, and village-making. When Piro people mobilize the agency of shamans to tame these powers, they actualize a relation with generic forces that lie in the background of experience.

The background/foreground relationship can thus illuminate how alterity feeds into social life and place-making, in the sense that everyday practice and sameness (as foreground) appear against a background imaginary pervaded by alterity. It is of crucial importance in this respect that among many Indigenous Amazonian peoples, alterity is epitomized by guardian spirits, masters of the land, and species owners: foreign, white, and urban (see, e.g., Kohn 2007; Overing 1996, 63–69; Santos-Granero and Barclay 2011). Although such metahumans are people in the sense that they are capable of social lives and possess subjectivity, they are not, like members of the group, real people, those who can be identified as "us, the [proper] human beings" or "the living ones" (Praet 2013, 15). Instead, they exhibit grisly physiques and inhuman qualities. While most spirit owners take care of their families and children, to the real humans they may also appear as roaming ogres and solitary cannibals. These spirits are, as Istvan Praet (2013, 39) suggests, monsters, in the sense that just as the production of humanity requires a specific effort, "monstrosity is always premised on a contrary effort."

For the Shuar, the forest is the vital space of various spirits (*iwianch*) and of giants, dead beings, and monsters (*nekas iwianch*). *Iwianch* are a class of spirits and dead beings of humanoid shape considered repulsive: they are typically oversized, hairy, and deformed. The myths often describe their bloodthirsty quest for human organs to repair their infirmity (Taylor 1993, 429–32; see also Mader 1999, 81; Pellizzaro 1978, 3–5). However, in everyday encounters they often appear normal to Shuar people, especially to lost women and children, and people only gradually take notice of their strangeness through their foreign body ornaments, physical deformities, and habits.

The *iwianch* that interest me in this section are usually Shuar-eaters and sport the clothes and tools of white, urban people: trousers, hats, boots, uniforms, and metal tools. Their conflict-ridden stories are perhaps the only oral record, alongside shamanic chants, where Shuar explicitly, or in encrypted form, speculate about colonial agency.[12] Their stories are also peculiar in their consistent emphasis on violence, coercion, cannibalism, and sexual and alimentary deviance, topics that offer important clues about how Shuar imagine the extraordinary power and unusual danger of white urbanites and their cities (for similar thoughts, see Overing 1996, 56; Santos-Granero, this volume). I have singled out four of these *iwianch* from the Shuar bestiary and discuss each of them in turn.

Jurijuri

This category of Shuar-eaters inhabits rocky areas and tree holes in the forest. Jurijuri are bearded and have a second mouth that lies behind their hairy neck, which conceals protruding sharp teeth. Their powers are evident in their armature: clothed with military uniforms, including boots, hats, and ponchos, they resemble Spanish conquistadores or Ecuadorian soldiers. They march in troops to devour their victims under the lead of their captain-boss. They are considered game mothers, and so the Jurijuri mobilize to protect their domesticated animals when Shuar hunters hunt them in excess or subject them to humiliations. In a well-known myth, the Jurijuri kill a group of Shuar after the hunters of the group laugh at a tamed *chu* monkey that cried pitifully.

Some versions of this myth include a sort of metacommentary on the possible origin of the Jurijuri and the relationship between the interior and exterior. The version recounted here was narrated in 1975 by Pitiur, a thirty-five-year-old man from Chiwasa, to the Salesian missionary Siro Pellizzaro (1978, 102–26). One day before the attack, a Jurijuri appears to a hunter's wife who has been left behind and warns her about an imminent attack by the Jurijuri to punish the hunters' transgression (figure 4.3). When the woman communicates the warning to her husband, she refers to the strange visitor as an *apach* who wears a poncho. Ponchos are garments worn by highlanders and common attire among settlers in the early years of colonization of the lowlands, so, intrigued by the foreign appearance of the visitor, the woman queries her husband, "Perhaps the colonists occupied these lands before us?"

FIGURE 4.3 Illustration of the Jurijuri's visit to the Shuar woman. Drawn by Tonino Clemente, Salesian missionary, under the guidance of Shuar narrators. Originally printed in Siro Pellizzaro, *Iwianch* (Sucúa, Equador: Abya-Yala, 1978), 106.

But her husband rebuffs her warning with the telling remark, "Lies, how could the colonists inhabit this bushy forest?"

The events that follow force the listeners of the narrative to rethink their certainties. At twilight—a liminal time when Shuar expect disasters and sad news—the troop of Jurijuri set foot on the camp while eerily playing their clarinets; then, like leaf-cutting ants, they devour everything they find in their way. The narrator ends the story with the words, "Thus I say now, perhaps the Jurijuri could eat me as well? We better fear them for they truly abound in the rocky forest."

The myth thus brings to the foreground a scary potentiality augured by the recklessness of Shuar hunters: while now the *apach* and the forest appear incompatible, perhaps the urban *apach* inhabited the forest *before* the Shuar?

Tsunki

The underwater world of rivers is inhabited by the Tsunki, a class of aquatic beings. At first glance, the material and social lives of the Tsunki look like the underwater mirror image of the Shuar earthly lives. The architecture of the Tsunki household and its customs epitomize Shuar domestic relations and the etiquette that governs relations through marriage (Pellizzaro 1980, 1–7; Descola 1996, 124; Mader 1999, 90). But the similarity with the Shuar world is only superficial, and once we zoom in on the depths of the underwater world, we see a large background canvas of colonial alterity. The anacondas that lie fenced just outside the subaquatic Tsunki household are called "pigs." This is not just a casual reference. Pigs—or *kuchi*, an Andean-Hispanic name that derives from the Spanish *cochino*—are colonial animals, first introduced from the Andes in the 1500s (Gnerre 2003, 51). The hilly and stony rivers recall the Andean foothills, where colonial urban settlements have concentrated. River waves themselves appear as big extended ponchos, which, as we have seen earlier, metonymically identify the *apach*. One myth recounts that a Tsunki woman receives written letters (*papi*) from her sister on earth and that the underwater realm is traversed by big roads (Pellizzaro 1980, 107–8). Another explicitly refers to the presence of *apach*, who appear as "water wolves." More importantly, the Tsunki are also depicted as being repressive and punitive, expressing their fury with military strength. A well-known myth narrates the marriage of a Shuar man to a spirit Tsunki woman. When things turn awry, the Tsunki father punishes the man (who mistreated his daughter) by sending his anaconda soldiers to attack him. The pigs, the hills, the poncho, the letter, the roads, and the soldiers are distinctly foreign elements that reflect colonial urban power.

The river spirits are also the ultimate source of shamanic power. The shaman situates himself within alien locales of power, and his chants abound with references to dangerous outsiders and their landscapes.

Cortacabezas

The fears and dangers of urban worlds also concretize in figures located at the interface of the forest and the city. No other figure forces the Shuar so palpably into the position of prey as does the terrifying figure of the head-hunter or *cortacabeza*. During my fieldwork, rumors had it that nasty gringos interested in making a fortune selling expensive *tsantsas* (shrunken head trophies) in their countries had hired unscrupulous mestizo intermediaries who in turn recruited Shuar people to capture people from their communities. The chain of command and supply therefore started far away in Europe or North America, moved along mestizo intermediaries, and ultimately harvested its victims in Shuar territory. Once harvested, the heads and organs of the unsuspected victims were said to be sold abroad or in mestizo towns directly. "Have you seen the cart of the ice cream vendor who goes around Macas?" Shuar friends asked ominously. "People say that when you open the cart it doesn't have ice cream but eyes, heads, and human organs."

These rumors are neither new nor entirely fantastic. We know that at the end of the nineteenth century when migrants descended from the Andean highlands to settle in the Upano Valley, they not only traded manufactured goods (machetes and shotguns) for Shuar labor and forest products, but also sought *tsantsas*). As Steven Rubenstein (2007, 359) has argued, during this period *tsantsas* passed through Ecuadorian traders, tourists, Euro-American museum collectors, and other aficionados, causing an escalation of Shuar warring and head-hunting; the circulation of these ritual objects created a trail connecting "different people and political regimes." Presently, Shuar deliberately deploy the image of wildness evoked by head-hunting in confrontations with the *apach*—as if to remind the latter that the Shuar are still capable of reducing heads—yet, in their own narratives, the headhunter is now typically a predator Other, whereas they are the prey. Anxieties over colonial violence play out most prominently in situations of internal conflict and breakdown, as when communities split along factional lines and suspicions flare up. On such occasions, marginal individuals, or Shuar urbanites with fragile connections to the interior, are accused of being headhunters working for the gringos (*inkis*).[13]

Iwia

Except for the analogy between the Jurijuri and the Spanish conquistadores, Euro-American foreigners, locally known as gringos, are conspicuous for their absence in mythic urban imaginaries. This is probably because gringos only appeared on the scene in the second half of the nineteenth century, when a few Aénts Chicham men involved in rubber extraction heard English for the first time, and then only occasionally. Maurizio Gnerre (1999,

62) speculates that the word *inkis* entered the Shuar language from English to denote "a white (Caucasian) not Spanish-speaking person, likely to come from far away." Until then, the *apach*—a term that was originally used to describe the Spanish-speaking conquistadores—assumed most elements of foreignness.

Certain prototypical cannibals, the Iwia giants, qualify as being analogous to the gringos. The Iwia are described as tall, fat, hairy, and immoral; they kidnap the wives of Shuar people and eat the brains of their children. They also eat raw meat, including that of their own wives and the taboo deer meat, and deplete forest game. In the cycle of myths depicting the Shuar fight against these cannibal giants, an Iwia always sets traps to harvest the Shuar and carries an axe and a bag to collect the people he kills. The Shuar keep moving farther and farther away to avoid the giant, while the Iwia keeps clearing jungle and opening roads into their territory. The Iwia is also wont to make others work for him and habitually gives them orders; interestingly, he calls his workers "grandsons," just as his workers call him "grandfather," though the relationship between them is marked by abuse and deceit, rather than care and respect.[14]

The story goes more or less along the lines of the following myth, which was told to me by Chuint, an elderly interlocutor, when he wanted to illustrate the greediness and foolishness of foreigners:

The Shuar people, who appeared as Kunamp [Squirrel] and Tsere [Spider Monkey], planted a grove of delicious fruit trees, called *yaasu* [Sp. *caimito*]. Then they built a vine bridge across the canyon alongside the fruit trees, and lying on it, they climbed to fill their baskets with the fruit. One day that Iwia was on his way to see if he could catch any Shuar in his trap, he asked, "Grandchildren, what are you doing in those trees?" The Shuar people answered, "Since the *yaasu* fruit are good and ripe we are picking and eating some." When Iwia asked to try one, they gave him a nice ripe fruit, and since Iwia wanted more, the Shuar people [Squirrel and Spider Monkey] slyly suggested that he go and invite others of his kind so they too could enjoy the fruit. Iwia readily accepted and soon returned with many of his people. But the squirrel man quickly loosened some of the vines with his teeth, so it was barely strong enough for the heavy Iwia to get across the canyon. The Iwia were fearful and asked if the vines were safe. "Oh yes," said the Shuar people [Squirrel], and to reassure them, they, with their little squirrels fastened to them, ran easily back and forth. So, the Iwia crossed over too, and filled their baskets with fruit. But when they crossed back, the vine bridge broke and sent them tumbling downward. At this point, the spider monkey, Tsere, crawled down the bank crying loudly—but feigning sadness—"My little grandfather, grandfather!" [*Apachrusé! Apachrusé*], as he went from one bashed Iwia head to another, licking out the splattered brains.[15]

Like in many mythical encounters between the Shuar and the Iwia, the Shuar find ways despite their vulnerability to deceive the giants by inciting their lust for food and services. What is interesting about this myth is that both the Shuar and white people have drawn inspiration from this saga to highlight what it is about foreigners that Shuar people find so repulsive.

Thus, for instance, Marie Drown, an American missionary who spent thirty-seven years living with her husband among the Shuar of Makuma, was particularly intrigued by the implicit analogies that Shuar drew between Iwia and white people.[16] In one of her notebooks, circa 1948, Marie speculated on the pleasure Shuar derived from telling stories of Iwia:

Now [the myth] is still enjoyable to them because it enhances the delight they feel in the ability to get the best of anyone who attempts to dominate them. They still use patient, calm indifference, repeated delays, etc. to wear down the drive and exhaust the patience of any white man who tries to get him to do something outside of his traditional value system—be it road building under government direction, school building, cement work, shovel work. . . . Weeding gardens that produces food in the traditional ways is sensible and important to them, captures their imagination and harnesses their emotional drives. Other kinds of work done for the white man or for hard cash are much more difficult to carry on. (Drown 1977–78, 29)

Shuar people provide an interesting twist to the missionary's exegesis. The narrators who told me the myth of Kunamp, Tsere, and the Iwia ended the story explaining that because Tsere ate the brains of Iwia, he became crazy and overbearing like the *apach*. "The *apach* are like Tsere: bearded, hairy, and a little white [*un poco blanquito*]." So, although Tsere used to be a cun-

ning Shuar man who fought the giant Iwia, he became *apach*-like after he
went down the canyon to lick the brains of the Iwia, something only cannibal
giants do. This is perhaps the closest to an emic exegesis of the hierarchy of
alterity powers in the colonial frontier: the Iwia (*inkis*) recruit the *apach* and
Shuar to work for them, and when the Shuar switch sides and work for the
Iwia, or copy the latter's manners, they become like the *apach*, enriching
themselves at the expense of Shuar bodies.

What all these beastly figures share is excessive power put to perverse
ends: when they punish, they kill, when they play, they devour, and when
they request, they subdue. Whether ruthless or reckless, they always feature
as intruders who challenge the moral and territorial grounding of the Shuar,
as well as their vitality and self-determination. The intruders' foreignness is
conspicuously urban because colonization has presented itself with an urban
face to Shuar people. Inevitably, interethnic relations and wider structures of
power are deeply interwoven with the places Shuar consider native.

Conclusion: The Politics of Defiance

I began by noting the seemingly paradoxical Shuar act of urbanizing the
forest as a way of capturing the power of settlers' cities while simultaneously
policing the boundaries between the forested interior and the urbanized exterior. This attitude can be explained as a form of relationality premised on
defiance. Engagement with alterity, which is seen as paradigmatically urban
and is presently embodied in the figure of the *apach* invader or colonist, is
ultimately premised on differentiation and separation. What Shuar people
try to escape from is submission and death, which they associate with the
condition of suffering without combat or the possibility of meaningful response to aggression. The city is a place of suffering because it embodies
a contrary sociopolitical order, one of dominance and anonymity (forced
work), disaffection (isolation from kin), and deprivation (of proper food). But
this form of suffering is not unique to the market towns of the Ecuadorian
border; rather, it extends to Shuar locales in the interior. Shuar people also
suffer when they compare their villages in the forest with the powers and
goods the urban *apach* have access to. Suffering—both in the forest and
in town—derives from a social force of separation and disjunction that is
opposed in every respect to the connection and attachment that perpetuate
well-being among the living.[17] In this sense, the superhuman and monstrous

powers of the forest provide the background of all suffering, that is, death and submission under foreign powers.

In this respect, forest and city are mutually implicated and coproduced, not only in mythical discourse but also through Shuar people's own engagement in forest development. Village formation emerges out of the late colonial encounter with missionaries and state officials. And Shuar now continue this subtle process of integration of and differentiation from urban powers by urbanizing the forest as they construct villages as semiautonomous shelter zones of well-being. In this sense, Shuar create not so much a continuum from oppressive white-mestizo cities to their own improved cities of the forest, as a continuum of sociopolitical orders, ranging from cities as sites of exploitation, illness, and deprivation to cities as sites of empowerment, well-being, and abundance. Thus, ambiguous feelings concerning contemporary white-mestizo cities are also transposed to the forest and result in what the editors of this volume call "enchanted cities" brimming with superpowers that may have positive or negative connotations.

In Marie Drown's circa 1948 reflection about Shuar dislike of foreigners, the Shuar drag their feet to avoid forms of work that they consider antithetical to their social order, such as road building and urbanization. Much has changed since then, and now many Shuar actively promote the urbanization of the forest. Perhaps road development is not like garden-making, but it is certainly considered work worth doing, at least when Shuar are in control and can command mestizo contractors, and not the other way around. Similarly, when Shuar imagine the villages of the future, they dream of places that can lure the *apach* into dyadic relationships of temporary parity through tourism and commercial exchange. In this, they seek to invert the lack of control experienced in interactions with impersonal figures (doctors, officers, state functionaries) or even more personal relations with patronizing and overpowering bosses and colonels.

But Tsere's act of feigning sympathy for Iwia while eating his brains reminds us that the relationship with urban Others is not just one of repulsion: if Tsere managed to outdo the monster, ultimately he was corrupted in the process himself. In these myths, the Shuar are always intrigued by Iwia and try to spend time with him, whether to observe his ways, half-heartedly follow his orders, or slyly plot against him. At times, even after attempting to rid themselves of Iwia, they go back to where they left him (finding him alive again) in order to get access to the material things they need.

When engaging others and their ways of living in this way, the risks are multiple, as the elderly Chuint cautioned. Consider this final example. Between 2012 and 2015, a road was being built that would connect the territories of the interior with the market towns of the colonial frontier, and by extension the rest of the country. After more than thirty-two years of repeated interruptions and broken promises due to lack of public funding, a much-admired Shuar leader called Marcelino Chumpi, then prefect of the province, resumed construction of the road. Its construction became the main point of contention between the Shuar of Makuma and the Ecuadorian government. Marcelino's decision to resume construction was made in open defiance of the central government, which had reportedly been trying to bargain the provision of the road and a local hospital in exchange for allowing the extraction of oil in the interior.

Thus, for the Shuar of Makuma the road came to symbolize their capacity to use the resources of local governments to pursue urban development on their own terms, as well as their ability to sabotage the central government's intention to blackmail them into allowing oil extraction. Yet the more the road advanced, the more my Shuar friends fretted over the impending oil threat. Now that the road existed, I was told, oil developers could enter their territory at any time and negotiate with individual families. The anxieties of the period also gave rise to all sorts of rumors: President Correa was preparing the army to invade Shuar territory; socialist Latin American presidents planned to vanquish Indigenous people using illnesses carried by bats incubated in laboratories; *cortacabezas* were recruiting aides all over the interior. Shuar villagers responded to these threats by reinforcing the security of their territory: they armed themselves with spears, arrested passersby who roamed around without authorization, and even ambushed a group of mestizo engineers patrolling the area. In other words, Shuar reacted by projecting back onto intruders the military power they so anxiously anticipated from (and have long associated with) their urban opponents.

This was a restless period, but one that brought about feelings of empowerment and fierceness rather than debilitation and humiliation. For one, Shuar were responding in a Shuar-like manner to conflict. Defiance allowed them to cultivate and affirm a confrontational stance they deeply value. This was possible as they exploited the conflicts engendered by urban development. So, if forest development has to do with mastering the power of the *apach* to pursue internal well-being, defiance capitalizes on this new form of power—which creates symbolic equality with the *apach*—to pursue a form of differentiating antagonism vis-à-vis the latter, as new targets of enmity. In this, Shuar people follow a well-known Aénts Chicham attitude toward alterity: to avoid becoming like outsiders, they instead aim at mastering the latter's sources of power and effectively "competing with them at their own game" (Taylor 2007, 134, 144–45). Presently, they do so by bringing to the foreground urban superpowers, even if, at the same time, they continue to separate themselves symbolically and materially from the lifeways of the city.

Acknowledgments

I am grateful to my Shuar friends and hosts in Makuma for everything they taught me about defiant village life. My gratitude also goes to Fernando Santos-Granero and Emanuele Fabiano for taking us this far, and finally to Hans Steinmüller for providing insightful comments on an early version of this chapter, and to Grégory Deshoulliere for offering invariably rigorous input and many conversations about Shuar urbanism.

Notes

1. All personal names in this chapter are pseudonyms.
2. I have conducted a total of twenty-four months of fieldwork in the southeastern Ecuadorian foothills in the province of Morona Santiago (2011–13 and 2018), within a network of villages in the Makuma area, and I settled in a village called Kuamar, which, in 2018, numbered approximately 220 people.
3. The *muraya shuar* include people living northwest of the Kutukú Mountains, in the settler towns of Sucúa and Macas. While the Kutukú Mountains rise to more than 8,000 feet above sea level, the Trans-Kutukú area itself is below 1,640 feet.
4. Shuar call the surrounding forest *kampúntin,* a term they connect with *kampui,* the trunks of gigantic trees that grow deep in the forest. The latter term bears an uncanny resemblance to *campo,* the Spanish name for countryside. Shuar are aware that the *apach* perceive *campo* as a remote place of domestic animals, cultivation, and shabby huts lacking in proper urbanization. For them, by contrast, the forest is domestic in the sense that it is always the domus of someone—species owners and a range of nonhumans—rather than being *terra nullius* (Descola 1986).
5. In addition to material enactments of the intercultural city that have emerged in the twenty-first century (see Durán Calisto 2019), they probably have in mind the community-led ecotourist model that has operated successfully among the Achuar (but see Carpentier 2011).
6. Of course, to do this Shuar must also manage the complex challenges of urban development (see Buitron 2020).

7. The Shuar strongly associate exterior urban life and mestizo otherness. Unlike many other Indigenous Amazonian peoples, though not uniquely, the Shuar keenly distinguish themselves and seek to control undue influence from mestizo Others, emphasizing the latter's bodily and moral inferiority.

8. Mestizo towns are also places where people can purchase books of magic through which they can establish pacts with the devil. The devil is a powerful yet oppressive supernatural being associated with the esoteric practices of the *apach* (Grégory Deshoulliere, pers. comm.).

9. In previous work (Buitron 2016b), I describe in more detail some gendered implications of youths' frightening yet desirable encounters with cities and urban beasts.

10. In 1963, the Summer Institute of Linguistics introduced a system of bilingual education training for Amazonian Indigenous peoples at the Pedagogical Institute of Limoncocha in Napo Province.

11. The Aénts Chicham linguistic family also includes the Achuar, Awajún, Shiwiar, and Wampis (see Deshoulliere and Utitiaj 2019 for the change of name).

12. Aénts Chicham historiography excludes conflicts with white outsiders (Taylor 2007, 2014). However, both the Shuar and mestizos living in the Upano Valley tell a story, largely legendary and typical of frontier areas, concerning an army of thousands of Shuar warriors commanded by a chief called Kiruba. The climax of the story recalls that the Indigenous army completely devastated the flourishing cities of Logroño and Sevilla del Oro, and Kiruba poured molten gold into the mouth of the Spanish *gobernador* (governor).

13. The accusation of being a hidden sorcerer or dealing with urban magic books is, however, the most frequent reason to expel villagers from interior communities. This has led to a concentration of marginals in shantytowns (for an example among the Awajún of Peru, see Garra 2019).

14. This is a curious expression since the word *apach*, which Shuar use for mestizo people, resembles the term *apách* (grandfather) (Pellizzaro 2005, 138).

15. For other versions of this myth and similar ones in which the Shuar cunningly kill Iwia, see Rueda and Tankamash (1987, 249–61).

16. Frank and Marie Drown (2002) are also the authors of *Mission to the Headhunters: How God's Forgiveness Transformed Tribal Enemies*, first published in 1961.

17. See also Cova (2021) for Shuar fantasies of kinless suffering in situations of crisis.

References

Albert, Bruce, and Alcida Ramos, eds. 2000. *Pacificando o branco: cosmologias do contato no norte-amazônico*. São Paulo: Editora da Universidade Estadual Paulista.

Buitron, Natalia. 2016a. "The Attraction of Unity: Power, Knowledge and Community Among the Shuar of Ecuadorian Amazonia." PhD diss., London School of Economics and Political Science.

Buitron, Natalia. 2016b. "Paths to the Unfamiliar: Journeying with Children in Ecuadorian Amazonia." In *Children: Anthropological Encounters*, edited by Catherine Allerton, 45–58. London: Bloomsbury Press.

Buitron, Natalia. 2020. "Autonomy, Productiveness and Community: The Rise of Inequality in an Amazonian Society." *Journal of the Royal Anthropological Institute* 26 (1): 48–66.

Candea, Matei, Joanna Cook, Catherine Trundle, and Thomas Yarrow, eds. 2015. *Detachment: Essays on the Limits of Relational Thinking*. Manchester: Manchester University Press.

Carpentier, Julie. 2011. "Tourisme communautaire, conflits internes et *développement local*." *Bulletin de l'Institut Français d'Études Andines* 40 (2): 349–73.

Chio, Jenny. 2017. "Introduction: Rural as Space and Sociality." *Critique of Anthropology* 37 (4): 361–63.

Cova, Victor. 2021. "Thinking the End: Desiring Death and the Undead in the Ecuadorian Upper Amazon." *Ethnos*. Published ahead of print, May 25, 2021. https://doi.org/10.1080/00141844.2020.1867607.

Descola, Philippe. 1986. *La Nature Domestique: Symbolisme et praxis dans l'écologie des Achuar*. Paris: Maison des Sciences de l'Homme.

Descola, Philippe. 1996. *In the Society of Nature: A Native Ecology in Amazonia*. Cambridge: Cambridge University Press.

Deshoulliere, Grégory. 2017. "Chamanismo, desarrollo económico y políticas estatales: notas de investigación desde una asociación de chamanes shuar (Ecuador)." In *Iniciativas empresariales y culturales: estudios de casos en América indígena*, edited by Anne-Gaël Bilhaut and Silvia Macedo, 175–210. Quito: Abya-Yala.

Deshoulliere, Grégory, and Santiago Utitiaj. 2019. "Acerca de la declaración sobre el cambio de nombre del conjunto Jívaro." *Journal de la Société des Américanistes* 105 (2): 167–79.

Drown, Frank, and Marie Drown. 2002. *Mission to the Headhunters: How God's Forgiveness Transformed Tribal Enemies*. Fearn: Christian Focus.

Drown, Marie. 1977–78. "Toward Understanding the Mythology of Jivaroan Tribal Groups in Ecuador." Notebook, Wheaton College independent study. In the author's possession.

Durán Calisto, Ana María. 2019. "For the Persistence of the Indigenous Commune in Amazonia." *E-flux Architecture*, February 2019. https://www.e-flux.com/architecture/overgrowth/221618/.

Fausto, Carlos. 2007. "Feasting on People: Eating Animals and Humans in Amazonia." *Current Anthropology* 48 (4): 497–530.

Fausto, Carlos, and Michael Heckenberger, eds. 2007. *Time and Memory in Indigenous Amazonia: Anthropological Perspectives*. Gainesville: University Press of Florida.

Garra, Simone. 2019. *Los brujos sentenciados: chamanismo y mutación en el mundo Awajún*. Quito: Abya-Yala.

Gnerre, Maurizio. 1999. "Ii jintí, 'Our Way': An English Textbook from the Amazon." *Anglistica* 1 (3): 59–78.

Gnerre, Maurizio. 2003. *La saggezza dei fiumi: miti, nomi e figure dei corsi d'acqua amazzonici*. Roma: Meltemi.

Gordon, Cesar. 2006. *Economia selvagem: ritual e mercadoria entre os índios Xibrin-Mebêngôkre*. São Paulo: Editora da Universidade Estadual Paulista.

Gow, Peter. 1995. "Land, People and Paper in Western Amazonia." In Hirsch and O'Hanlon 1995, 43–62.

Hirsch, Eric, and Michael O'Hanlon. 1995. *The Anthropology of Landscape: Perspectives on Place and Space*. Oxford: Clarendon Press.

Kelly, José Antonio. 2011. *State Healthcare and Yanomami Transformations: A Symmetrical Ethnography*. Tucson: University of Arizona Press.

Killick, Evan. 2008. "Creating Community: Land, Titling, Education, and Settlement Formation Among the Ashéninka of Peruvian Amazonia." *Journal of Latin American and Caribbean Anthropology* 13 (1): 22–47.

Kohn, Eduardo. 2007. "Animal Masters and the Ecological Embedding of History Among the Avila Runa of Ecuador." In Fausto and Heckenberger 2007, 106–29.

Lévi-Strauss, Claude. 1995. *The Story of Lynx*. Chicago: University of Chicago Press.

Mader, Elke. 1999. *Metamorfosis del poder: persona, mito y visión en la sociedad Shuar y Achuar (Ecuador, Perú)*. Quito: Abya-Yala.

Overing, Joanna. 1996. "Who Is the Mightiest of Them All? Jaguar and Conquistador in Piaroa Images of Alterity and Identity." In *Monsters, Tricksters, and Sacred Cows: Animal Tales and American Identities*, edited by James Arnold, 50–79. Charlottesville: University Press of Virginia.

Pellizzaro, Siro. 1978. *Iwianch*. Sucúa, Equador: Abya-Yala.

Pellizzaro, Siro. 1980. *El mundo del agua y los poderes de la fecundación*. Sucúa, Equador: Abya-Yala.

Pellizzaro, Siro. 2005. *Chicham Diccionario Shuar–Castellano*. Quito: Abya-Yala.

Peluso, Daniela. 2015. "Circulating Between Rural and Urban Communities: Multisited Dwellings in Amazonian Frontiers." In "Indigenous Urbanization: The Circulation of Peoples Between Rural and Urban Amazonian Spaces," edited by Daniela Peluso, special issue of *Journal of Latin American and Caribbean Anthropology* 20 (1): 57–79.

Peluso, Daniela, and Miguel Alexiades. 2005. "Urban Ethnogenesis Begins at Home: The Making of Self and Place Amidst Amazonia's Environmental Economy." *Traditional Dwellings and Settlements Review* 16 (2): 1–10.

Praet, Istvan. 2013. *Animism and the Question of Life*. New York: Routledge.

Rival, Laura. 2002. *Trekking Through History: The Huaorani of Amazonian Ecuador*. New York: Columbia University Press.

Rubenstein, Steven. 2007. "Circulation, Accumulation, and the Power of Shuar Shrunken Heads." *Cultural Anthropology* 22 (3): 357–99.

Rueda, Marco Vinicio, and Miguel Tankamash. 1987. *Setenta "mitos shuar."* Quito: Abya-Yala.

Santos-Granero, Fernando. 2009. *Vital Enemies: Slavery, Predation, and the Amerindian Political Economy of Life*. Austin: University of Texas Press.

Santos-Granero, Fernando, and Frederica Barclay. 2011. "Bundles, Stampers, and Flying Gringos: Amazonian Perceptions of Capitalist Violence." *Journal of Latin American and Caribbean Anthropology* 16 (1): 143–67.

Stasch, Rupert. 2013. "The Poetics of Village Space When Villages Are New: Settlement Form as History Making in Papua, Indonesia." *American Ethnologist* 40 (3): 555–70.

Stasch, Rupert. 2016. "Singapore, Big Village of the Dead: Cities as Figures of Desire, Domination, and Rupture Among Korowai of Indonesian Papua." *American Anthropologist* 118 (2): 258–69.

Stasch, Rupert. 2017. "Afterword: Village Space and the Experience of Difference and Hierarchy Between Normative Orders." *Critique of Anthropology* 37 (4): 440–56.

Taylor, Anne-Christine. 1993. "Des fantômes stupéfiants: langage et croyance dans la pensée Achuar." *L'Homme* 33 (126): 429–47.

Taylor, Anne-Christine. 2007. "Sick of History: Contrasting Regimes of Historicity in the Upper Amazon." In Fausto and Heckenberger 2007, 133–68.

Taylor, Anne-Christine. 2014. "Healing Translations: Moving Between Worlds in Achuar Shamanism." *HAU: Journal of Ethnographic Theory* 4 (2): 95–118.

Vallejo, Ivette, Natalia Valdivieso, Cristina Cielo, and Fernando García. 2016. "Ciudades del milenio: ¿inclusión o exclusión en una nueva Amazonía?" In *Nada dura para siempre: neo-extractivismo tras el boom de las materias primas*, edited by Hans-Jürgen Burchardt, Rafael Domínguez, Carlos Larrea, and Stefan Peters, 281–316. Quito: Abya-Yala.

Vilaça, Aparecida. 2010. *Strange Enemies: Indigenous Agency and Scenes of Encounters in Amazonia*. Durham, N.C.: Duke University Press.

Wilson, Japhy, and Manuel Bayón. 2017. *La selva de los elefantes blancos: megaproyectos y extractivismos en la Amazonía ecuatoriana*. Quito: Abya-Yala.

CHAPTER 5

Sublime Cities

Ethnographic Fabulations on Plant Beings Among the Jarawara of Brazil

FABIANA MAIZZA

As their oral accounts indicate, the Jarawara people of Southwest Amazonia have a history of intense struggle, death, and flight. The life of these people and their ancestors was deeply marked, and indeed destroyed, by the two rubber-extraction fronts whose terrifying advance—in search of seringa (*Hevea brasiliensis*) and caucho (*Castilla elastica*), from the opposite directions of the Brazilian Northeast and Peru, respectively—caused a slaughter among Indigenous peoples. The rubber boom's consequences are still felt today, as is the case for most of the Indigenous peoples referred to in this volume (see Fabiano and Buitron, for instance). At the end of the rubber boom, Christian missions entered the region, many of which remain active in the villages of diverse peoples. Thus, what we could call "contact with the world of white people" spans a period of more than one hundred years of losses, traumas, and inventions (in Roy Wagner's [1975] sense of the term) related to what the anthropological literature has described as the end of the world (Danowski and Viveiros de Castro 2014).

Jarawara shamanic activity is filled with references to the "white world," found side by side with references to the many Others in the Jarawara world. If we wish to think of something called an urban imaginary, it would be just one of many imaginaries accessed and lived by shamans in their interactions with otherworlds: knife beings, peach palm beings, peccary beings, sorubim catfish beings, sky beings. . . . There is no exclusivity to the urban imaginary; it is simply one among diverse other possible worlds. What I investigate in this chapter are aspects of the Jarawara world that, seen from the viewpoint of our Western logic, may appear contradictory—an appearance that highlights our latent difficulty in "experiencing another imagination" (Viveiros de Castro 2002, 123) but also indicates just how important it is for us to *speculate with* other creativities (Puig de la Bellacasa 2017; Haraway 2016).

As I have discussed elsewhere (Maizza 2014, 2017), in the Jarawara world, the souls (*abono*) of plants, which have a human appearance, leave their bodies to be raised (*nayana*) in the upper layer (*neme*) by other plant beings. At the same time, shamans, who periodically visit the *neme*, say that some places in this upper layer are similar to the cities of the white people. As the shaman Batebiri recounts: "I've already seen it, I like it up there [*nemeya*], it's like Lábrea, a city. It's big, there are a lot of cars, planes, a full river." Thus, the postmortem world, the upper layer—or, as among diverse other Indigenous peoples, the "better world"—is a world we could describe as one of plant people who live in cities and hold festivals (*marina*) frequently, if not the whole time. Here, I *speculate with* the idea of an eco/urban/festive world, where kinship is made mainly through raising, and *speculate with* the questions that this world poses for us.[1]

This chapter, as its title suggests, is a writing experiment where anthropology and feminism "each constitutes a position from which to regard a counter position," as Marilyn Strathern (2004, 35) has taught us to do. I begin with a descriptive section, presenting the Jarawara shamans' songs as they wander through the worlds of many kinds of beings and bring back new knowledge. I then talk about the Brazilian village of Lábrea, where Jarawara people often go to buy white people's things; after which I discuss human-plant relations among the Jarawara and the ways those relations can be understood through Donna Haraway's (1998) provocation about borders in her "Cyborg Manifesto." In brief, I conduct some feminist experimentation with my ethnographic material while at the same time trying to stay faithful to the Jarawara people and to their teachings during all the years that we have been friends.

Nemeya Aesthetics

I begin by exploring several tales and songs of the Jarawara shamans that I collected during my doctoral field research and after, in order to think about the aesthetics of the Jarawara upper layer, the *neme*, including its urban dimension but also its danger as well as its connection to raising and caring. Rather than providing a linear and synthetic description of the *neme*, I turn to various accounts given by Jarawara shamans and use their voice, whether in conversations or in songs (translated with the help of Jarawara collaborator friends), to evoke the multiplicity of the *neme*—a multiplicity also encountered in the terrestrial layer, where different types of beings live in different locations in their own villages.[2]

As we learn from the shamanic accounts of Davi Kopenawa (Kopenawa and Albert 2013), shamans seem to travel to diverse space-times, without time and space being dissociable as they are for us Westerners. In one shamanic voyage, for example, taken after consuming *yakoana*, Kopenawa arrived at the place of a specific Yanomami myth, at the precise moment when it was happening. The *ayaka* songs of the Jarawara shamans—likewise performed after consumption of a plant, in this case tobacco snuff (*sina*)—also describe this move to diverse space-times. In parallel with the concept of travel, central to the Jarawara shamans' narratives, is the idea of the *inamati*, also an important concept. In the Jarawara language, *inamati* signifies something whose existential quality remains opaque to us: a being, a thing, some kind of stuff. But it is more commonly used to refer to those souls that are not of someone who died, or someone known to the Jarawara (in which case, the word *kanamori* would be used). Above all, it refers to the souls of plants, reflecting the fact that plants maintain close relations with shamans. The Jarawara include in what the anthropological literature denominates as the shaman's "auxiliary spirits" the souls of cultivated plants—called, among other names, *inamati*.

The types of people who live in the places to which shamans travel seem to encompass—in the Strathernian sense—other characteristics, such that place is marked by the mode of being of the type of people who live there.[3] At the same time, though, the characteristics of those who live there reflect the type of place occupied, in a complex relationship that again evokes Strathern's concept of encompassment. Hence, the shaman Batebiri speaks about a place "there above," as partially quoted earlier in this chapter:

> I've already seen it, I like it up there, it's like Lábrea, a city. It's big, there are a lot of cars, planes, a full river. I saw thunder [*bahi*] in the *neme*. A lot of thunder, like people from the city, they used a rubber hat like police officers, like police chiefs, they were talking, there were a lot of

people. . . . When the thunder spoke with force, it shot bullets to kill the large trees [*awa ehebote*]. The tree fell in the river because of the thunder's bullets. The thunder's wife is like you, a woman from the city; there are lots of women, I think.[4]

The same shaman recounts that:

A long time ago, the *neme* fell and killed various people, but a shaman who was very wise did not die, he took the payment [*manakone*] and since then the *inamati* have been holding up the *neme* with a length of rope, they're not going to let go again.

The shaman Batisawa sings in his *ayaka*:

The *neme* stopped. People approached the *neme*, they said: "I want to spy on the *neme*. I'm going to look." They had looked from a distance, now they went closer. Our kin went close to the *neme* and returned.

Batebiri also tells that:

I had never gone *nemeya*. One day I went *nemeya*, I met the *inamati* and spoke to him. . . . I spoke to the soul of Labiwawi [Labiwawi *kana-mori*]. . . . I came back, *inamati* carried me on his back, he brought me back. *Inamati* brought me on his back, then placed me on the ground, "You can go," he returned to his own house. I wanted to sleep. I climbed the ladder to my house, grabbed my hammock, and laid down.

In a song of another shaman, Kowisari, he said:

Did you see me? You know me, you're not going to speak any more. You're going to talk, but not me.

Below, we can read the *ayaka* song of Batebiri about the knife people, performing festivals in the *neme*:

Dyimakisanisawi carries a large machete, he carries it on his shoulder. Dyimakosisawi and Dyimakosinisawi carry a machete in their hand.

Dyimakosinisawi has a machete with two blades. "You can go, I'm going home too. When I get there, I'm going to work," Dyimakosinisawi said. "I'm going there, I'm going to work, I'm going to clean/tidy [*namosa*] the *neme*. We're going to tidy our father's *neme*. My father lives *nemeya*, he makes a noise in the *neme*. He lives in the *neme*. We live in the *neme*. The noise from the *neme* is like this: *tataroro*."

"We're going to see them in the *neme*. We're going to see what they're doing in the *neme*. Listen to the noise they're making in the *neme*. Listen to the noise, *kisi kisi*. Our father is making a noise in the *neme*, *kisi kisi*. Let's go to the *neme* to watch. Every day in the *neme*, the work makes that noise, *kisi kisi*."

The soul of the large rock called me. "Let's give him some food." The soul of the *paúba* [*boko abono*, a plant species] came. Nobody had seen the jaguar. She arrived, everyone saw her, a female jaguar, she ate the bones, the bone got stuck in her throat, she spat it out and made a noise.

Later in the same song, Batebiri speaks of the *neme* people, the Nemefe:

At the end of the *neme* [*neme matoniya*], a piece of *neme* came out, it came walking, traversing, changing direction. The Nemefe live in the *neme*, the folk of the *neme*.

In a story told by Batisawa, he said:

I'm going to travel; I'm going to travel to meet the *inamati*. If I go to the village of the *inamati*, I'll come back home afterward. I went, and went, and went, and went. I heard the *inamati* playing. They were playing. They were making a lot of noise. There were a lot of people. They were making a lot of noise; you could hear them from afar on the path. They said: "Someone's coming [*inamati kake ka*], who is it?" Only one person came to greet me: "Grandfather [*iti*], why did you come?" "I came to visit, to see you." "You came traveling to see us? You can look. We're playing. We're playing with our [unmarried] women, the women of our village." Now a jaguar came, their jaguar, they played with their jaguar. A large jaguar. . . . The jaguar left. I stayed to watch the *inamati* playing. When they stopped playing, I left. I returned home.

Through these shamanic songs and accounts it becomes clear that *neme* refers, in fact, to diverse places—not just one—and that there is no clear idea about how these places look. The only common characteristic is the position they occupy vis-à-vis the terrestrial layer: all of them are above the earth. In this sense, we could say that the *neme* can only be "defined" in relation to the earth, as *nemeya*, "there above." It is necessary for the shamans to visit these places alone to learn about their characteristics and their inhabitants. The shaman is carried on the back of an *inamati* to reach the *neme* and then see where he is, and with whom. These journeys lead the shaman to acquire knowledge that is linked uniquely to itself and his experience (see Coelho de Souza 2010). The *neme* reflects the multiplicity of the Jarawara world. On each trip, a shaman discovers one of the many places of the *neme* and its residents. Sometimes he returns to places he already knows, sometimes not. Importantly, when the shaman arrives somewhere different, it might be dangerous: the people there may be wild and may not want the shaman to visit. The danger forms part of a shaman's acquisition of knowledge and wisdom.

Batisawa and Batebiri each offer a narrative of how such danger manifests in the shamans' journeys to the *neme*. In an *ayaka* song, Batisawa narrates various tensions:

The noise of the *neme* is like soft rain falling. "It's me making the noise from the *neme*, I live in the *neme*." I'm sweating because the *neme* is hot. My grandmother fanned me. The *neme* is hot. There's a hole in the *neme*. There's hot water in the *neme*. Hot rain falling. The water of the *neme* spoke to me. The hole of the *neme* is bad. Look at the people who live in the *neme*, at the end of the *neme* [*neme yowitiwa*]. "Did you see the people at the end of the *neme*?" The *neme* is hot, I went to the *neme*, I know that there it is hot, the *neme* is hot. When we go to the *neme*, it's bad, it's very hot.

I went to see my grandmother. My grandmother talked to me. I went to see the *neme*. The *neme* is hot, now I sweated.

In the *neme* there is another, different land. I don't think the *neme* is any good. I heard the beast bellowing in the *neme*. The beast that lives in the *neme* makes a lot of noise. "Don't go there, let the beast live there. If we go there, the beast will eat us." We never went there where the beast lives, we never saw the beast [*yama*].

In this narrative, danger comes from a beast (*yama*) that bellows, makes a noise, and, if someone approaches, eats them. Batebiri narrates another account of danger:

> "Wash the *neme*," they said, now I know. "Did you see the end of the *neme*?" We cannot see anything of it. Who were you speaking to? They were all wild. They were all angry. They were angry about their mother. "We're angry because our mother died." We've arrived. "We came here to go there." "You can go." "We'll return afterward, it will take some time."

In this example, danger comes from beings who have just lost their mother and are angry: an encounter with them may prove fatal for the shaman if badly handled. Thus, what we see as dangerous in the upper layer, as in the terrestrial layer, are ill-fated encounters that can cost a person's life, including that of shamans during their "celestial" journeys.

Some details make the upper-layer villages allied with the shaman somewhat different from places on earth. To begin with, everyone is young, and nobody becomes sick. Above, the hunters are stronger and can, for example, carry hunted game without help, even tapirs. The plants in the swiddens are larger and more beautiful; the rivers are full and the trees tall. Nobody ever goes hungry. There are lots of food, abundant fruit, much money, a lot of tobacco snuff. Furthermore, when residents of the *neme* go to the city to make purchases, rather than traveling on foot or by canoe, they use their cars and airplanes, and can buy whatever they want. In fact, the villages of the *neme* look like the city of Lábrea, with streets, markets, cars, motorbikes, bicycles, and many people. They are very much like the enchanted cities described in this volume by Fernando Santos-Granero and Daniela Peluso, who argue that relating the afterlife to urbanity is not a recent phenomenon, but a timeless Amerindian process of speculating about cities. It is also worth remembering, as Philippe Erikson points out in this volume, that many contemporary Amazonian cities are located in the exact same place where Amerindian settlements once stood. The people in the *neme* spend a lot of time together, holding festivals. The *kisi kisi*, a sound characteristic of many places of the *neme*, is the noise made by the clatter of shell shin rattles, used solely on *marina* days. Therefore, like the games cited by the shaman Batisawa in one of his stories above ("We're playing. We're playing with our [unmarried] women, the women of our village"), it is characteristic of the closure of the *marina* rituals.

It is here that it becomes interesting to consider the urban qualities of the *neme*. As we saw in the first account that I cited (Batebiri's narrative of the place "there above"), parts of the sky, or some places of the *neme*, are a city. Not a city exactly like Lábrea, but a city similar to Lábrea, and better. In the *neme*, there are cars, airplanes, and motorbikes that allow people to travel around with ease, but there is no negative side, such as accidents with pedestrians or a high cost of gasoline. In the *neme*, nobody needs to pay exorbitant prices for merchandise or carry their weight. Moreover, there are lots of easy-to-purchase goods, while garbage does not seem to exist. There are lots of people in the *neme*, and this too seems to be a quality connected to the image of cities.[5] Thus, we can see how some places in the *neme* present this double aesthetic: a hyper–Indigenous village (tidy, clean, and beautiful, with constant festivals in which everyone is appropriately adorned), and a hyper–white city (with lots of merchandise and no garbage). In other words, the *neme* is a Jarawara reading of our cities, a reading of how our cities could be good were they conceived through the Indigenous imagination. It is a reminder that the correct way to live is among kin. The cities of white people would be good if they were Jarawara villages (figures 5.1, 5.2, and 5.3), a notion similar to that of the Shuar, who seek to "urbanize the forest" (see Buitron, this volume). The cities in the *neme* are just so. . . . Which is why they are sublime cities.

Lábrea City

The Jarawara travel regularly to the city of Lábrea, on monthly trips lasting about two days.[6] All the people from different Jarawara villages have at least one house where they can stay for their short periods in the city. No Jarawara person, therefore, must stay in a hotel, as I have seen other Indigenous people doing in the city. Every Jarawara village has at least one person who owns a house in the city. The city is depicted as a place with many people, goods, cars, bicycles, and motorbikes, where it is good to be when you have money. If not, it is better to stay in the village. The monthly trips to Lábrea are pleasurable moments when people are not working but are "visiting," buying what they need before returning to the village. They are also a time to see relatives who reside in the city and others who are also visiting. These

FIGURE 5.1 Casa Nova village, 2014. Photo by Fabiana Maizza.

FIGURE 5.2 Casa Nova school, 2014. Photo by Fabiana Maizza.

FIGURE 5.3 Jarawara women, 2014. Photo by Fabiana Maizza.

meetings of different people in the same place undoubtedly recall the *marina*, where people from different villages meet up in one place for a short period of time, chat, see one another, and cook and eat lavish meals.

Some women have also married white men and established their homes, and lives, in the city. They acquire a double life in the process: with relatives in the villages, and relatives in the city, relations that emerge through marriage. The relatives of their husbands end up forming relations with Jarawara persons who live in the villages and visit the latter on festive occasions. These women (at present, I know of four) of different ages maintain close ties to the villages, going to spend long periods with their Jarawara relatives, with or without their spouses. They also welcome with open arms and much hospitality those who arrive from the villages to spend time in Lábrea. They are highly effective in facilitating the communication between their Jarawara relatives and the merchants and other services in Lábrea, like banks, social welfare, and the postal service.

However, the city is also considered a place of imminent aggression (see Fabiano and Santos-Granero, this volume, for similar perceptions among the Urarina and the Southern Arawak, respectively). Many Jarawara have been assaulted in Lábrea: their houses have been broken into when they were away, their canoes have been stolen from the port, and their pockets are often picked without them noticing. In most cases they do everything they can to find the thief and recover the lost goods, threatening them with phrases like, "I'm a real wild Indian, like my father, if you steal here again, I'll kill you," as a friend said to scare a man who had stolen his TV set. On the other hand, for a village chief, a *cacique*, it is important to have and maintain good relations in the city. Jarawara chiefs feel at ease in Lábrea and know a lot of white people with whom they chat and joke, and who invite them to their houses, birthday parties, and so on.

Lábrea can be, however, an inhospitable place for the Jarawara. It is a place where they may experience racism and physical aggression, based solely on an immense and uncontrolled disdain for Indigenous peoples in Brazil, which is most felt in cities that were historically important for the conquest and invasion of Amazonia, as is the case of Lábrea. In 2014, to take just one example, four youths, returning from a party early in the morning, decided to stop at a bar close to their home.[7] Following an unfriendly look and exchange of words, they found themselves under attack by various non-Indigenous men armed with lengths of wood and knives. Two of them escaped, but the other two woke up hours later in the Lábrea municipal hospital, where they remained for several days. Even today they feel the aftereffects of the gratuitous and criminal attack, which the authorities never investigated. The violence to which young Jarawara people are exposed in the city is a threat to their lives, and they know this. For this reason, they never walk alone and only go out in groups at night. Young women avoid being in the open at night, and whenever they go out during the day they are always accompanied by other family members.

While the older generations were constantly tricked by Lábrea's traders, young people, fully versed in mathematics and fluent in Portuguese, suffer less from this kind of problem. They calculate prices with ease, including installments, and also know how to handle money, both their own and that of their parents. Over the last fifteen years (since 2004), therefore, I have seen these young people acquire what they need to live comfortably in their villages—items such as outboard motors, radios, boats, and mobile phones—often making long-term plans for payment in installments.

These young generations are more widely educated than their parents. For those young people who graduated from high school in 2017, for exam-

ple, many continued studying through a partnership with the Secretaria de
Estado de Educação (SEDUC, State Education Department), which provided
the infrastructure and hired a teacher to teach higher education courses in
Casa Nova village through the Technology-Mediated Secondary Education
program developed by SEDUC's Educational Media Center and run by the
Amazonas state government (Maximiano, Fonseca, and Mitidieri 2020).
The classes were given in Manaus studios and transmitted live via satellite.
The students were assisted by an on-site teacher at certain moments during
the more than three hours of classes held every evening. She would answer
questions and help the students complete their exercises. Each day of the
week was dedicated to a different subject. Many problems exist in relation
to "nondifferential" (standard national curriculum) teaching for Indigenous
communities, including for example the lack of suitable content and the fast
pace of the work, when many students are in fact seeing the material for the
first time. However, secondary education in Casa Nova met the demands of
the young people, who had neither the inclination nor the money to move
to the city. Many young people and adults who graduate from high school
immediately enroll in the Technical Course in Forestry for Jarawara people,
offered by the Instituto Federal do Amazonas (Federal Institute of Amazonas), where they are making exemplary progress in their academic studies.

In sum, Lábrea is not just a place that foments the Jarawara urban imaginary. It is also a real place with relations, people, and encounters both good
and bad, where those who opt to live in the village can visit and have periodic
experiences in the world of white people, experiences that most of the time
constitute an interlude to their lives in the village. White people always are,
and always will be, distrusted by the Jarawara. For the latter, the best place
to live is among kin on their own land. For this reason, the Jarawara urban
imaginary is perhaps more perceptible through the relations they cultivate
with the plant world.

Sublimating: The World of Plants

As I have described in detail elsewhere (Maizza 2014, 2017), when the plants
that the Jarawara cultivate in their swiddens grow and emerge from the soil,
their souls also emerge. These souls, according to shamans, possess the appearance of a human baby. Shamans refer to them as *inamati* of the *neme*
and take them to be raised in a village "there above," where they will forge

kinship ties with their "foster" parents—those who raise the children in the *neme*. The person who sowed the plant is also considered to be the parent of the plant child raised in the *neme*. This parent will not have relations with the *neme* soul, though, but will care for the plant being through constant actions of clearing, talking to, looking after, and tidying the swidden.

When a Jarawara person dies, their body is buried and their soul emerges, to be fetched and taken to the *neme* to live in the village of their plant kin: a child, niece/nephew, or another type of kin. The soul rejuvenates, literally becoming a youth (not a child) again, and thus remains without ever aging, marrying someone good and beautiful with whom to raise plant children, who will in turn be born in the Jarawara swiddens. Growing swiddens is how human-plant ties are established beyond the present, enabling maintenance of the relations between the Jarawara and the *inamati* beings through the daily care of cultivated plants.

The beings closest to the Jarawara who live in the *neme* are their plant children, as well as their dead kin, who have gone to live in the villages of the plant people related to their swiddens. Shamans know these villages and the people who live in them, but they also know many more beings in the *neme*. Anyone who is not a shaman will also know diverse beings through the shamans' songs, but will only maintain relations of care with their own swiddens and their plants (their plant children). If we speculate on this idea, therefore, the city aesthetic of the *neme* throws into question our worn-out nature/culture dichotomy, showing how it continues to be, despite everything, an epistemological barrier to our imagination. For us, the idea that plant beings live in high-technology cities may appear contradictory. However, as Emanuele Fabiano shows in this volume for the Urarina case, this is not uncommon in native Amazonian urban imaginaries (although, unlike Jarawara plant cities, which connect people through marriage and child-rearing ties, Urarina arboreal cities are characterized by their hierarchical and coercive relations).

From a Jarawara perspective, plant beings have a human appearance, live in crowded cities, and have cars, motorbikes, airplanes, electricity, brick houses, knives, and every other type of merchandise. In these cities, everything functions smoothly; there is no garbage, no traffic, no pollution, no violence, and no social inequality. Everyone lives well, is married, and is beautiful. Adapted to our own imagination, it might correspond to a work of science fiction, a type of future city where plant beings benefit from technology in a fair and equitable manner, without harming what we call the environment.

Critically, the notion that fiction has nothing to teach us forms part of the very same Western thought that separates nature from culture. Speculative feminism or speculative fiction, however, have shown us that both beliefs are wrong: fiction can teach us much, and nature is not so separate from culture. Recently, the filming of *The Handmaid's Tale* (1985) by Margaret Atwood as a TV series (2017–) has reinvigorated the force of this type of feminist narrative. Ursula K. Le Guin and Octavia Butler are other central names here. These authors began writing in the late 1960s and 1970s, but this type of literature continues to be an important arena for younger generations, for feminist imaginings of the real, the possible, the limits of the imagination. The idea is to propose new futures, possible futures, and implausible but real presents (Haraway 2016, 136).

In her book *Staying with the Trouble*, Donna Haraway (2016, 137–38) also engages in an experiment of speculative fiction, through her final chapter, called "The Camille Stories: Children of Compost." In "The Camille Stories," Haraway encourages us to "Make Kin Not Babies"—that is, to think about forms of kinship centered not on the heterosexual man-woman relation or on reproduction, but on what the author calls *oddkin*, which includes human and nonhuman relations and makes us *become with* Others and other forms of life. In Haraway's tales of feminist speculation, the world is in ruins and the "Children of Compost" must deal with the problem of living in such a world. Making kin in innovative ways is one answer. Each child should have at least three parents; children should be considered rare and precious and should possess an animal symbiont, which is part of the person; and kinship relations can be formed at any moment of life and can include newly arrived immigrants. We are thus talking about anticolonial, antiracist, and proqueer worlds. In these worlds, creating kinship is a means of reducing the number of humans and their demands on the earth and, at the same time, increasing the number of creatures (human or not) that prosper with the energies invested in these dispersed emergent worlds (Haraway 2016, 138).

Thinking about the relations of Jarawara people in such terms, I observe that my friends' creativity dialogues in surprising ways with Haraway's speculative fiction. In some ways, the Jarawara world is closer to the world of the "Children of Compost" than my own world as I conceive it today, starting with the fact that Jarawara people are survivors of the genocides resulting from the rubber booms that took place in Southwest Amazonia throughout the late nineteenth and early twentieth century. I see features in contemporary Jarawara kinship that push the boundaries of our conception of kinship and make us aware of what Haraway calls *becoming with*—and more-than-human worlds. As I have discussed elsewhere (Maizza 2017), among the Jarawara, many children possess more than one father, as is well known in the Americanist literature. But there also exists a fairly original form of action that we could call multimaternity. Finally, among the Jarawara, people have diverse children; some are human while others are plants. This is possible within a system of nurture (*nayana*) in which children and plants are raised by individuals who are not their "biological" parents—and who sometimes do not even form a couple.[8]

Back to the *neme*: what seems to be posed by Jarawara creativity is that plant beings possess qualities beyond what we normally attribute to these types of beings (that is, the characteristics that we consider, according to our nature/culture divide, as belonging to nature). Here, in Jarawara shamanic speculation, there is an urban way of plant existence. The Yanomami shaman Davi Kopenawa (Kopenawa and Albert 2013, 344–45), on a journey to work in Paris when he saw the Eiffel Tower for the first time, asserted with a disconcerting conviction that it was a house of spirits. If we consider that the Eiffel Tower is one symbol of the project of Western modernity, then the boundaries that the "moderns" (in Bruno Latour's [1993] sense of the term) have established for themselves and within which we constantly operate—such as nature/culture, body/mind, science/fiction, rural/urban, man/woman—are disconfigured and definitively decomposed by Indigenous thought. The idea that plant beings live in sublime cities in the upper layer is not contradictory for the Jarawara. On the contrary, it is the experience of these cities that inspires the Jarawara urban imaginary, and not the sporadic visits to the city of Lábrea, as one might have initially thought.

Thinking and qualifying Jarawara human-plant relations seem to me central here. While the cities of the upper layer are inhabited by plant people, they reflect the relations that humans establish with their swiddens and plant children. As I have described in other works (Maizza 2014, 2017), there exists an everyday practice of persuasion and care that permeates people's relations with all the beings with whom they wish to establish some kind of kinship connection. The Jarawara world is a world in which "magic," as we might think it, is not excluded from knowledge, from knowing, from gardening practices, or from relationships with other beings. This makes all the difference to the dimensions of care, which are in themselves indications that in this world Jarawara persons *compose with* diverse types of beings (Haraway 2016).

For Jarawara people, to consider the act of caring as something exclusively human would be unthinkable—as would seeing it as something that does not require phenomenal efforts to cultivate relations in diversity and very often in dissidence (Puig de la Bellacasa 2017, 79). Thus, it would not be wrong to assert that caring is what organizes Jarawara relations, whether these relations are with what we qualify as humans or nonhumans. In terms of Jarawara relations, this divide seems inoperative. It is also worth noting that Jarawara shamans are described as "great carers"; living close to them means being under their care.

Some poststructuralist feminist academics, if we can use this label, have been working toward removing the concept of care from an exclusively human sphere. Haraway's (2016) idea of *composing with* is one pointer in this direction. For a long time, care has been one of our most powerful self-descriptions to subjugate the feminine world, approximating women to nature. Thus, for instance, it is natural—an instinct—for the mother (and only the mother) to care for her offspring. As Rosi Braidotti (2006, 270) tells us: "Women were classified alongside natives, animals and others as referents of a generative force that was reduced to a mere biological function and deprived of political and ethical relevance." The notion of care has been reappropriated today by feminist intellectual thought and given new meaning, applied both to the sphere of politics and to an ethics of other-than-human relations. Caring, thus, becomes an experiment in thinking about a world where people make decisions in the presence of those who will face the resulting consequences (Haraway 2016, 12), something that Isabelle Stengers (2012) calls cosmopolitics. Along the lines of contemporary feminist thought, here the term *care* also becomes a provocation.

If we return to the "Cyborg Manifesto" and use it to think about the concept of care, we can see that the resignification of care—as proposed by contemporary poststructuralist feminists like Rosi Braidotti, Maria Puig de la Bellacasa, Anna Tsing, Vinciane Despret, Elizabeth Grosz, and Claire Colebrook—is analogous to the cyborg beings proposed by Haraway (1998). Pushing this speculation to one of its limits, we can say that cyborg beings care by *becoming with* other cyborg beings. It is this multiplicity of partial relations that connects and disconnects various types of beings, who are in turn hybrid beings, made from parts without a whole, which breach our epistemological borders like the nature/culture dichotomy itself. In this way, we can see how the Jarawara *neme*, with its plant beings, sublime cities, everyday care, and festivals, tells us about such composite beings and their relations. The Jarawara urban imaginary is connected to the reading that they make of our cities, our urban space, but which, inversely, they rethink and improve in a movement that we could define as sublimation, since it passes from one state to another without intermediation. In other words, the urban becomes Indigenous, which translates into clean, ecological, and joyful cities, characterized by their calm and abundance, where one lives with kin, and which are, therefore, more human.

If there is one thing that Yanomami shaman Davi Kopenawa, in partnership with Bruce Albert (2013), tells us strikingly, it is that there is nothing in the world of white people and in the Indigenous-white encounter that Indigenous peoples would miss. As we know, from the Indigenous viewpoint this encounter has been lamentable (Krenak 1999). In a long discussion on what lies behind his desire to purchase goods, Kopenawa tells us that he only purchases goods to give to kin and to the kin of kin, so that his name travels and is spoken in distant lands. This evokes something known to us in the anthropological literature on Polynesian chiefs through the concept of *mana*. In this sense, and as we have always known, these foreign goods only make the Yanomami become more Yanomami. Likewise, the cities of the Jarawara *neme* only make the Jarawara more Jarawara.

The Jarawara urban imaginary tells us about the life of plants and about living among kin. It tells us, in sum, about the Jarawara model of beauty, care, and living well. But it tells us also that the villages where the Jarawara go on their monthly trips, the sublime cities of the plant people, and other *neme* villages visited by the shamans, are places where people or shamans should be alert. The Jarawara urban imaginary fits with what westerners would think of the notion of multiplicity in the Jarawara world, being both very beautiful and very dangerous.

Notes

1. This is an ethnographic chapter, and I apologize for the absence of comparisons with other Indigenous societies whose ethnographic descriptions bear similarities to the Jarawara.
2. Here I especially thank Bibiri, who spent hours on end helping me translate diverse accounts, and Dyimayanici, who made the transcriptions with me. I also

thank the research support received from the Conselho Nacional de Desenvolvimento Científico e Tecnológico (Brazilian National Council for Scientific and Technological Development) and the Fundação de Amparo à Pesquisa do Estado de São Paulo (São Paulo Research Foundation) during my doctorate and postdoctorate, respectively.

3. "The one viewpoint is also contained within the other. Such is the condition I call encompassment" (Strathern 1988, 242).

4. Here the term *city* was given in Portuguese (*cidade*), the same as *hat, bullet, police chief, car,* and *plane.*

5. White-lipped peccaries are another group of beings likened to an agglomeration of people, just like the plants in the swiddens.

6. The other city that some Jarawara visit frequently is Porto Velho, especially beginning in the 2000s, when some people participated in teacher training courses organized by JOCUM (Jovens Com Uma Missão), a Christian youth mission. In such visits, however, they were kept in locales distant from the city center and had no direct contact with white people outside of the organization. The Jarawara who become sick and cannot be treated in Lábrea are taken to Manaus—where they stay at the hospital or at the CASAI (Casa de Saúde Indígena, an Indigenous hostel)—or to Porto Velho. Some elderly men also say that they once worked for rubber bosses in Boca do Acre. These are the four cities that the Jarawara know best, but they have also heard of various other remote regions where *yara* (white people) live. These places have been described to them by Catholic or Evangelical missionaries, linguists, and anthropologists.

7. Unfortunately, I could list various additional instances, including the brutal murder of a young woman.

8. Jarawara parenthood, like other aspects of Amerindian worlds, evokes a multiplicity of forms that destabilize the understandings of kinship and gender traditionally held by anthropologists. I discuss this in more detail elsewhere (Maizza 2017).

References

Braidotti, Rosi. 2006. *Transpositions: On Nomadic Ethics.* Cambridge: Polity Press.

Coelho de Souza, Marcela Stockler. 2010. "A cultura do invisível: conhecimento indígena e patrimônio immaterial." *Anuário Antropológico* 1:149–74.

Danowski, Débora, and Eduardo Viveiros de Castro. 2014. *Há um mundo por vir? Ensaio sobre os medos e os fins.* São Paulo: Instituto Socioambiental.

Haraway, Donna. 1998. "A Cyborg Manifesto: Science, Technology, and Socialist-Feminism in the Late Twentieth Century" (1985). In *Simians, Cyborgs, and Women: The Reinvention of Nature,* by Donna Haraway, 149–81. London: Free Association.

Haraway, Donna. 2016. *Staying with the Trouble: Making Kin in the Chthulucene.* Durham, N.C.: Duke University Press.

Kopenawa, Davi, and Bruce Albert. 2013. *The Falling Sky: Words of a Yanomami Shaman*. Cambridge, Mass.: Harvard University Press.

Krenak, Ailton. 1999. "O eterno retorno do encontro." In *A outra margem do Ocidente*, edited by Adauto Novaes, 23–31. São Paulo: Minc, FUNARTE.

Latour, Bruno. 1993. *We Have Never Been Modern*. Cambridge, Mass.: Harvard University Press.

Maizza, Fabiana. 2014. "Sobre as crianças-planta: o cuidar e o seduzir no parentesco Jarawara." *Mana* 20 (3): 491–518.

Maizza, Fabiana. 2017. "Persuasive Kinship: Human-Plant Relations in Southwest Amazonia." *Tipití: Journal of the Society for the Anthropology of Lowland South America* 15 (2): 206–20.

Maximiano, Claudina Azevedo, Alessandra de Souza Fonseca, and Marco Antônio Cordeiro Mitidieri. 2020. "Aprender o nome das árvores na língua dos yara: relato de experiência do curso técnico em florestas para o povo Jarawara." *Abatirá: Revista de Ciências Humanas e Linguagens* 6 (2): 616–48.

Puig de la Bellacasa, María. 2017. *Matters of Care: Speculative Ethics in More Than Human Worlds*. Minneapolis: University of Minnesota Press.

Stengers, Isabelle. 2012. "Reclaiming Animism." *E-flux Journal* 36. https://www.e-flux.com/journal/36/61245/.

Strathern, Marilyn. 1988. *The Gender of the Gift: Problems with Women, Problems with Society in Melanesia*. Berkeley: University of California Press.

Strathern, Marilyn. 2004. *Partial Connections*. Walnut Creek, Calif.: Altamira Press.

Viveiros de Castro, Eduardo. 2002. "O nativo relativo." *Mana* 8 (1): 113–48.

Wagner, Roy. 1975. *The Invention of Culture*. Chicago: University of Chicago Press.

PART III

Urban Imaginaries
Through Time

CHAPTER 6

"Originally, Riberalta Was Called Xëbiya and It Was Ruled by Mawa Maxokiri . . ."

Urban Imaginaries and Urban Migration Among the Chacobo of Beni, Bolivia

PHILIPPE ERIKSON

Some years ago, in the early 1990s, I overheard a group of Chacobo from Alto Ivon, Bolivia, making fun of one of their relatives who lives on the banks of the Yata River, a few days by boat from a border town called Guajará Mirim on the Brazilian side and Guayaramerín on the Bolivian side. They were laughing because the man, drinking with a group of mestizos and ashamed to admit his Indigenous descent, allegedly insisted: "Yo no soy chacobo, no; soy de Walalamili. . . . Wa-la-la-mi-li." Indeed, the town's name is a tongue twister and the mispronunciation quite funny, but there was more to the joke than the drunken fellow's self-contradicting phonetics. Its humorous effect was also increased by the tinge of indignation it triggered. Back then, far from denying their origins, most Chacobo were politically self-assertive (and they still are today). Pretending to be a "Walalamili" urbanite rather than a native son was therefore scornful as well as laughable. It was also amusing for being quite unlikely: in the 1990s, only a handful of Chacobo lived in cities, making the stuttering drunk man's preposterous assertion even more improbable.

Since then, the situation has changed drastically, and at an amazingly rapid speed, largely due to the improved infrastructure and increased job opportunities for Indigenous peoples brought about, in 2006, by the election of Evo Morales Ayma as Bolivia's first Indigenous president. As I discovered in 2015 when a young Chacobo erudite helped me pinpoint people's whereabouts on a store-bought city map, nearly one-third of the Chacobo population now spends a good part of the year in urban settings, especially in Riberalta, a provincial capital in Beni Department. Many families even own houses in town, where they live, intermittently at least, a substantial portion of the year. Thirty years ago, there were practically none.

This chapter is about Chacobo people's experience of urban settings. After setting out the facts regarding increased mobility and interconnectedness between town and village following the rapid expansion of the Bolivian road network, it moves on to discuss three aspects of Chacobo urban experiences. First, a historical section about Chacobo people and urban settings throughout the centuries shows that the Chacobo have enduring and deep relations to urban centers, and that the current context of urbanization is therefore not particularly new or unfamiliar to them. It might even be considered a leading factor in Chacobo ethnogenesis, as discussed in the subsequent section. A third section then describes some of the harsh realities presented by urban life, including the difficulties of finding lodging, employment (beyond the sector of labor in Indigenous representation), and sustenance. Here it is argued that Chacobo people endure these conditions not because they enjoy the experience of urban life, but because they hope these visits will lead to well-being in the future. What follows is a description of how Chacobo people consider the region's towns to be built on their land and how, even though dispossessed, they therefore feel at home anywhere in the region. Finally, in a concluding section, the chapter describes how Chacobo people bring the aesthetics and amenities of urban centers into their villages as a way of urbanizing the forest. Ultimately, their urban imaginaries appear as fully compatible with enhanced autonomy and ethnic pride.

Of Roads and Travel

As mentioned above, an impressive number of Chacobo families have recently moved to town, at least part-time. The improved road system seems to be the major explanatory factor for the trend (figure 6.1). As a matter of fact, many Chacobo have now established residence along the road itself: neither in town nor in the village, but somewhere midway. In that respect, the proximity of a mobile telephone relay antenna—on par with access to nearby fishing spots—appears to be a crucial criterion for the election of a new residence site, even on a roadside that would otherwise appear stranded in the middle of nowhere, surrounded by little more than barren pampa. The road itself is to some extent an extension of the city, and for those who have opted for part- or full-time residence in town, I would argue that improved infrastructure has been critical for more than merely allowing them to settle there. The importance of all-weather roads, rather, stems from the ease of to-ing and fro-ing they allow. Previous generations of Chacobo were perfectly able to migrate on foot or via bark canoes, but they weren't constantly moving back and forth as people tend to do nowadays. Rather than permanently settling down in town, many Chacobo tend to stay there only part-time, while keeping a strong foothold in the village. During harvesttime, they might also spend a few weeks or months in yet other locations. Similar patterns of constant circulation between urban and rural spaces—rather than outright urban migration—have also been noted for the Ese Eje (Peluso, this volume) and many other Amazonian groups (Andrade and Magnani 2013).

In the early 1990s, when the rainy season had set in and roads were inundated, traveling from Alto Ivon (the Chacobo people's main village) to Riberalta implied several days of tedious navigation—except for those, such as missionaries and anthropologists, rich enough to occasionally hire a light aircraft. Even in the dry season, motorized vehicles were often hindered by a lack of sturdy bridges, and before the government introduced heavy machinery, community work parties had to be organized several times a year to clear up the trails leading from the village to the main road. The airstrip and the bridges also had to be kept up on a regular basis. Fueled by manioc beer and armed with no more than machetes, axes, and sheer enthusiasm, people did their best to open the territory (Oporto Ordóñez 1988). Nowadays, non-floodable roads are open year-round, making travel incomparably easier: in 2010, I saw a man ride to town and back in the same day on his motorcycle, just to buy a birthday cake for his daughter. Similar trends have been noted elsewhere. In the Upper Xingu, for instance, there is a clear link between improved infrastructure and increased urban migration among Indigenous people (Horta 2017).

Means of transportation have obviously evolved along the way. When I first met the Chacobo, in 1991, only one man owned a motorbike, and a rather shattered one to be honest. Most everyone went on foot. To enjoy a minimum of social life, people living farthest away from Alto Ivon would leave their homes on Sunday morning before daybreak to make it on time for church at ten o'clock followed by the soccer game at one, and then head

FIGURE 6.1 Travelers fixing the road from Alto Ivon to Riberalta to get their bus across a swampy section during the rainy season, 2019. Photo by Philippe Erikson.

back again to make it home by nightfall, thus having to walk eight or nine hours in one day. By the end of the twentieth century, ordinary bicycles had been massively introduced. Nearly everyone owned an inexpensive model of the Phoenix brand, imported from China. But that fad only lasted a few years, until the roads really began to improve. Then came the era of motorcycles.

FIGURE 6.2 Motorcycles have become the favorite means of transportation between village and city, 2019. Photo by Philippe Erikson.

Motorcycles have now swarmed, to the extent that the younger generation seems to consider walking a mostly useless, last-resort, and somewhat archaic mode of locomotion (figure 6.2). Families of up to six are sometimes seen stacked on a single bike, which certainly reflects alignment with urban manners, Riberalta being known as "la ciudad de las motos" (the city of motorcycles), where cars have only recently begun to circulate, and people cruise around the main plaza at slow motion on their bikes just as their elders used to do on foot for the evening paseo.

An even more recent phenomenon, circa 2015, is the introduction of Indigenous-owned trucks, usually acquired via a government- or NGO-sponsored project, and typically operated by a younger member of one of the most influential families, designated for the office of driver. Even though only a handful of Chacobo presently know how to drive a car (somewhat recklessly and without a license in most cases), intermediaries are no longer necessary to transport marketable forest products such as palm hearts or Brazil nuts to urban wholesalers. There is even a taxi station in Alto Ivon, and rides to town are now available on a daily basis, thereby creating what Daniela Peluso (2015, 59) aptly refers to as "a wide series of active links between cities and communities of origin." All these phenomena are of course very much interconnected: the economic opportunities offered by roads are precisely what allow people to generate the income needed to purchase vehicles to market their products.

This chapter concentrates on how the above-mentioned changes came to happen, how they have affected daily lives, and how they relate to Chacobo urban imaginaries. Rather than being attracted by the city lights or urban life of nearby towns such as Riberalta or Guayaramérin, the Chacobo are attracted by urbanization as a concept—that is, the improved living conditions they might hopefully achieve in the future. In other words, Chacobo people might go to town hoping for a better life, yet not expect to find it immediately on location. Their relationship with towns is tinged with a mixture of political reclamation and dreams of a better future. It paradoxically combines claims to autochthony with yearning for better access to modern technology and commodities. Cities are said to have been built on the precise spots where former Chacobo strongholds once stood, and this lays the ground for great expectations: gaining what the towns have to offer without departing from their own core identity. However, there is a price to pay, the urban experience being, in practical terms, a rather painful one, as the following sections show after a brief historical review of Chacobo past urban encounters.

Deep-Seated Familiarity with Urban Settings

As noted by Jack D. Forbes (2002, 5), "it may well be that the Americas witnessed a greater process of urban development in pre-1500 C.E. time than did any other continent, with the growth of the most elaborate planned cities found anywhere." Admittedly, however, the proto-Chacobo history of urban encounters does not reach back in time as far as that of other peoples, such as the proto-Apurinã/Manxineru or the proto–Southern Arawak, discussed in this volume by Pirjo Kristiina Virtanen and Fernando Santos-Granero, respectively. Unlike the latter, it is most unlikely to predate the emergence of the Wari Empire, and unlike what has been reported for the former, it certainly does not extend all the way back to mythological times. And, even if it did, what imprint could it have left on Chacobo urban imaginaries? Yet, the Chacobo have not had to wait until the twenty-first century to get acquainted with town life. Records of their familiarity with permanent settlements—on the banks of the Beni River—can be traced back at the very least to the founding days of Misión Cavinas, in the second half of the eighteenth century (Armentia 1903).

Back then, most of the proto-Chacobo people's interaction with neighboring groups and missions was openly hostile. They were perceived as marginal "savages," whose territories marked the limits of "civilized" (i.e., mission-controlled) lands. As a matter of fact, Cavinas was founded high upstream precisely to stay as far away as possible from the hostile Pacaguara, as the forebears of Panoan-speaking groups such as the Chacobo were then called. Obviously, few proto-Chacobo chose to live in missions, but there were always times when scattered dissident groups settled down with the enemy, if only for a few years, and such episodes brought about close contact with neighboring groups such as the Cayubaba and the Tacana-speaking Cavineño (Ciuret 1838–60; Tabo Amapo 2008, 104–12).

Such interactions have had a profound impact and long-lasting effects on Southern Panoans. Even though the proto-Chacobo were generally considered averse to missionary subjugation, some aspects of their ritual life have nonetheless been obviously influenced by Christianity.[1] The now-bygone *shi-ati* ritual, for instance, is stunningly reminiscent of Holy Communion, especially an episode involving a shaman feeding a few drops of "blessed" manioc beer and a tiny piece of meat directly into the mouth of those deemed worthy or mature enough to be thus honored (Prost 1970, 40–41). In a similar vein, Erland Nordenskiöld (1924, 146) noted that "the old literature speaks of a number of Indians who went naked, but who have since taken to wearing these [bark] shirts. The Chacobo and Cayubaba have the same word for a bark cloth shirt. The former say *moru*, the latter *i-moro*. This shows that it was possibly from the Cayubaba that the Chacobo first learnt the use of this garment."

As early as the mid-1800s, a dozen proto-Chacobo, then known as Pacaguara, were already listed as permanent residents of Exaltación, on the banks on the Mamoré River, while many of those living in the vicinity of that town were reported to visit at least once a year for the patronal feast (Orbigny 1839, 262). A generation later, José Cardús (1888, 290) also mentioned Indigenous presence in Exaltación, this time referring to Chacobo rather than Pacaguara—a blanket term for all the closely related Panoan-speaking groups, including Sinabo, Capuibo, Caripuna, and others, as well as Chacobo (on Southern Panoan ethnonyms, see Córdoba and Villar 2010). In 1864, thirteen "Chacobo" were taken to Trinidad for what seems to have been the first recorded visit of representatives from that group.[2] This long-standing history of contact with missionized groups certainly explains the cultural similarities and political alliances uniting the Chacobo and Cavineño, even today.

Urban Zones as Marshaling Yards for Chacobo Ethnogenesis

A wide array of Southern Panoan groups once controlled vast tracts of land north of the Llanos de Moxos, bounded by the Beni River to the west and by the Mamoré to the east. Since those bygone days of their past splendor, following a tragically common pattern, the various politically autonomous and then dispersed Chacobo-Pacaguara groups have gone through considerably harsh times and suffered massive depopulation. Some were hunted down, some joined mainstream Bolivian or Brazilian society, and some were felled by internal warfare and epidemics. Survivors of several remnant groups ended up merging, so that the contemporary population identified as Chacobo (now numbering around 1,600 people) can be seen as the remnants of a cluster of formerly numerous Panoan-speaking groups of which the northernmost ones were mostly wiped out, whereas the southerners migrated northward: as the macaw flies, Exaltación is 166 miles (268 kilometers) south of Riberalta and only slightly closer to Guayaramérin, which sits to the east of Riberalta.[3]

In the late 1960s, the Chacobo were living on the banks of the Benecito and Yata Rivers, both affluents of the Mamoré River. Back then, the most accessible towns for them were therefore the twin cities of Guayaramerín and Guajará Mirim (terminus of the Madeira-Mamoré Railroad). Although a few families remained behind and still live in those parts (on the Yata and Benecito), most Chacobo migrated westward in 1964, to settle in a more remote location in the headwater areas of the Ivon River (Erikson 2022). Consequently, the town where one is most likely to find Chacobo people is now Riberalta, which is only 87 miles (140 kilometers) from Alto Ivon and can therefore be reached by truck or by motorcycle in just about five or six hours (or two or three days in a boat or on a bicycle, but of course no one ever does that anymore).

In the era during which their ethnogenesitic exodus occurred, most Southern Panoan groups simply disappeared, or ended by merging with the mestizo population. This course of events led some isolated surviving groups to move closer to towns. One family, for instance, is reputed to have been discovered by chance in the 1960s, at a time when most of the various Chacobo groups were being united by the combined effort of a charismatic leader (Capitán Paë) and Summer Institute of Linguistics (SIL) missionaries (Erikson 2022). Named after their former boss (Roca), family members were wandering in Guayaramerín, unaware that other people speaking their language were still to be found, until they stumbled across other Chacobo, who invited them to join up with the larger group. Members of this family, because they had been employed by cattle herders, are known for their ability to deal with livestock, which is rather unusual by Chacobo standards.

Occasionally, Chacobo men who travel to Pando or along the Mamoré River to harvest Brazil nuts or for any other reason come back with exciting stories of chance encounters with unknown people whose language is reportedly similar to theirs. Usually, only overheard nocturnal conversations are recounted, but face-to-face interaction is sometimes also involved. I have witnessed such occurrences twice over the past thirty years. In one instance, it even led me and a group of Chacobo friends on a fascinating but ultimately unsuccessful wild-goose chase for "lost relatives." Interestingly, such tales are reminiscent of those involving *nohiria* (lit. "people"), supernatural beings who appear exactly like the Chacobo of yesteryear, complete with bows and arrows, bark shirts, long ponytails, capybara-toothed ear pendants, monkey teeth collars, head crowns, and toucan feather nose plugs. *Nohiria* are often heard roaming around at night, and—although this has not occurred in several decades now—they reportedly occasionally abduct people, especially teenagers, who disappear for a few days. Such spirits are similar to those the Shipibo-Conibo call *chai coni* (Morin 2007), or those the Chimane call "inside people" (Daillant 1998). They emerge as glorious but somewhat gloomy incarnations of past mores; attractive, admirable, but nevertheless dangerous entities with whom shamans are likely to have sex and found parallel families; and fleeting metaphorical resurrections of bygone times and traditions that somehow still lurk around.

It is of course impossible to determine whether rumors of meetings with unknown Chacobo speakers in modern attire echo those of encounters with *nohiria* beings in traditional garment, or whether they instead echo the historical fact that Panoan speakers in the region were once more numerous, dispersed, and eager for reunification. But whatever the case, far from being unrepresentative, the Roca family's fate seems to provide a telling illustration of what must have happened to many Indigenous peoples in the first half of the twentieth century, especially in those parts most affected by the rubber boom (1870–1910). After the great recession in the years immediately following the First World War, a tremendous number of the Indigenous people who had been put to work on the rubber *estradas* ended up in local towns rather than returning to forest life, causing hamlets to swell to considerable proportions, and at tremendous speed. With the influx of former *barraca* workers after the rubber boom collapse, places such as Puerto Maldonado turned into rather large cities practically overnight (Portillo 1914). Between 1897 and 1911, Riberalta's population expanded from a total of merely 646 inhabitants to more than 4,000 (Sánchez 1897; López Beltrán 2007, 318).[4] The Chacobo, Pacaguara, Sinabo, and Caripuna were obviously not spared from the common plight, and many Indigenous people ended up stranded in towns for lack of better options (Vallvé 2010). Some, like the Roca—and a few other families such as the Soria (Hanke 1958)—managed to retain their Indigenous status by reuniting with more autonomous groups, but they might just as easily have lost it and, in any case, have been strongly affected by their past urban experience.

Another historical factor worth mentioning is the long-standing Pacaguara-Chacobo tradition of incorporating refugees who were trying to escape the harshness of life in (successively) Franciscan missions, rubber estates, or Brazil's Far West. Based on observations made in 1866, Nicolás Armentia (1903, 106) wrote of the Chacobo that "they have relations with the Cayuvaba Indians, and there still exist among the Chacobos several Indians of this race from Exaltación and even Mobimas from Santa Ana, who have hidden in the forest or have returned to a savage life." A certain familiarity with the outside world (including its urban forms) has therefore arisen from people coming in to live with the Chacobo, rather than from Chacobo directly experiencing urbanity themselves.

Interestingly, women have played a prominent role in such cases, with many prominent Chacobo leaders owing much of their power to successful marriages with Spanish-speaking wives. Such was the case with the semilegendary Capitán Paë and his Movima wife, Mama Tohë, in the 1950s (Hanke 1958). Such is also the case with the Ortiz family, whose rise to power is clearly linked to a shrewd strategy in which a group of brothers married a group of Spanish-speaking sisters who came to live in Alto Ivon. This allowed them to avoid the strict constraints of uxorilocality (i.e., matrilocality), to flatter the SIL missionaries' obsession with virilocality (i.e., patrilocality), and, above all, to act as middlemen when dealing with the outside Spanish-speaking world (Erikson 2017, 2018).[5]

Because of this long-term history of interaction with the outside world, most Chacobo do not find urban life particularly bewildering. This is strikingly different from the situation among many other Amazonian people, such as the Matis, who have spent several decades in voluntary isolation. In the early stages of contact, when forced to go to town for medical reasons, the Matis would spend most of the day huddled up in a corner, as if expecting an imminent doomsday. And if sent to a megalopolis for advanced treatment (rather than just being left to die as more frequently occurred), they would return with the impression that Manaus was no different than Atalaia do Norte. Both places were similarly swarming with terrifying numbers of strangers, more numerous than ants; their threshold of tolerance for crowds could be superseded by a few hundred Atalaienses as easily as by several million Paulistas. For historical reasons, the Chacobo have a totally different—and obviously much more placid—relationship with urbanity.[6] However, as previously stated, neither older Chacobo nor their children seem to consider cities to be the quintessential locus of modernity, or *the* place to be. To them, cities rather seem to stand for a place of suffering one must temporarily endure in hopes of a better future.

Enduring Cities: The Hardships of Urban Life

Remarkably, most Chacobo who spend time in town do so with the future in mind. They go to receive medical attention and return home cured; to hold political office and work for the general benefit to come; to ensure better formal education for their children so they might ultimately get a salaried job and improve their economic situation; or to attend Bible classes, with eternal salvation in mind. But as far as I know, no one seems to go to seek immediate reward or to enjoy city life for its own sake. The pleasures of strolling around buzzing markets are rather limited when one is penniless, and most Chacobo clearly see cities as places of economic hardship rather than economic opportunities. In fact, the major source of monetary income for the Chacobo is by far the harvest of Brazil nuts, a seasonal occupation that mainly takes place deep in the forest.

For the Chacobo, cities are so systematically associated with suffering and grief that some people decide to escape there after the painful loss of a child or partner, wishing to get away from places associated with exceedingly painful memories. One man thus told me that after losing the wife he had spent most of his adult life with, he felt compelled to move to town, the most adequate place for mourning. When asked how he was faring out there, he sadly responded: "Just wandering around pathetically, from one relative's house to the next, like one of those numerous stray dogs in Riberalta." In another instance I witnessed, a young woman ran away from an unhappy marriage, and everyone suspected the best place to go searching for her was Guayaramerín, where her husband's namesake—involved because of the onomastic connection between them—sent someone out to retrieve her.

Lodging Problems

The first problem faced by Chacobo who go to town is that of lodging. Where can one sleep? I have been told that several decades ago, when rubber tapping still generated good income, people coming to town to sell their produce could afford to stay in hotels (those of the lesser price range, at least). The premises of the Misión Evangélica Suiza offer another option, but generally the missionaries only host the sick, those who work for them, or those attending the Bible classes or the training courses that they supervise. They seem otherwise hostile to the idea of Indigenous people coming to town, where the risks of perdition are, in their eyes, widely increased.

In 1991, finding a place to stay for those going to Riberalta was high on the agenda of the Chacobo leaders. After completing my first year among their people, I was asked to help obtain funds from the French embassy to acquire a communal house in the suburbs. Once built, this became the very first urban property owned by the group, much to the missionaries' dismay. Yet, this did not solve the accommodation predicament. The "Hotel Chacobo" never really served its function, both because it was too far removed from the town center (and this was before the era of generalized motorcycles) and because would-be occupants were reluctant to disturb those designated as caretakers of the house: a Chacobo woman and her Spanish-speaking mestizo husband, who ended up staying there for their own account on a more or less permanent basis.

Interestingly, despite the seriousness of this lodging crisis, I have never seen or heard of Chacobo sleeping in the streets or on riverbank beaches, although members of neighboring Indigenous groups might do so, as is so nicely illustrated by Peluso's chapters on the Ese Eja in this volume. Neither do the Chacobo, while in town, openly resort to panhandling or scavenging in trash cans as a temporary means of subsistence. Likewise, prostitution is apparently quite rare: over the past thirty years, I have only heard of one man engaging two of his daughters in the sex trade (and that occurred in the fluvial port district rather than directly in town). Urban survival strategies are clearly culture bound, and those the Chacobo resort to are noticeably different from those of other Indigenous peoples who spend time in Riberalta, such as the Araona, Cavineño, and Ese Eja. Members of each group adhere to their own norms and rely on their own networks to get around urban hardships.

As previously stated, nearly a third of Chacobo families now have their own place in town (mainly used as a secondary residence), which solves the lodging problem to some extent. Rather than buying a ready-made house, most families can only afford to buy a cheap plot of land, dig their own well in the courtyard, and build their own house using whatever materials they can gather, which usually means wooden planks and palm fronds rather than bricks and roof tiles. Youth pursuing higher education (i.e., high school) now also have the option of staying in a dormitory, which is a brick building constructed in the late 2010s under the auspices of the Central Indígena de la Región Amazónica de Bolivia (CIRABO, Indigenous Union of the Amazonian Region of Bolivia). Theoretically, this accommodation was meant for Indigenous youth of all the affiliated ethnic groups, but the last time I visited there (December 2019), it was mainly occupied by Chacobo youth. Those from other groups had been expelled on the grounds that their behavior was deemed unsatisfactory (although it is tempting to believe they have simply been barred access because CIRABO's main leaders are Chacobo themselves and have no qualms about treating their own kinspeople in the most favorable manner). Obviously, the demand for these dorm rooms far exceeds their availability. To make matters worse, the *internado* (residence) was partially destroyed by fire in the aftermath of the political turmoil surrounding Bolivia's 2019 electoral campaign.[7]

Job Opportunities

In the wake of Evo Morales's accession to power in 2006, with official efforts to turn Bolivia into a "Plurinational State" (per the 2009 Constitution), a few salaried positions did indeed open up for Indigenous persons—working for the government-sponsored Instituto Plurinacional de Estudio de Lenguas y Culturas (Plurinational Institute for the Study of Languages and Cultures), for instance. In the past fifteen years, several Chacobo have started working in places such as the Comité Civico (Civic Committee), the Census Bureau, or the Defensoría del Pueblo (Ombudsman's Office). A number of bilingual teachers have spent some years in Riberalta to improve their literacy and pedagogical skills, and a few have even been assigned to urban employment. Some jobs or training programs have even brought people for a time to larger cities, such as Trinidad, Cochabamba, Santa Cruz, or even La Paz. Sustainable development programs, funded by NGOs but strictly monitored by government agencies and managed at the local level by CIRABO, also offer salaried positions, which usually imply moving to town for a few years. However, such opportunities are scarce, available only to the few young people (mostly male) who have graduated from high school. Furthermore, they tend to be assigned to those belonging to the affluent and influential families who corner most of the political positions under CIRABO's thumb, thereby leaving graduates from most families without many prospects of employment in town.

Although greatly expanding in number (there were none a few decades ago), institutional urban jobs are nonetheless scarce. Further, because it is totally cut off from the tourist circuit, Riberalta doesn't offer any opportunities for the sale of Indigenous handicrafts or other means of marketing indigeneity. Even as spiritual guidance and shamanic pharmaceuticals seem to be booming across Latin American, offering abundant financial opportunities for Indigenous enterprise, such is absolutely not the case in Riberalta. The only instance I have ever come across of someone making a living as an urban native therapist was a man from a remote Yata River community, whose quite unusual profile was further enhanced by his being intersex.[8] In other words, little if anything is done in Riberalta to advertise local people's Indigenous background for commercial purposes. Unlike Rio Branco (farther north in Brazil), whose pavement is inspired by traditional Huni Kuin graphics and whose walls are covered with street art glorifying its Indigenous heritage (figure 6.3), Riberalta seems quite neutral, even barren of any outward signs of indigeneity.

Urban life in Riberalta can thus be exacting for those who do not benefit from one of the rare salaried jobs recently opened for representatives

FIGURE 6.3 Streets of Rio Branco paved with Indigenous (Panoan) motifs and booming with Indigenous street art, 2019. Photo by Philippe Erikson.

of Indigenous peoples. When ordinary Chacobo are compelled to spend extended amounts of time in town, they have very few options. If they want their children to benefit from Riberalta's better schools, for instance, they must seek low-paid jobs as construction workers, or as dockers, earning barely enough for mere survival. One Chacobo friend of mine tried to make money working as a moto-taxi driver but to do so, not owning his own vehicle, had to rent one from a military serviceman. His earnings, by the time he had paid the daily rent and gasoline expenses, were barely positive. Job opportunities for women are equally rare, seasonal, and underpaid. They are mainly restricted to breaking nuts in Riberalta's numerous *beneficiadoras de Almendras* (nut processing factories), Riberalta being a hot spot for the export of Bolivian Brazil nuts.

Scarce Food, Illness, Economic Hardship, and Social Deprivation

Difficulty in finding enough to eat is another hardship encountered in town. A Chacobo friend of mine once explained that his earnings from his city job as a bricklayer only allowed for the purchase of twenty-five grams of meat a day per person to mix with the rice he and his family lived on (that is, less than one ounce, or one-fifth the amount of meat in a standard McDonald's hamburger). Considering how difficult it is to earn enough money to feed one's family in town, much of what is eaten in Riberalta understandably comes from the villages rather than from the local market. Whenever a truck leaves from Alto Ivon to go to town, it is filled with bags of oranges, mangoes, bananas, manioc roots, and sometimes even piglets or live chickens for family members "stranded" in town. A few families who live in town on a more permanent basis try to maintain swidden gardens in the suburbs, which they tend over the weekend or whenever they can. But, because such plots are difficult to conceal, theft is a recurring problem for those who try to grow staple foods close to town. Transportation of bulky products such as manioc, maize, and bananas is also a problem, and harvesting, especially for rice, is time consuming and requires a full-time presence when the produce ripens.

To sum up: Riberalta stands out as a place of suffering, and sometimes of near starvation. Because most trees have been cut down, it is tremendously hot, and bathing in the river is not even an option. But worst of all from a Chacobo perspective, people staying there are deprived of manioc beer, which is a staple in Alto Ivon and nearly impossible to brew in town, for lack of sufficient firewood and access to manioc roots. This leads to an impoverished social life, which has also political repercussions. I was once told that the lack of manioc beer was one of the major challenges the president of CIRABO had to face. Without manioc beer to act as social lubricant, and due to the prohibitively high price of industrial beer, it is nearly impossible to hold political meetings in town to mobilize his followers.

Because of the deprivation the Chacobo suffer in town, one Chacobo leader told me he was reluctant to visit his friends and relatives who were also living in Riberalta, because that might lead to gossip and resentment. Though he himself was rather well off by Indigenous standards, other people would nonetheless say he only came to visit to be offered food or, more likely, manioc beer, as would be expected from people with strong traditions of hospitality, people for whom social life is intrinsically associated with the sharing of the home brew known as *chicha* in local Spanish or *jënëria* in Chacobo (Erikson 2009b). In rural settings, social visits only last as long as the host's supply of beverage does. Once the last drop is finished, staying would merely reflect bad manners. Such traditions are impossible to maintain in an urban environment. Clearly, rural exodus leads to much deprivation, and such economic hardship also affects social lives.

Poverty's negative effects on social life even have indirect repercussions in the village itself. When I visited the Chacobo in 2019, Alto Ivon was rather depressingly empty, and the annual soccer tournament, which is usually a major event, turned out to be a major flop: most of the youngsters and the best players were in town, and therefore unavailable to take part in the local tournament. This offers a striking contrast with the situation just a few years prior. In 2010, for instance, the very few players who lived in town decided to return to play in Alto Ivon, at the cost of missing an opportunity to watch the televised World Cup semifinals, which were scheduled at the same time and difficult to watch in Alto Ivon. In just a few years, the situation had drastically changed: watching television is now rather easier than it used to be, but the local tournament has lost most of its attractiveness.

Health problems brought about by the harshness of urban life are another issue that takes a heavy toll on the population's well-being. Though I have no precise statistics to rely on, I feel confident enough, based on personal experience, to say that diabetes is becoming more widespread, due to reduced exercise (because of motorbikes), impoverished and unbalanced diets, and easier access to refined sugar. Years ago, children regarded any candy brought to Alto Ivon as a treat, and very few if any seemed to be overweight. Such is no longer the case, and over the 2010s, the number of Chacobo friends and acquaintances who lost a limb or even their lives to diabetes is tragically high. Urban migration, however, has only been an aggravating factor, since impoverished diets, especially in terms of protein resources, have been a major problem for several decades now for those of the Chacobo who live in Alto Ivon.[9] This settlement was founded in 1964, and once-bountiful fishing and hunting have long since become unproductive.

To a certain extent, the vast majority of the Chacobo—those settled along the banks of the Ivon River—were familiar with at least one major facet of urbanization long before urban migration settled in. They have experienced sedentariness for more than half a century. In any case, the vicinity was deforested long before Alto Ivon started showing its first signs of "urbanization." Sadly, the original place name, Tapaya, or "the place where Brazil nut trees abound," has nowadays lost most of its relevance, the once-abundant and majestic specimens that earned the place its name having all been chopped down by people or blown down by the wind years and years ago.

Recovering Cities, Urban Migration: A Return to Former Splendor?

As we have seen, life in Riberalta is often quite challenging, and most Chacobo find it difficult to feel totally comfortable there. Yet, from a purely discursive point of view, there is a clear feeling of belonging and connection with the past most anywhere in the former Southern Panoan territory, urban spaces included. Surprisingly, the notion that urban spaces should be the white man's realm by contrast with Indigenous peoples' forests and pampas does not at all reflect the point of view of most of the Chacobo I have interacted with. In fact, their elders and leaders proudly insist that the locations of present-day Bolivian or Brazilian towns such as Guayaramerín, Riberalta, and Cobija were once Chacobo strongholds, led by leaders of great renown, whose names are still remembered. "Originally, Riberalta was called Xëbiya and it was ruled by Mawa Maxokiri . . ." is but one of a long series of similar assertions I have heard since I began to work with the Chacobo, in the early 1990s. Admittedly, claiming the original grounds as part of one's heritage does not alleviate the harsh realities of city life and the disruptive effects of mass urban migration, but it certainly offers some form of consolation.

Chacobo oral tradition recalls times when large villages (*yacata*) were led by paramount leaders (*chama chamaria*) whose depictions strikingly depart from the typical image of Amazonian leaders "à la Pierre Clastres" (Erikson 2009a). Many generations have passed since those days, and the tremendous authority ascribed to such chiefs may have been retrospectively exaggerated (Villar 2013), or perhaps influenced by oral traditions pertaining to other former chiefdoms from the Llanos de Mojos.[10] Yet, the names of these long-departed strong chiefs are still remembered today, often in association with present-day settlements no longer considered to be Indigenous. Riberalta, for example, the capital of Vaca Diéz Province, with a population of close to one hundred thousand people, is said to have once been known as Xëbiya and ruled by Mawa Maxokiri.[11] The twin towns of Guayaramerín in Bolivia (population of thirty-nine thousand) and Guajará Mirim in Rondônia, Brazil (population of forty-six thousand), were originally called Jënë-Shiniya, and their last Chacobo leader was reportedly known as Mawa Tëwi Tëtëka.[12] Yet another politically significant claim is that Tumichucua—the place where SIL missionaries had their Bolivian base—was once known as Pamahuaya and led by a man called Boca.[13]

Geographically speaking, there is little wonder that contemporary cities would be located in the very same places Indigenous communities once stood. Riberalta is situated on the elevated (and therefore nonfloodable) south bank of the Beni River, where it joins with the Madre de Dios River. The twin cities of Guayaramerín and Guajará Mirim also occupy a strategic location, on the Mamoré River, as reflected by the Tupian etymology of their shared name: "little waterfalls." And Tumichucua, for its part, is ideally situated near a magnificent oxbow lake where archaeological ruins are found in the form of raised fields and ditches, which the Chacobo formerly used for ritual purposes (Erikson 2014). Historically speaking, these places might, or might not, have been Chacobo strongholds. They might just as well have been temporarily occupied by rather small groups. Rhetorically speaking, however, in terms of their urban imaginary, present-day cities are clearly perceived as built on the very sites where ancient Chacobo large village sites once stood, before being taken over by the Rëquë Josho (lit. "white noses"), a derogatory nickname given to Spanish speakers, also known as Carayana, following a more widespread Bolivian usage. And thus, even though dispossessed, the Chacobo are clearly entitled to feel "at home" anywhere in the region, in ways somewhat similar to those depicted by José Agnello Alves Dias de Andrade (2020) regarding the Sateré-Mawé's frequent assertion that since the land was once all theirs, they should be allowed to live there now.

Onomastics is one of the means available to the Chacobo to symbolically reclaim ancestral rights on urban spaces, thereby "speaking with names" as aptly phrased by Keith H. Basso (1988) and others after him (e.g., Webster 2017). Since 2009—when the new constitution officially established the country as Estado Plurinacional de Bolivia (the Plurinational State of Bolivia)—more than thirty Indigenous languages have gained official status. These languages are now being used for signage, on par with Spanish, in a great number of public locations such as airports and government offices (especially those directed toward Indigenous people) (figure 6.4). Nameplates in Riberalta's teacher training college were, at one point, all translated into Chacobo, at the cost of sometimes rather cumbersome paraphrases for terms such as *toilets* or *secretarial office*. In areas where large sectors of the population speak a non-European but majority language such as Aymara, Kichwa, or Guarani, choosing what language to use to highlight the region's plurinationality is rather easy. But the situation is more complex in Riberalta, where most of the population is of Tacana descent (even though absolutely no one speaks Tacana), and where Chacobo (spoken by less than 1 percent of the regional population) is at odds with other minority languages, such as Cavineña and Ese Eja.

Surprisingly, however, the Chacobo never seem to insist on using the native name Tapaya to refer to Alto Ivon, despite the obviously foreign origin of the latter name, and despite the numerous traces of former occupation by people sharing the same material culture as theirs encountered by the contemporary Chacobo when they collectively moved there from the Yata-Benecito region in 1964.[14] Bull-roarers stuck in trees and decorated pottery similar to theirs gave abundant proof that they were not the first of their group to hold parties there. Historical archives also confirm that the Ivon is traditionally Chacobo. Yet, the group currently living there uses imported names to designate Alto Ivon and its surroundings. Thus, one settlement situated an hour's walk away from Alto Ivon is called Núcleo, which is the name of a settlement formerly situated on the Benecito River; and a group of houses located a short distance from Alto Ivon's center is commonly referred to as La Misión, because it is close to but not exactly part of Alto Ivon, just

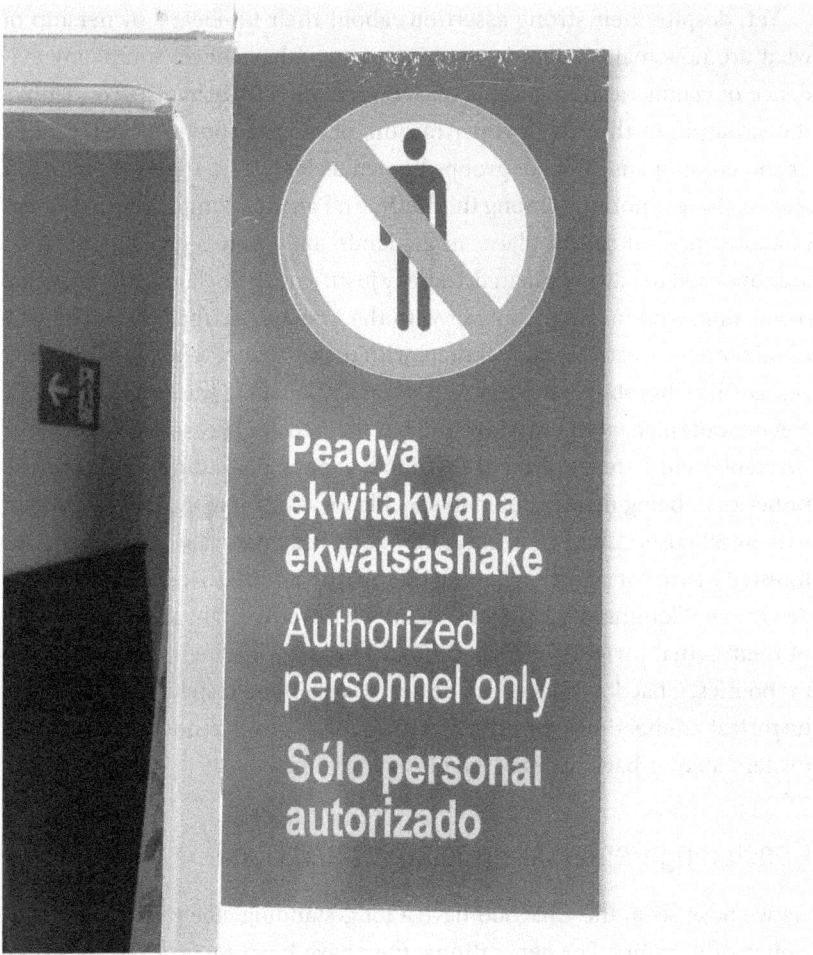

FIGURE 6.4 Overhead signs in one of Bolivia's Indigenous languages at Cobija's Capitán Aníbal Arab airport. The signs are in Cavineña, although no speakers live in the vicinity, 2019. Photo by Philippe Erikson.

like the Misión Evangélica Suiza is close to but not exactly part of Riberalta. This seems to be a way of metaphorically stressing ongoing connections with other parts of the region, be they urban or bygone, connections that are even integrated into the group's eschatology. As I have argued in a previous publication (Erikson 2022), the souls of those who die in Alto Ivon are compelled to head back toward the Benecito and Yata areas.

Yet, despite their strong assertions about their forebears' ownership of what are now major Spanish-speaking towns, I have never found any evidence of claims regarding a spiritual connection with urban spaces. Unlike the situation in the Northwest Amazon, or among some Arawak groups or the cultural ensemble of groups known as People-of-the-Center, for instance, there is nothing among the Southern Panoans comparable to "places of emergence," or salient places in the landscape where a group's ancestors are supposed to have originated, thereby justifying their claims for perpetual ownership. And in sharp contrast with the Manxineru, there is no rhetoric of sacredness, of strong connections with urban spaces related to inherited rights. The Chacobo might very well state that Riberalta was originally called Xëbiya and ruled by Mawa Maxokiri, but their cosmology seems to be of the "portable" kind, their spirits likely to follow people around like wind gusts rather than being firmly rooted in specific locations one must keep contact with at all costs. Chacobo leaders are, quite pragmatically, much more interested in securing and expanding their hard-acquired Tierra Comunitaria de Orígen (Community Land of Origin) wherever it might stand, regardless of their actual "origin," and via ordinary political means rather than cosmopolitics. Chacobo leaders can be heard reclaiming respect based on their historical connections with the native soil, but never requesting exclusive ownership of urban spaces based on such grounds.

Concluding Remarks: Bringing It Back Home

As we have seen, the Chacobo have a long-standing albeit vicarious experience of urbanity. For generations, they have been incorporating people from the outside, from refugees fleeing mission posts in the eighteenth century, to fugitives escaping abusive bosses in the late nineteenth and early twentieth centuries. Following this tradition, in more recent years, a man seeking refuge from Brazilian hit men was hosted for several decades by the Chacobo of Alto Ivon, before eventually being put to death on the grounds of alleged witchcraft (Erikson 2016). Over the past fifty years, several Bolivian Carayana whose children have learned to speak Chacobo have also been allowed to settle in the vicinity of Alto Ivon. All these interactions have greatly contributed to the circulation of knowledge and indirect experience of the outside world.

The Chacobo people's indirect familiarity with urban manners was also enhanced by the educational policy adopted, in the late 1960s, by the SIL missionary Gilbert Prost, who, in order to train them as future leaders for their community, selected a group of promising youth to be sent to a boarding school run by Norwegians in the nearby town of Gonzalo Moreno. The results were rather positive. Despite much suffering in the boarding school due to racism, bullying, linguistic insecurity, culture shock, and longing for the family back home, these youngsters all learned to speak excellent Spanish and completed their education, thereby acquiring numerous useful skills. Unlike what tragically occurred in other parts of the Americas, the idea was not to "kill the Indian in the child" by cutting youngsters from their communities (Barker 1997). The missionaries' goals were rather to change the communities via the education of future leaders. And this seems to have produced good results. Strikingly, rather than moving out, all the youngsters trained at the boarding school returned to live with their people, where they filled important roles as teachers, paramedics, commercial intermediaries, political leaders, and more. Only recently, reaching retirement age, have they (and some of their children) chosen to settle more or less permanently in town.

Recently, a Chacobo friend of mine shared his speculations about what might happen once his people's undisputed leader, Rabi Ortiz, ends the political mandate that has kept him in Riberalta since 2006 as president of CIRABO (Erikson 2017). Two of CIRABO's previous presidents had also been Chacobo, and none ever returned to their village after completing their term. Yet, my friend had high expectations that Rabi might come back to settle permanently in Alto Ivon, where he could act more like a "traditional" *chama chamaria*, a role he had been trained for as a young man, learning how to successfully host the manioc beer parties that were once the quintessence of Northern Panoan political and ceremonial life. This, my friend said, is the reason why Rabi is so keen on having Alto Ivon become an autonomous *municipalidad* (municipality) rather than just a *distrito indígena* (Indigenous district). That administrative upgrade would imply having a mayor, a position perfectly suited for Rabi, offering him (and his community) excellent prospects for the future. Admittedly, my friend has always been somewhat of a romantic, and his hope for the imminent and simultaneous return of both Rabi and the good old days seems unlikely to ever turn true. Time will tell, but in any case, Chacobo leaders display a manifest willingness to transform Alto Ivon into a city of sorts. The last time I interviewed Rabi, in March 2022, he told me of his intention, upon retirement, of improving the living conditions of the more remote segments of the Chacobo population (those living in the Benecito and Yata region) by helping them upgrade their infrastructure.

Rabi's brother, whose official title is *capitán grande* (big captain) of the Chacobo, once opened up his dreams to me. Shortly after the passing of Bosi Yaco, in December 2012, he told me of plans to have a statue of her erected in the village, to honor this great figure, last of the original group of Pacaguara who were "rescued" by the SIL and brought to live with the Chacobo in the late 1960s. He told me of his hopes to see the soccer field—which had for decades been the village's center and main point of attraction—turned into a central plaza surrounded by shops, in the middle of which the statue could be placed. People would go there to socialize and relax in the evening, strolling around the plaza in Alto Ivon just as they do in Riberalta. I was then quite skeptical, finding the project rather unrealistic and, above all, disconnected from local conditions. Much to my surprise, however, I returned a few years later to see that the project had indeed partially turned into reality. There were no shops or statues, but the soccer field had been moved to a remote location and replaced, in the village center, by little brick structures and benches in imitation of those found in Riberalta's main plaza (figure 6.5).

For decades, Alto Ivon consisted of thatched houses surrounding a soccer field, each house having front and backyards for socialization. It now has running water (albeit in the form of outdoor faucets that bring about unsanitary quagmires), a relay antenna, and brick structures for the school and medical center. Diesel-fueled generators and a few solar panels provide minimal electrification. The main gathering house has a corrugated iron sheet roof, and there are even a few rows of tiny brick houses piled up one next to the other. Though these houses were built by a government program with little regard for local standards, and despite the artificially crowded conditions they produce, some younger people have chosen to live in them. Just like with the Ese Eja and the Aénts Chicham (formerly Jivaro), discussed by Peluso and Natalia Buitron in other chapters of this book, the Chacobo ideal seems to be bringing the amenities of city life to the villages, rather than migrating to town. This strategy of indigenization of urbanity will or will not succeed, but whatever the case, let us hope it brings satisfaction to the future generations of Chacobo.

FIGURE 6.5 The new plaza in Alto Ivon, akin to those found in Riberalta, 2019. Photo by Philippe Erikson.

Acknowledgments

A preliminary version of this chapter was presented in June 2019 at the Society for the Anthropology of Lowland South America Twelfth Sesquiannual Conference in Vienna, Austria, on the panel "Urban Imaginaries in Native Amazonia," organized by Fernando Santos-Granero and Emanuele Fabiano. Lively discussions with the organizers and other participants provided great inspiration for developing this chapter, which also includes data obtained during fieldwork conducted in December 2019 and March 2022, with generous funding from the Agence Nationale de la Recherche (research project Amaz-ANR-17-CE41-0013). While taking full responsibility for any errors or shortcomings, the author gratefully acknowledges the help provided by the editors and the two anonymous reviewers, whose suggestions have greatly contributed to improving this chapter. My gratitude also extends to Jessica Hinds-Bond, for her meticulous proofreading, and to my Bolivianist friends and colleagues Mickaël Brohan, Lorena Córdoba, Vincent Hirtzel, and Diego Villar, for their useful comments on earlier drafts.

Notes

1.   José María Ciuret (1838–60, 4) wrote that "Los Cavinas convertidos en nuevos
     cristianos, fueron el blanco de los Pacaguaras. Los Pacaguaras es la gente que
     tiene todos los vicios y ninguna virtud" (The Cavinas, after converting to Chris-
     tianity, became the Pacaguaras' target. The Pacaguaras are people who have all
     of the vices and none of the virtues). This reputation of ungrudging fierceness
     was still ongoing during the rubber boom (Córdoba 2015), and to some extent
     still pervades: during political rallies, the Chacobo reputedly lose their temper
     quicker than do members of other Indigenous peoples (a stereotype they will-
     ingly adhere to).

2.   "En marzo del 64, el cacique Domingo Avaroma condujo a Trinidad trece chaco-
     bos. Los salvajes fueron bien recibidos por el pueblo: la prefectura abrió audien-
     cia pública para contemplar a estos hijos de la selva y se obtuvo la promesa de
     que los chacobos entreguen seis niños para educarlos en Trinidad" (In March
     1864, the chief Domingo Avaroma brought thirteen Chacobo to Trinidad. These
     savages were well received: the local authorities organized a public meeting so
     that everyone could contemplate these children of the forest, and the Chacobo
     were made to promise they would surrender six children to be educated in
     Trinidad) (Limpias Saucedo 1942, 172-73).

3.   The Sinabo, for instance, have totally disappeared as an ethnic group, and
     Wanda Hanke (1949) seems to have met the very last Panoan-Caripuna speak-
     ers, roaming in the town of Jaci Paraná in the 1940s. Despite recurring rumors
     of uncontacted Pacaguara in voluntary isolation in the northernmost forest of
     Bolivia, the small group of Pacaguara contacted in the late 1960s by Summer
     Institute of Linguistics (SIL) missionaries guided by Chacobo interpreters seems
     to be the only Northern Panoan group to have avoided extinction. This handful
     of survivors settled among the Chacobo, with whom they have intermarried and
     among whom their descendants still live. These descendants seem to have some-
     what artificially retained a distinct ethnic identity for mainly political reasons.
     When it comes to electing tribal representatives, for instance, two "nations"
     open two slots, one for the Chacobo and one for the Pacaguara (Villar 2014).

4.   I am grateful to Mickäel Brohan for drawing my attention to this point, as well
     as for providing useful references.

5.   José Pimenta (2017) provides comparable data concerning local Ashaninka
     headmen, who owed much of their power to strategic marriages with daughters
     of Spanish-speaking colonists rather than bilateral cross-cousins, thus gaining
     better access to the outside world.

6.   Admittedly, even the most ingrained familiarity with the Western world does
     not prevent Indigenous people who have spent most of their lives in the Am-
     azon forest from experiencing a certain awe when visiting megapolises. When
     a group of Wayana from French Guiana came to Paris for a collaborative re-
     search project (Vapnarsky 2019), one of our guests claimed that he sometimes

doubted that he was actually living this experience, rather than just dreaming it. Artificial bank stabilization (implying tons and tons of concrete to channel such a large river as the Seine) and the extended amount of time Parisians spend underground (in tunnels, subways, etc.) were listed among the major causes of this eeriness and resulted in Frenchmen being jokingly referred to as *tatuyana* (armadillo people).

7. This happened during the riots that took place in the aftermath of the mass street protests and counterprotests that occurred in response to claims of electoral fraud by Evo Morales's party in November 2019. CIRABO's main office was ransacked as well, which goes to show that bigotry is yet another obstacle to overcome for Indigenous people living in Bolivian towns. The counterriots are said to have been largely led by members of the *sindicato de transporte* (the transporters' union).

8. Originally, this person was identified as female and consequently given a girl's name. But as they grew up, the child also appeared to have a penis, which led to changing the first consonant of their name to account for this peculiarity. In March 2022, I was told this person no longer worked in town as a shaman, having been hired to care for a local rancher's livestock.

9. Protein scarcity is much less of an issue for those Chacobo living on the Benecito and Yata Rivers. Improved infrastructure and generalized access to motorized vehicles have encouraged urban migration but also increased, or rather renewed, contact between the Chacobo living in Alto Ivon and those of the Yata-Benecito region, from whom they had been more or less cut off in the previous decades.

10. The Chacobo oral tradition of strong chiefs is clearly reminiscent of eighteenth-century descriptions of Bauré hereditary strong chiefs (Eder [1772] 1985, 84–85).

11. Xëbiya means "the place abounding with *xëbini* palms" (*Scheleea princeps*; Sp. *motacú*). Mawa is a man's given name, and Maxokiri might be rendered as "strong headed."

12. Jënë-Shiniya could be translated as "Red Waters" or "the Red River," and the name Mawa Tëwi Tëtëka as "long-collared Mawa" (*tëwi* = collar; *tëtëka* = tall, long).

13. *Pama* is a generic name for the frequently encountered trees of the *Pseudolmedia* family, known as *nui* in local Spanish. Pamahuaya, therefore, simply means, "the place where large *pama* trees abound."

14. The Ivon River was named after the brother of the explorer Edwin R. Heath, and the Chacobo have been known to live there since at least the late nineteenth century: "Los Pacaguaras, también se llaman Chacobos, de los cuales hay algunas familias en las cabeceras del arroyo Ivon (en el Beni), picando goma, en los nuevos trabajos de un señor Pardo" (The Pacaguaras, also known as Chacobos, of whom a few families live upstream on the Ivon River [in Beni], tapping rubber, in the new estate of one mister Pardo) (Sanjinés 1895, 61; see also Armentia 1897, 42–43, 82–83; Heath 1883).

References

Andrade, José Agnello Alves Dias de. 2020. "'Se isso um dia isso foi do povo sateré-mawé, nós também temos direito de ter uma casa pra morar': notas sobre a presença sateré-mawé na cidade de Parintins-AM." *Ponto Urbe* 26. http://journals.openedition.org/pontourbe/7996.

Andrade, José Agnello Alves Dias de, and José Guilherme C. Magnani. 2013. "Uma experiência de etnologia urbana: a presença indígena em cidades da Amazônia." In *Paisagens ameríndias: lugares, circuitos e modos de vida na Amazônia*, edited by Marta Rosa Amoroso and Gilton Mendes dos Santos, 45–74. São Paulo: Editora Terceiro Nome.

Armentia, Nicolás. 1897. *Límites de Bolivia con el Perú por la parte de Caupolicán.* La Paz: Imprenta El Telégrafo.

Armentia, Nicolás. 1903. *Relación histórica de las misiones franciscanas de Apolobamba por otro nombre Frontera de Caupolicán.* La Paz: Imprenta del Estado.

Barker, Debra. 1997. "'Kill the Indian, Save the Child': Cultural Genocide and the Boarding School." In *American Indian Studies: An Interdisciplinary Approach to Contemporary Issues*, edited by Dane Anthony Morrison, 47–68. New York: Peter Lang.

Basso, Keith H. 1988. "'Speaking with Names': Language and Landscape Among the Western Apache." *Cultural Anthropology* 3 (2): 99–130.

Cardús, José. 1888. *Las misiones franciscanas entre los infieles de Bolivia: descripción del estado de ellas en 1883 y 1884.* Barcelona: Librería de la Inmaculada Concepción.

Ciuret, José María. 1838–60. *Historia de las misiones musetenas.* Vol. 4, *La de Cavinas por el P. José María Ciuret.* La Paz: Archivo de la Recoleta, Colegio Apostólico de S. S. José.

Córdoba, Lorena. 2015. "Barbarie en plural: percepciones del indígena en el auge cauchero boliviano." *Journal de la Société des Américanistes* 101 (1–2): 173–202.

Córdoba, Lorena, and Diego Villar. 2010. "Relaciones interétnicas, etnonimia y espacialidad: el caso de los panos meridionales." *Boletín Americanista* 60:33–49.

Daillant, Isabelle. 1998. "'Ils sont comme nous, mais . . .': relations de parenté et de genre entre Chimane et 'gens de dedans.'" *Anthropologie et Sociétés* 22 (2): 75–97.

Eder, Francisco S. J. (1772) 1985. *Breve descripción de las reducciones de Mojos ca. 1772.* Cochabamba: Historia Boliviana.

Erikson, Philippe. 2009a. "Diálogos à flor da pele . . . Nota sobre as saudações na Amazônia." *Campos, Revista de Antropologia Social* (Curitiba) 10 (1): 9–27.

Erikson, Philippe. 2009b. "Jënë jënëria: la chicha chacobo." *Revista Socio-Lógicas* 7:95–109.

Erikson, Philippe. 2014. "El ritual como máquina del tiempo: ejemplos chacobo (Amazonía boliviana)." In *Antes de Orellana. Actas del 3er Encuentro Internacional de Arqueología Amazónica*, edited by Stephen Rostain, 399–406. Lima: Instituto Francés de Estudios Andinos.

Erikson, Philippe. 2016. "'Si matamos a un brasileño, ¿en qué le concierne al gobierno?': análisis de un caso de brujería entre los chácobo." In *Apus, caciques y presidentes: Estado y política indígena en los países andinos*, edited by David Jabin, Oscar Espinosa, and Alexandre Surrallés, 179–94. Copenhagen: International Work Group for Indigenous Affairs.

Erikson, Philippe. 2017. "La carrera política de un líder chácobo de la Amazonia boliviana o de cómo Rabi 'Yobëca' se volvió Alberto 'Toro' Ortiz." In *Política y poder en la Amazonia: estrategias de los pueblos indígenas en los nuevos escenarios de los países andinos*, edited by François Correa, Philippe Erikson, and Alexandre Surrallés, 146–61. Bogotá: Centro Editorial de la Facultad de Ciencias Humanas de la Universidad Nacional de Colombia.

Erikson, Philippe. 2018. "Traductores, pastores, conversos . . . ¿jefes?: reflexiones sobre el fundamento evangélico del poder político entre los chácobo (Amazonía boliviana)." *Bulletin de l'Institut Français d'Etudes Andines* 47 (3): 335–48.

Erikson, Philippe. 2022. "Where Past and Future Meet . . . : Abandoned Village Sites as Cruxes of Political, Historical, and Eschatological Narratives Among the Chacobo of Bolivian Amazonia." In *Living Ruins: Native Engagements with Past Materialities in Contemporary Mesoamerica, Amazonia, and the Andes*, edited by Philippe Erikson and Valentina Vapnarsky, 169–98. Louisville: University Press of Colorado.

Forbes, Jack D. 2002. "The Urban Tradition Among Native Americans." In *American Indians and the Urban Experience*, edited by Kurt Peters and Susan Lobo, 5–25. Walnut Creek, Calif.: Altamira Press.

Hanke, Wanda. 1949. "Algumas voces do idioma karipuna." *Arquivos, Coletanea de Documentos para a historia da Amazonia* 10:5–12.

Hanke, Wanda. 1958. "The Chacobo in Bolivia." *Ethnos* 23:100–125.

Heath, Edwin R. 1883. "Exploration of the River Beni in 1880–1881." *Proceedings of the Royal Geographical Society* 5:327–47.

Horta, Amanda. 2017. "Indígenas em Canarana." *Revista de Antropología* 60 (1): 216–41.

Limpias Saucedo, Manuel. 1942. *Los gobernadores de Mojos*. La Paz: Escuela Tipográfica Salesiana.

López Beltrán, Clara. 2007. "Un imaginado banquete comercial: una historia de Riberalta (Bolivia), 1890–1920." In *Estado, región y poder local en América Latina, siglos XIX–XX: algunas miradas sobre el Estado, el poder y la participación política*, edited by Pilar García Jordán, 305–27. Barcelona: Universitat de Barcelona.

Morin, Françoise. 2007. "Genre, alliance et filiation dans les relations chamanes-esprits chez les Shipibo-Conibo: un itinéraire de recherche conjointe et multisituée." *Anthropologie et Sociétés* 31 (3): 87–106.

Nordenskiöld, Erland. 1924. *The Ethnography of South America seen from Mojos in Bolivia*. London: Oxford University Press.

Oporto Ordóñez, Luis. 1988. "Alto Ivón o la decisión de vencer: la comunidad de los chácobo en la coyuntura actual." *Etnología* 9 (14): 33–44.

Orbigny, Alcide d'. 1839. *L'homme américain (de l'Amérique méridionale) considéré sous ses rapports physiologiques et moraux*. Paris: Pitois-Levrault.

Peluso, Daniela. 2015. "Circulating Between Rural and Urban Communities: Multisited Dwellings in Amazonian Frontiers." In "Indigenous Urbanization: The Circulation of Peoples Between Rural and Urban Amazonian Spaces," edited by Daniela Peluso, special issue of *Journal of Latin American and Caribbean Anthropology* 20 (1): 59–79.

Pimenta, José. 2017. "'All Together': Leadership and Community Among the Asháninka (Brazilian Amazon)." In *Creating Dialogues: Indigenous Perceptions and Changing Forms of Leadership in Amazonia*, edited by Hanne Veber and Pirjo Kristiina Virtanen, 169–96. Boulder: University Press of Colorado.

Portillo, Pedro. 1914. "Departamento del Madre de Dios." *Sociedad Geográfica de Lima* 30:139–87.

Prost, Marianne. 1970. *Costumbres, habilidades y cuadro de la vida humana entre los chacobos*. Riberalta, Bolivia: Instituto Lingüístico de Verano.

Sánchez, Dámaso. 1897. *Informe anual del señor delegado nacional en los territorios del Noroeste de la República*. Riberalta, Bolivia: Edición Oficial, Imp. Hamond.

Sanjinés, Fernando de María. 1895. *Ligeros apuntes de viaje*. La Paz.

Tabo Amapo, Alfredo. 2008. *El eco de las voces olvidadas: una etnohistoria y una etnografía de los Cavineños de la Amazonía boliviana*. Edited and with commentary by Mickaël Brohan and Enrique Herrera. Copenhagen: International Work Group for Indigenous Affairs.

Vallvé, Frederic. 2010. "The Impact of the Rubber Boom on the Indigenous Peoples of the Bolivian Lowlands (1850–1920)." PhD diss., Georgetown University.

Vapnarsky, Valentina. 2019. "Petites aventures et grands défis de la restitution patrimoniale interculturelle: quelques réflexions à partir d'une expérience wayana (Guyanes)." In *Les patrimoines en recherche(s) d'avenir*, edited by Etienne Anheim, Anne-Julie Etter, Ghislaine Glasson-Deschaumes, and Pascal Liévaux, 91–105. Nanterre: Presses Universitaires de Paris Nanterre.

Villar, Diego. 2013. "Modelos de liderazgo amerindio: una crítica etnológica." In *Al pie de los Andes: estudios de etnología, arqueología e historia*, edited by Pablo Sendón and Diego Villar, 11–31. Cochabamba, Bolivia: Itinerarios.

Villar, Diego. 2014. "¿Los últimos pacaguaras?" *Caravelle: Cahiers du Monde Hispanique et Luso-brésilien* 103:51–65.

Webster, Anthony K. 2017. "Why Tséhootsooí Does Not Equal 'Kit Carson Drive.'" *Anthropological Linguistics* 59 (3): 239–62.

CHAPTER 7

Urbanity in Ancient and Present-Day Southwestern Amazonia

Human-Environment Collectives, Cycles of Generosity, and Their Ruptures

PIRJO KRISTIINA VIRTANEN

Contemporary Latin America is among the most urbanized regions in the world. Modern Amazonian cities have been designed, over time, by a range of colonial agents including the nation-state, the church, and diverse actors seeking, extracting, and trading in natural resources. In colonial thinking Indigenous nations were inferior on many levels, particularly because of their belief systems and lack of writing systems. Nonetheless, colonial agents regarded Indigenous populations as potential subjects worthy of being assimilated into the nation-state and converted to Christianity, although little space was allocated to Indigenous agency. Indeed, to be considered a "good Indian" required the individual to contribute labor to economic production, serve the state, and participate in church activities. As is typical of coloniality/modernity efforts (Mignolo 2000; Maldonado-Torres 2007), in the eyes of the early colonizers and the first rulers of independent Brazil, Indigenous traditions and languages were regarded as hindering development and progress and, thus, had to be weeded out (Gomes 2000, 56–77).

Latin American history of the city mentions Inca, Maya, and Aztec urban systems (Gilbert 1998; Clark 2013). It has also been noted that precolonial polities in Central Amazonia comprised regional clusters of ritual and political centers, forming a social network of both mobile and more settled peoples (Heckenberger 2006). Furthermore, it has been recorded that low-density early urbanity existed in Southwestern Amazonia (Iriarte et al. 2020; Pärssinen and Ranzi 2020). This essay addresses the latter region—namely, the Upper Purus area, which hosts numerous precolonial earthwork sites (geoglyphs) and road structures—with a specific focus on how urbanity is imagined in the long term by its local Indigenous inhabitants.

Today, this region is inhabited by the Arawakan-speaking Apurinã (Pupỹkary) and Manxineru (Manchineri), who are mostly clustered around the Upper and Central Purus River, whereas the Arawá-speaking Paumari and Jamamadi are found in the Central Purus region and the Panoan-speaking Huni Kuin are located closer to its headwaters. These are among the peoples that appear in the historical records of the Purus River (e.g., Chandless 1866).

Currently, the Apurinã, with a population of over ten thousand, inhabit an area that stretches from the southern tip of the State of Amazonas through Boca do Acre to Manaus. Most live in villages in over twenty demarcated Indigenous reserves, but sizable numbers also live in the urban areas of Tapauá, Lábrea, Pauini, and Boca do Acre in the State of Amazonas, and Rio Branco in the State of Acre. Apurinã society includes diverse communities and, in the past, contained several subgroups organized in exogamous moieties.[1] In earlier times Apurinã also inhabited the Abunã and Iquiri Rivers—the area containing the precolonial earthworks—in the states of Acre and Amazonas, and were highly mobile intermediaries and organizers of large ceremonies and meetings. In this they resemble the Manxineru, who live in the State of Acre, along the Iaco River, a tributary of the Upper Purus. The Manxineru, one of several subgroups of the so-called Yine (lit. "humans"; also called the Piro) in contemporary Peruvian Amazonia, number some one thousand people and live mostly in the Mamoadate reserve, situated along the Iaco River.[2] They have also settled in cities such as Assis Brasil, Sena Madureira, and Rio Branco.

In 2003 I started to collaborate with the Apurinã and Manxineru, examining their youthhood; their leadership and the generosity required of it; their circulation between rural and urban areas aimed at incorporating new knowledge; and, in collaboration with archaeology colleagues, the sociopolitico-philosophical systems of precolonial, earthwork-constructing societies. Here I address the deep history of Amazonian urbanity through the lens of recent archaeological findings on precolonial human concentrations, coupled with my ethnographic material and oral histories of how urbanity is represented in my interlocutors' contemporary imaginaries. I begin by examining precolonial urbanity with the aid of the archaeological evidence, showing how the systems of precolonial earthwork-building societies highlighted the generosity of rulers, the integration of different peoples, and human-environment relationality. These are among the keys to understanding the motivations behind the construction of these societies and are still central concepts in contemporary Amazonian Indigenous social life. I then address how the Manxineru and Apurinã ancestors' encounters with the world of spirits in the past are imagined in the present time, before discussing parallel narratives of interaction with the spirit world and power in urban areas. This is followed by ethnography produced in urban areas revealing the domestication and indigenization of contemporary cities through Indigenous cosmopolitics, social organization, and spatial and ritual concepts. Last, I argue that for Southwestern Amazonian Indigenous societies, urbanity is not just a modern, Western phenomenon; it is also typical of ancient Indigenous and other-than-human social organization, the difference being that contemporary urban centers ruled by non-Indigenous peoples display an absence of the past generosity and the seamless human/environment continuum that was typical of precolonial human concentrations.

Amazonian Early Urbanity and the Ancient Continuum with Other-Than-Human Beings

Despite modern Amazonian cities being "new" for most of their Indigenous residents, and thus requiring domestication, recent archaeological studies have shown rich evidence of early urbanity in the region. This is apparent, for instance, in the circular fortified villages and roads of Central Amazonia— also called galactic clusters—with their territorial polities (Heckenberger 2005; Heckenberger et al. 2008), as well as in the chiefdoms and mound sites in the Marajó area (Roosevelt 1991). Furthermore, the mounds in Ecuadorian Amazonia (e.g., McMichael et al. 2012) and the raised fields and large landscapes of movement with their straight lines in Bolivian Amazonia (Erickson 2009) are also associated with early human concentrations.

The area where I have carried out my ethnographic fieldwork exhibits special cultural traditions of monumentality that constitute the material expression of an extensive system of precolonial Indigenous populations in Southwestern Amazonia. The Upper Purus region is known for over eight hundred monumental geometric earthwork complexes (also called geoglyphs), mostly located in the interfluves (figure 7.1). Most ditched earthworks are circular or square, although there are also octagonal, hexagonal, rectangular, oval, and

FIGURE 7.1 Geometric earthworks in the Jacó Sá and Seu Chiquinho farms along the BR-317 highway, Brazil. Photo by Sanna Saunaluoma.

U- and D-shaped earthworks of varying sizes, often accompanied by contiguous exterior embankments. The road system also indicates the closely connected organization of several sites. Ancient roads, delineated by low banks, frequently connect the separate earthworks, or lead to them; some such roads are avenues of up to 330 feet (100 meters) in width. The ditches forming the geometric structures can be 65 feet (20 meters) wide and 10 feet (3 meters) deep, with diameters of a thousand feet (or a few hundred meters) (Schaan et al. 2010; Saunaluoma and Schaan 2012; Saunaluoma and Virtanen 2015; Virtanen and Saunaluoma 2017). After deforestation by farms, roads, and settlers, an area of 15 acres (60,000 square kilometers) of this precolonial human earthworks has been revealed, with a largely heterarchical (nonhierarchical) system of organization (Pärssinen and Ranzi 2020). Deforestation and satellite and lidar technologies constantly reveal new sites.

These ditched and embanked earthwork structures date back three thousand years and were in use until the fourteenth century (Saunaluoma, Pärssinen, and Schaan 2018; Pärssinen and Ranzi 2020). Previous archaeological studies have concluded that these were ceremonial centers, based on the absence of residential areas, the elaborate forms and designs of the ceramics found in them, and the earthworks' fine spatial planning. Domestic pottery, bowls, and serving vessels—finely decorated and painted with motifs of animal figures—have been identified, usually next to the main entrances or in nearby ditches (Pärssinen 2021; Pärssinen, Schaan, and Ranzi 2009; Virtanen and Saunaluoma 2017; Saunaluoma, Pärssinen, and Schaan 2018). These latter finds point to the earthworks as the loci of frequent feasting. In addition to their ceremonial use, the earthworks might have also been constructed for functional purposes, and their different forms could have been used for defense, trade, political gatherings, and so forth.

There are few residential sites dating to the same period as the ditched earthwork structures, and no burial sites have been found. Yet, although residential evidence is scarce in the geoglyph sites, a few neighboring mounds have been identified, all of them situated close to the current BR-317 highway in the State of Acre: near the Severino Calazans and Tequinho earthworks (the names derive from the owners of the cattle farm where they were found), and even inside of the earthwork formation at Fazenda Colorado. These mounds with their rich ceramic density imply cultural features of offerings as well as practices of serving and maintaining the sites, requiring significant physical labor, planning, and guidance for their use (Pärssinen and Ranzi 2020; Saunaluoma, Pärssinen, and Schaan 2018). Members of earthwork-building societies must have lived close by with their gardens, managing palm trees and many other domesticated and semidomesticated species that have been identified in Southwestern Amazonia's archaeological sites (Watling et al. 2015; Pärssinen et al. 2021).

Furthermore, more recent precolonial residential mounds have been found in the region, some even adjacent to the older earthworks (figure 7.2), with rich domestic layers whose ceramics indicate their more secular use. These more permanent sites were circular and rectangular mound formations, connected by several entrance roads and a road network system. There are also walled enclosures that, like the mound villages, are more recent than the geoglyph sites and were inhabited until the colonial period (Saunaluoma, Pärssinen, and Schaan 2018; Saunaluoma et al. 2020; Iriarte et al. 2020).

An interesting feature of these geometric earthworks, which extend from contemporary northern Bolivia to the State of Amazonas in Brazil, is that they form a system of diverse spaces, mostly circular and square types, connected by a road system (figure 7.3). Clusters of earthworks can be identified, yet the main features of the hierarchy are demonstrated by separated

FIGURE 7.2 Square-form geoglyph with double embankments and ring village from a later period, with their road systems. Fonte Boa farm site, 2008. Photo by Diego Gurgel.

FIGURE 7.3 Tequinho site with its ceremonial roads. Photo by Martti Pärssinen.

spaces, sections, and forms within the individual sites (Saunaluoma and Schaan 2012; Saunaluoma and Virtanen 2015), and in the size of ceremonial entrance roads, which differ in width and length (Pärssinen and Ranzi 2020, 321–22). The geoglyphs are not hierarchically spatialized in location or size (Schaan et al. 2010, 36–37; Riris 2020). Rather, they form an interacting multicentered entity. This polity system of groups sharing a similar sociocosmology points to continuous movement between different sites and within the site complexes.

The peoples that built these sites operated in social units that planned the sites and managed how they were to be used and visited. In fact, the regional system of precolonial earthworks met many of the Western criteria for urban settings: a complex division of labor, large-scale public works, social hierarchy, trading, special skills (like the knowledge of engineering and astronomy evident in the material forms of the structures), and the presence of fine arts such as decorated pottery. These are among the first criteria that were established to distinguish early cities from villages (Childe 1950). The earthwork structures and the ceramic designs are also ways of recording and documenting, even if not numerical or comparable to the writing systems in use at the time in other parts of worlds.

Temporary habitation and exchange relations between the people and their leaders may have worked in the precolonial Purus River earthworks in much the same way as in the Andes under Inca rule. Some researchers have noted that the provincial capitals of the Inca Empire had few houses, only becoming populated when a leader or chief of the polity issued invitations to gather there, or on special occasions, such as the death of the leader (Morris 1982, 162–68; Morris and Thompson 1985, 83–96; Murra 1980, 121–31; Pärssinen 1992, 275). Thus, they constituted centers for the display of generosity, evidenced in the archeological finds of feasting artifacts such as *chicha* (fermented maize beer) jars. The Inca rulers fed the incoming visitors, who then contributed to the system with their labor by building the city's material structures. Thus, these provincial capitals became centers of social interaction and redistribution, which at certain times became the sites of great ceremonies where food was offered and marriages, trading, and political alliances were arranged. This dynamic was crucial because, through their invitations, leaders could display their wealth and the fact that they were sharing it with the people, thereby demonstrating their generosity and reinforcing their prestige. Although people did not build houses in the vicinity of the provincial capitals, they acknowledged and confirmed their allegiance to their leaders through these means of exchange. When their services were no longer required, the people moved on, living mobile lives (Morris 1982, 162–68; Morris and Thompson 1985, 83–96; Murra 1980, 121–34; Pärssinen 1992, 274–77).

While most early precolonial settlements and plazas in Central Amazonia are circular (Heckenberger 2005; Heckenberger et al. 2008), earthwork ditches in Southwestern Amazonia might be square or circular, along with, less often, many other geometric patterns. As I've discussed elsewhere (Virtanen and Saunaluoma 2017; Saunaluoma and Virtanen 2015), the spatial patterns and designs of these earthworks reveal a visible and invisible relationality—an ecology of relations—involving both the humans and the more-than-humans who have channeled the spatial setting and construction of the sites. The spatial layout pointed in the cardinal directions, while constellations, solar and lunar phases, and a number of other-than-human beings were probably taken into consideration in the actions and interactions that organized social and political lives. It has been argued that Amazonian patterned designs are about engaging and establishing relations with other beings (Severi and Lagrou 2013; Lagrou 2019). Their making (on surface, body, objects, etc.) is a process of becoming with other beings, as designs play with the ideas of inside/outside, and thus with the notion of incorporating other perspectives (Gow 1999). Beings on their own lose their vitality, but designs bring life, insofar as "being" in Amazonia is considered to be relational, formed by clusters of beings. Thus, the guiding principle of geometric architecture in the Upper Purus was activated by the life-giving and life-protecting forces incorporated by the architects and builders, contributing to people- and community-making. These ideas, revealed in the architecture of the precolonial sites, must have been a central part of the early precolonial urban experience.[3]

In addition, the sacred and transformative character of these encounter sites makes it apparent why ceremonial roads were needed: they prepared visitors for ritual meetings at the geometric sites and were thus markers of liminal time and space (Virtanen and Saunaluoma 2017; see also Erickson 2009 on paths). Thus, it can be argued that the monumental, public architecture of these early, low-density urban systems took into account interactions with the other-than-human world, which was the field of expertise of some of its specialists. While the geometric earthworks might have been used for diverse purposes, they constitute the material expression of the animist ontologies of their constructors and users.

Ancestors' Settlements and the Urbanity of the More-Than-Human World

The social system of earthwork-building polities in Southwestern Amazonia collapsed before the colonial era, perhaps due to climate change or the arrival of diseases brought by newcomers. Mound villages, however, continued to exist (Saunaluoma, Pärssinen, and Schaan 2018; Iriarte et al. 2020), and in the Central Purus there are several locations that need more in-depth studies in order to understand the region's transformations and their impact on other regions. The changes were radical, yet oral histories of earthwork-building technical processes are no longer extant.

The oldest places of ancestral residence that are remembered in the Manxineru reserve of Mamoadate are located in interfluvial areas along the smaller tributaries of the Iaco River, upstream in the direction of Peru, and were known to display ancient gardens and ceramics, although mostly in the form of shards. Besides the material evidence, these ancestors' settlements were mentioned in the stories of contact, as the Manxineru and other Yine subgroups were attacked in these places by colonists and taken captive to work in rubber extraction or on the farms established in the region. There are also stories of massacres recounted by those who managed to escape. The ancient, managed banana and palm trees that I visited together with my Manxineru friends when I lived with them in 2005, and the ceramic shards in the vicinity, were the only material reminders of the past.

The time of the ancestors is referred to as one of large communal meetings of the subgroups (with competitions, games, rituals with dances, and singing), a time of strong shaman-chiefs who guided their societies in human and other-than-human interactions. These narratives highlight the large number of people who attended these ceremonies, and the cleanliness of the ceremonial plazas along with the paths leading to these places, which were carefully tended and prepared for the festivities. Similar ideas are important to the Apurinã, and typical of their ceremonial preparations is the cleaning of ceremonial terrain, both small and large, depending on the size of the community.

Years after my stay in the Manxineru villages, we visited the geoglyph sites in a deforested area far from their Mamoadate reserve, one hour's drive along the BR-317 highway from the federal capital of Rio Branco. Today, cattle farms have displaced forest, and the earthworks discovered in the deforested area are known only by the names of their owners. While we were visiting a few of them, my Manxineru collaborators observed that these places were used for specific ritual purposes, including attempts to incorporate the powers of diverse other-than-human beings. The designs and motifs of other-than-human beings found in the precolonial pottery also evidence the relational dimension of these sites and their ceramics. The earthworks' monumental features are consistent with oral histories passed on to the Manxineru that mentioned the large communal rituals and gatherings during which generous quantities of food and beverages were consumed (see Virtanen and Saunaluoma 2017). Yet such geometric earthworks are unknown in the contemporary Manxineru reserve, which is fully forested.

When we were analyzing the geometric designs of the rich pottery found in these precolonial earthworks in the Upper Purus (figure 7.4), my Manxineru research collaborators interpreted the decorative incised or painted motifs on the ceramic bowls in the light of their current knowledge of design diversity. Some they had seen and knew about, while others they still used as part of their design repertoire. The purpose of the geometric pottery designs is to materialize and influence interactions with the worlds of powerful more-than-human beings, thus conferring on people resistance, strength, health, and a long life. The designs are used in ceramic art and body paintings, but they also appear in mental visions during healing rituals (Virtanen and Saunaluoma 2017).

Even today, Indigenous meeting spaces have fluid boundaries between the sacred and the profane. Thus, for instance, in the political encounters in which I have participated over the years in different Indigenous reserves, other-than-human actors, materialized through the use of plant substances, dances, songs, and corporeal body paintings, are key actors in cosmopolitical relations. The events involve a great number of people, including kin, potential affines, and allies, who arrive from different directions and gather in large numbers in the meeting places. Ritual encounters are also, however, about trade, social exchange, and political alliances.

The Apurinã close to Boca do Acre refer to the geometric earthworks situated in their territory by the generic term *kymyrury*, which is also used

FIGURE 7.4 Some of the ceramics from the Tequinho site analyzed with Manxineru collaborators. Photo by Martti Pärssinen.

to refer to other transformative places, generally those that are homes to diverse master spirits and ancestor spirits, which are highly respected and should be avoided. These places are considered to be inhabited by more-than-human beings and shamans from past times, who are thought to have been transformed into different entities that still interact with the living, controlling resources and life forces. Their powers can even cause death. For this reason, as I have described in a previous work (Virtanen 2019), *kymyrury* are shrouded in secrecy, which has enabled the Apurinã to resist and survive colonization and subsequent periods of assimilation and domination (see also Apurinã 2019). These stories, shared among kin, are closely linked with other community events and the deep history of generations of Apurinã who have inhabited the area. Indeed, some earthworks in the lands of the Apurinã were known by the specific names of their shamans. Meanwhile, although the Apurinã of the past moved from site to site, the dead were buried in diverse locations that were not visited and were rarely talked about.

Ancient *kymyrury* are also located in the contemporary urban area of Boca do Acre—and its Piquiá district, as satellite images indicate—outside the Apurinã's present-day reserves.[4] Apurinã elders recount that their large ancient villages were also situated in the area of Piquiá, meaning that in earlier times the *kymyrury* were not as hidden as they are today, but, rather, were places of transformative powers located not far from residential areas. Apurinã narratives about the *kymyrury* resonate with Michael Heckenberger's (2005, 224–27) descriptions of the circular plazas of Central Amazonia as places of the ancestors that contain considerable power. He notes that in the Upper Xingu, "history is expressed, produced, and reproduced in a historically defined landscape of greater and lesser places, special settings, spaces, and locales, tied together through time and space by specifiable actions of discrete humans and other beings" (226). In the Xinguano landscape, the central plazas were owned by chiefs, in a hierarchical pattern that is closely related to the sociopolitical and agricultural system that Heckenberger and colleagues (2008) call "garden cities": galactic clusters with independent satellite polities, forests, and agricultural lands.

Most earthwork excavations have been carried out in the Upper Purus, but findings of precolonial sites have also been made by locals in the Central Purus, with numerous decorated ceramic shards being unearthed in the urban areas of Lábrea and Pauini. Even if detailed stories of the places no longer exist, the places are known by many Apurinã.[5] Manxineru and Apurinã imaginaries of the past rarely refer to their ancestors' ideas of urbanity, but such ideas are more clearly present in relation to the worlds of spirits. The oral histories and narratives of these peoples share ideas about the urban locations of master spirits—guardians, chiefs, or owners of animals and plants—which appear in their human forms in dreams and visions. The Manxineru recount how certain trees and the chief of peccaries, among other beings, are considered to live in their own cities. My research collaborators asserted that when one is able to see the spirit world, for instance, after consuming *kamalampi* (ayahuasca) in ritualized spaces, the master spirits' places appear as vast plazas with numerous dwellings around them.

Cities imagined in the subterranean world have been mentioned in various Amazonian ethnographies. Peter Gow (2011) recounts a story told to him by the Yine people of the Urubamba River of an underworld of white streets and fenced enclosures where the white-lipped peccaries live. He argues that Indigenous models for cities can be found in myths and other narratives, even though their relation to history is by no means straightforward. In the Manxineru and Apurinã imaginaries, the urban worlds of diverse master spirits have various locations, not only in the underworld. They move from these worlds to humans' places, appearing in their animal and plant bodies, while in their own world they live like humans, as is typical of perspectival thinking (Viveiros de Castro 2012).

The spirit world is thus a galactic system with its own special entry points composed of diverse social units that comprise the domains of different master spirits and guardians. Its entrances can be physical places, such as holes or elevations in the land, but also locations in mental imaginaries that are in fact paths. These are often manifested as geometric designs, also present in *kamalampi* ceremonies. Specific transitional lines, transitory spaces, and substances enable access to the worlds of master spirits. One master spirit often mentioned in these narratives is the chief of peccaries, who is considered to be the protector of forest resources. An older Manxineru teacher in the Mamoadate reserve once commented of this being, "He is a person, and when he wants, he enters a hole [in the land]. Like that he can move around. It's like when we leave for a trip: we go to Rio Branco [the capital of the State of Acre], and from there we go to other places." The imaginaries of master spirits and contemporary urban areas thus share similarities: both are relational places with their own sources of power and protection. In the follow-

ing sections, I address the main differences between the urbanity described
so far and urban areas governed by non-Indigenous people.

The Alterity of Cities and Parallel
Narratives of Transformability

Today, the cities of Brazilian Amazonia are home to substantial Indigenous populations, as becomes evident from research conducted in Manaus,
Belem, Boa Vista, São Gabriel da Cachoeira, and Rio Branco, as well as in
northeastern Brazil. Earlier anthropological accounts of these areas paid attention to the cultural transformation experienced by Indigenous societies
as a result of the process of industrialization and the subsequent accelera-
tion of urbanization (Oliveira 1968). Although the proportion of Indigenous
Amazonian peoples inhabiting different urban areas varies, scholars have
observed many similarities in terms of residential practice. Several studies
have identified and underlined the continuous exchanges and mobility between urban and rural areas (Andrello 2006; Cesarino 2008; Peluso 2015;
Virtanen 2012, 2017), while others have looked at the new territorialities,
collectivities, and spatiality generated in urban areas (Peña Márquez 2008;
Chernela 2015). Ethnographic inquiries have also emphasized the alterity
of cities, Indigenous attempts to appropriate the power of urban areas, and
Indigenous agency in urban transformation processes (Cunha 1998; Lasmar
2005; Andrello 2006; Cesarino 2008; Virtanen 2012, 2017).

Despite the increased Indigenous presence in urban areas, during my first
year of work with the Manxineru in the Mamoadate reserve, in 2005, they
rarely visited the cities. For those Apurinã and Manxineru who spent most
of their time in rural villages, urban areas offered major contrasts in terms
of food, the use of currency, means of transportation, nonfamiliar faces, and
violence. When we discussed their visits to and ideas about urban areas, I often heard them say that they did not feel good about the city, largely because
everything there had to be bought with money, which they only had in very
small amounts, and thus it lacked generosity and reciprocal relations. Cities
were imagined as places of pollution where it was easy to fall ill or experience
a range of threats, prejudice, and accidents linked to the large number of
vehicles—cars, motorbikes, trucks, and so forth (see Maizza, this volume,
for similar ideas among the Jarawara).

Yet, despite the alterity of cities, they are needed and valued by those living in forest areas. The variety of their shops and commodities are admired,

even though, because of the lack of financial resources, people can only buy the most crucial things with the income obtained from the sale of various kinds of produce or from state benefits. Important information can be received from the authorities and civil and public servants concerning health, land, education issues, NGO representatives, and so on. Cities also boast mobile telephone coverage, widespread TV use, modern technologies, and new means of transportation. Concomitantly, when my Apurinã research collaborators in villages far from contemporary urban areas dream of cars, airplanes, lights, speedboats, and cities, they say it presages the arrival of urban non-Indigenous people to the village. In 2015, for instance, an Apurinã friend in a Tumiã River settlement without radio connection told me that he had known about my visit in advance because he had had a beautiful dream about walking in the city. Closer to the date of my arrival, he had dreamed of cars, a motorcycle, and promenaders on a street. Dreaming of cattle is also considered to be an indication of the arrival of people from the city.

Generally, non-Indigenous people hold the dominant positions in the legal system, school administration, and production of industrial commodities. For the Manxineru and Apurinã, merchandise obtained in urban areas can be exchanged and shared in the villages, and the information, skills, and tools accumulated in the cities have the power to produce new relations and capacities. Through access to the non-Indigenous system, Indigenous communities not only improve production for their families and make their relational bodies, but also protect themselves from invasion and destruction of their lands (Virtanen 2017). Visits to urban areas also offer opportunities to access power other than that derived from the worlds of master spirits and other spirit entities.

Geraldo Andrello (2006, 270) notes that for the Tariano and Tukano of Northwest Amazonia, white people's instruments, clothes, and money are regarded as weapons and sources of protection and are therefore considered to have shamanic powers. Cristiane Lasmar (2005) has discussed how Indigenous people in the Rio Negro area associate transformative capacities with non-Indigenous people and urban areas, which can be accessed through strategic methods. In their attempts to understand and control political institutions and knowledge resources in urban worlds, Indigenous people often rely on bodily changes (Seeger, DaMatta, and Viveiros de Castro 1987) and parallel discourses associated with shamanic travel and the incorporation of power through diverse other-than-human actors, such as the master spirits of plants and animals (Vilaça 2007; Virtanen 2016, 2017; see also Cunha 1998; Cesarino 2008), rather than becoming integrated into the dominant society. For my research collaborators, the parallels between these narratives can be seen in the transformative capacities gained through their dedication to learning and mastering urban decision-making mechanisms, bureaucratic procedures, and digital technologies, which can eventually lead to better living conditions, education, and health at a more collective level (Virtanen 2017). Furthermore, bodily changes require considerable effort, as what is considered proper or moral behavior in forest areas is embodied early in the life course, and often differs greatly from modern urban mores. The social body exists even before birth, and children learn to think through the body and with its help: "The representation of the body constitutes a package of ideas, images, symbols, emotions, and value judgments that in every culture serve not only to think but to control," as Maurice Godelier and Michel Panoff (1998, 26) argue. For those living in the rain forests, with their specific kinship systems built on generosity and reciprocity (Overing and Passes 2000), the contemporary urban environment can be an unknown world, a place of alterity, which requires a different way of living to cope with its verbal and nonverbal communication, rules, messages, and codes.

Just like undertaking shamanic initiation and forest training, spending temporary periods in urban schools, new types of urban employment, offices, or simply the urban world can lead to special expertise that assists Indigenous peoples in mastering relations with the Other, that is, with those responsible for state services and decision-making, as well as the governmental and nongovernmental workers "bringing" projects to the villages. Such expertise also facilitates dealings with missionaries and researchers, which can result in the obtainment of valued resources and better economic and political opportunities to fashion the present and future in a more autonomous way. This is why Apurinã and Manxineru actors take the risk of distancing themselves from their communities and kin. Urban areas and their actors are crucial for today's life-making, establishing health and education services in villages, land protection, and community economic projects.

Contemporary urbanity can be, however, as dangerous as the urbanity of the spirit world, since in both cases the person is dealing with transformative powers. Apurinã and Manxineru village spokespeople, who spend longer periods of time in urban areas, often say that contemporary cities make their mindful bodies dangerously weak, even though they also offer new skills and access to societal decision-making (see Virtanen 2017, 270–71; Buitron, this volume). Urban diets are different, and a number of practices and rituals that involve relating with other-than-human beings cannot be meaningfully carried out in contemporary urban areas. After years of dedication, some Manxineru and Apurinã actors have in recent years attained employment and influential positions in the education and health sectors of local governments, among other fields. Despite their benefits, cities have been experienced since the colonial period as places where relations with non-Indigenous people are devoid of generosity and reciprocity, elements that are crucial for the construction of kin relations, leader/follower dynamics, and, indeed, any mastery relationship. Amazonian Indigenous peoples' sociophilosophies and values differ greatly from those of contemporary modern urbanity, something frequently reflected in the ways my Indigenous research collaborators perceive and refer to cities.

Indigenous Domestication of Urban Areas Through Reterritorialization

The domestication of urban areas has become a major mode of Indigenous resistance to modern and contemporary urban political institutions, their production of relationships, and dichotomous categories. Rather than just adapting their bodies and practices to the new place, Indigenous people have made urban areas into a home, a domestication that occurs in diverse ways based on Indigenous practices of sociality (sharing and reciprocity) that contribute to Indigenous society- and community-making processes. Connection between those living in distant reserve villages and those in urban areas is maintained and manifested through the exchange of goods, healing substances, and information. The size and population density of a city, as well as the diversity permitted by local politics, affect the processes of domestication and indigenization in different ways. At present, several Apurinã families have their own houses in the smaller towns of Pauini or Lábrea, which are only a few days' travel from Apurinã territories and, consequently, can be visited quite frequently. This has given these more settled urban families greater independence in terms of preparing their own foods and medicines in the city. Furthermore, the small houses provide temporary accommodation for members of the younger generation if they wish to continue their studies in a local town. The links between the Manxineru and the town of Assis, Brazil, only a one-day journey from the Mamoadate reserve, produce similar relations.

Unarguably, Apurinã and Manxineru villages in the Purus River region have become closely interconnected with modern urban areas due to state-centric practices, such as registering births and collecting pensions, as well as receiving other government benefits that involve negotiating with state officials, but also as a result of access to new means of transportation. For many of those coming from the villages, extended stays in the city lessen their fear of being physically harmed, robbed, or injured in traffic accidents. Cities can gradually become familiar through everyday activities and lived experience (see Saito 2017). Furthermore, social media has changed the means of communication, radio and satellite telephone connections between Indigenous territories and urban areas have improved, TV sets are now more common in the villages, and it is not rare to own and use mobile phones while in urban areas. Despite these adjustments, most village Apurinã and Manxineru, whatever their age or gender, do not wish to live in a city, although they may frequent an urban center on a monthly basis to make purchases. There are also those who only visit a city once or twice a year, those who travel there frequently, and those who have moved to live in the city and spend most of their time there.

Social rules and principles of social organization between kin persist in urban areas. Among other continuities, notions of territoriality prevalent in Indigenous villages have simply been transposed (Peña Márquez 2008, 205–6). Among the Apurinã, people from certain river areas often live in the same urban neighborhoods, while those who have left the village due to conflict with kin tend to live apart from other members of their Indigenous group. Depending on the situation and the size of the city across southern Amazonas and the State of Acre, there might be separate Indigenous districts, or Apurinã and Manxineru houses might be scattered among those of non-Indigenous urban dwellers.

The clusters of families or social units along the tributaries of the Purus River, as well as in urban areas, are all called *awapukutxi*. As the term can be used for both village and urban contexts, it points to a system that does not differentiate between urban and rural, as is the case in Western thinking. Indeed, the Apurinã and Manxineru (re)territorialize spatial elements of cities via their ideas of movement, which can be seen in the conceptual similarities they perceive between forest paths and urban paved roads, both of which they call *kimapury*, meaning paths of continuous circulation. Manxineru social units, Apurinã moieties, and other internal social hierarchies are also reproduced in cities, shaping social life in urban areas. Among the Apurinã living in cities, moieties still define potential marriage partners, territoriality, and place of residence. This conforms with what Juan Carlos Peña Márquez (2008, 165–69) has noted for the Vaupés area (Colombia), where traditional marriage structures and language learning affect relations with others. Given these developments, there is a wide range of modes of experiencing urbanity—and of experiencing imaginaries concerning urban areas—which differ from those held by Indigenous people who have been born in cities.

Yet even those who are born in urban areas often become familiar with social practices that include other-than-human beings, insofar as in urban areas the Apurinã and Manxineru continue to experience and nurture such relationality. Imaginaries and actions are directed at a heterogenous group of animal, plant, and ancestor spirits, often through the use of plants that have a special role in their history. For example, among the Manxineru and Apurinã there is a story that describes how the shamanic plants *awiri* (tobacco) and *katsupari* (coca) were born from the body of an ancient shaman, while *kamalampi*, among other plants, was born from the body of a man who had killed several sisters and was about to eat them. Although ancestral forests and homes may be distant, these substances continue to be imported to urban areas. The Apurinã's *awiri* snuff, prepared from tobacco leaves and the ashes of a specific tree, chewed with coca leaves and two other plants, and the Manxineru's *kamalampi* are the most common means used to enter the worlds of ancestors, spirits, animals, and plants. These plant substances create links both with the ancestors and with the world of spirits, as well as with their own social and moral principles, and constitute the material mediators in the production of certain types of discourses and communication. Apurinã men gathering privately in their urban houses send photos of *katsupari* bowls to their kin in group WhatsApp messages, which often receive positive comments and jokes asking to be invited to the gatherings, or requests for the *katsupari* consumers to send them some. The same goes for pictures of traditional foods that kin living in villages with mobile coverage send to their WhatsApp groups. Among the medicinal plants, *katsupari* and *awiri* are increasingly used in today's interethnic political spaces, as they are thought to make mindful bodies stronger. These plants also offer a sense of self-determination while enhancing the consumers' immaterial and material cultural heritage.

Manxineru's *kamalampi* rituals are private and usually occur at night. Organized in both urban and forest spaces, these rituals enable participants to enter the world of spirits, remember and learn things, and obtain guidance for their actions. In my early discussions about the times of the ancestors with a Manxineru man, since deceased, who often led *kamalampi* ceremonies, he commented, "When we take *kamalampi*, we remember. *Kamalampi* indeed teaches you." He also explained how the ancestors discovered the capacities provided by *kamalampi* to speak with the water, the land, the moon, and so forth, and asserted that the same happens today.

Not only plants but ancient songs lead participants to the spirit world. Teachings are received by means of songs or visions, with the ceremony leader announcing when a song that may affect participants intensely is about to be sung. On one occasion, for instance, the above-mentioned Manxineru elder said, after a quiet moment during a night ceremony in a Rio Branco neighborhood, "Now we all go with god." Then he started to sing a specific song that strongly affected the participants, their visions, and their bodies, by generating a close connection with the intentionality of the other-than-human beings—the master spirits—involved. The spirits also lend a hand in relating with different actors, including the social worlds governed by non-Indigenous people, while plant substances are thought to contribute to producing mindful bodies, thus offering tools for acquiring personhood. During these ceremonies, Manxineru participants also receive names from the spirits. Ultimately, medicinal and ancestral substances contribute to the domestication of urban spaces by guiding and teaching on different issues, such as work, politics, relationships, and studies, illuminating the path one should take forward (Virtanen 2012).

However, contemporary cities change the relationality with other-than-human beings more than that between humans. Human-environment interactions are largely absent from the official economic and political discourses of non-Indigenous actors. Manxineru and Apurinã people often draw attention to efforts by urban non-Indigenous leaders to exploit natural resources and promote technological advancements that harness natural resources without any moral limitations, thus supporting the dominant belief that humans are ultimately in control of the environment. In the views of the Manxineru and Apurinã, in contrast, reciprocal relations with other-than-human beings are the bedrock of sustainable relations and futures. Humans have a social and moral responsibility to act so that trees, plants, and animals also partake of the good life; otherwise, they may punish the transgressors (see

Cadena 2015 on the Andes). Urban areas are also domesticated by bringing this Indigenous articulation of ideas into different spaces, from Indigenous movements to urban academia, which is also slowly being indigenized.

When I started my fieldwork in Acre in 2003, this process of domestication of urban spaces could be seen in the local government's introduction and building of Indigenous cultural centers and museums based on Indigenous architecture. This was an important element of creating alliances with Indigenous peoples and recognizing Indigenous pasts and presents in the state capital, a trend increased by Indigenous museum guides telling their versions of history to visitors. Today, however, due to the current political situation, these places have been closed or are not receiving state funding.

Lack of Human-Environment Relationality and Generosity in Contemporary Urban Areas

When urbanity in Southwestern Amazonia is examined in the long term, it becomes apparent that Indigenous urban residents do not exclude other-than-human subjects from urban processes. Early human concentrations established and counted on the inclusivity of different beings and their relationality in diverse social spaces. Today, other-than-human beings are not excluded from contemporary urban areas; indeed, they are still imagined as living in their own cities. Rather than merely becoming accustomed to new types of modern non-Indigenous cities, Indigenous residents have indigenized and domesticated them.

The deep history of urbanity in Southwestern Amazonia shows how people in precolonial urban centers oriented their lives through their close relations with one another and with other-than-human beings, rather than excluding the latter as is the case in Western thinking. As the archaeological evidence on the lives of the ancient peoples of the Upper Purus demonstrates, the locations and designs of the network of enclosures and their material culture reflect a shared thought of a continuum between humans and other-than-humans, the importance of investments in healthy relations and unity, and the generosity of leaders in sponsoring and organizing gatherings (Saunaluoma and Virtanen 2015; Virtanen and Saunaluoma 2017). It seems that people circulated through and inhabited these galactic clusters of earthworks only temporarily. Overall, early urbanity took seriously not only notions of reciprocity, protection, and power, but also moral links with other-than-human agencies. Although these features do not fit with the

Western definition of the polis, which highlights economic production and population growth, there can be no doubt that Southwestern Amazonian galactic clusters qualify as early forms of urbanity.

In Apurinã and Manxineru views, modern urban areas ruled by non-Indigenous people are categorically different, given that the overall conception of living well in their biopolitics and epistemological approaches differs substantially from Western ways (see Santos-Granero 2015). Since the birth of Christianity, in the West, humans have been considered as being above all other life-forms, with specific racial and ethnic attributes taking precedence over and dominating others (Mignolo 2000). This notion was reinforced during the Enlightenment. Modern urban areas in Latin America have followed the Western model of the city as society's polis (see Madsen 2002, 1–3), a place of justice and development, further lessening Indigenous agency. These ideas draw from the Euro-American vision of humanity—embedded in the hierarchical structures of urban state offices, universities, hospitals, museums, and prisons (Foucault 1975)—which still exemplifies and regulates how modern people should think about their relations with others and among themselves. Finally, urban institutions, including those in Latin America, rarely take into account human-environment relationality and its moral aspects. Modern cities are built based on a logic that elides these relational social systems, as shown by the locating of urban areas on hills, by water sources, in valleys, or in other protected environments. This is true even in those cases in which Western artists and architects have drawn inspiration from the environment.

In the meantime, the Apurinã and Manxineru, like many other Indigenous peoples, continue to resist, diversifying urban spaces by domesticating and indigenizing the social, economic, and political structures of cities and importing their models of social life, knowledge, and ideas of relationality between humans and the environment, with their different materializations, discourses, and values. In Indigenous imaginaries, contemporary urbanity leads to a process of incorporation of skills and tools, similar to that which takes place in their relationships with the worlds of spirits, as previous research has shown (Lasmar 2005; Cesarino 2008; Virtanen 2017; see also Santos-Granero, this volume). Here I have shown that the parallel discourses on contemporary cities and the spirit worlds draw from the same logic of negotiation with the Other and incorporation of the Other's power in order to master the necessary transformative resources for people- and life-making.

This, in turn, seems to be not very different from the social system of the precolonial builders of Southwestern Amazonian galactic clusters. In fact, from my interlocutors' point of view, urbanity is still strongly present in the galactic system of spirits.

While the notion that humans should be researched in relation to other species rather than in isolation is becoming more prominent in academia (e.g., Morton 2010), contemporary cities continue to play a big role in the Anthropocene. Anna C. Roosevelt (2013) has shown that the Amazonian Anthropocene was instigated ten thousand years ago by precolonial Indigenous populations, and that the impacts of human-mediated disturbances have only become radical in the modern era. As she observes, "after the conquest and colonization of Amazonia by Europeans, the types and scales of human impacts changed. Management by colonial and post-colonial capitalist states has not been as broadly productive and sustainable as that by the Indigenous people" (83). Heckenberger and colleagues (2008) have noted that the variously sized, precolonial, dispersed garden cities of the Upper Xingu had their own agricultural production areas, and Xinguano landscape models should be acknowledged when discussing sustainability and ecological questions. Since the 1970s, Indigenous Amazonian peoples have been vocal in drawing attention to the human-environment balance. Furthermore, it seems unlikely that the recent environmental degradation of the Brazilian Amazon rainforest and the increasing population shift to its cities—resulting in more dramatic human-mediated disturbances—will be stopped unless Indigenous peoples are incorporated into the decision-making processes.

Acknowledgments

I am grateful to the hospitality offered to me by the Apurinã and Manxineru communities, as well as to the support of the Academy of Finland (grant number 297161). I also thank Fernando Santos-Granero, Emanuele Fabiano, Martti Pärssinen, Sanna Saunaluoma, and the anonymous reviewers for their comments.

Notes

1. In the past, these subgroups included, among others, the Iũpiriwakury (Japó Bird People), the Kỹỹrykywakury (Mouse People), the Ximakywakury (Fish People), the Kaikyrywakury (Caiman People), the Hãkitiwakury (Jaguar Peo-

ple), the Kemawakury (Tapir People), the Tsikutywakury (Capuchin Monkey People), the Kemapiri (Giant Armadillo People), the Tsuminerywakury (Worm People), and the Iuwatawakury (Bamboo People).

2.   Among the most commonly mentioned subgroups of the Yine are the Koshits-ineru (Koshitsineru Bird People), the Cocamoluneru (Woodpecker People), the Kiruneru (Peach Palm People), the Hahamluneru (Downriver People), the Hi-jwutaneru (Headwater People), the Himnuneru (Snake People), the Natshineru (Hungry People), and the Wenejeneru (Riverside People).

3.   In the future, archaeological evidence, such as research on pottery, will surely show us more about this relationality with personified other-than-humans and its effects on the design of the ceremonial sites.

4.   This is also a geographically important area as it is next to where the Acre trib-utary meets the Purus River. The highway has caused vast deforestation, which has revealed the geometric earthworks, still strongly regarded in Indigenous understandings as sacred ancestral places.

5.   The Central Purus has several precolonial sites, but they have been little archae-ologically studied.

References

Andrello, Geraldo. 2006. *Cidade do índio*. São Paulo: Editora da Universidade de São Paulo.

Apurinã, Francisco. 2019. "Os 'limites' da rodovia federal BR-317 e os povos indíge-nas: Do licenciamento ambiental à licença dos espíritos." PhD diss., University of Brasília.

Cadena, Marisol de la. 2015. *Earth Beings: Ecologies of Practice Across Andean Worlds*. Durham, N.C.: Duke University Press.

Cesarino, Pedro de Niemeyer. 2008. "¿Babel da floresta, cidades dos brancos?" *Novos Estudos* 82:133–48.

Chandless, William. 1866. "Ascent of the River Purus." *Journal of the Royal Geograph-ical Society* 36:86–118.

Chernela, Janet. 2015. "Directions of Existence: Indigenous Women Domestics in the Paris of the Tropics." *Journal of Latin American and Caribbean Anthropology* 20 (1): 201–29.

Childe, Gordon V. 1950. "The Urban Revolution." *Town Planning Review* 21 (1): 3–17.

Clark, Peter, ed. 2013. *The Oxford Handbook of Cities in World History*. Oxford: Ox-ford University Press.

Cunha, Manuela Carneiro da. 1998. "Pontos de vista sobre a loresta amazônica: Xam-anismo e tradução." *Mana: Estudos de Antropologia Social* 4 (1): 7–22.

Erickson, Clark L. 2009. "Agency, Causeways, Canals, and the Landscapes of Every-day Life in the Bolivian Amazon." In *Landscapes of Movements: Trails, Paths, and Roads in Anthropological Perspective*, edited by James E. Snead, Clark L. Erickson, and J. Andrew Darling, 204–31. Philadelphia: University of Pennsylvania Press.

Foucault, Michel. 1975. *Surveiller et punir: naissance de la prison.* Paris: Bibliothèque des Histoires.

Gilbert, Alan. 1998. *The Latin American City.* London: Latin American Bureau.

Godelier, Maurice, and Michel Panoff. 1998. Introduction to *Le corps humain: concu, supplicié, possédé, cannibalisé*, edited by Maurice Godelier and Michel Panoff, 13–27. Paris: CNRS Éditions.

Gomes, Marcelo P. 2000. *The Indians and Brazil.* Gainesville: University Press of Florida.

Gow, Peter. 1999. "Piro Designs: Painting as Meaningful Action in an Amazonian Lived World." *Journal of the Royal Anthropological Institute* 5 (2): 229–46.

Gow, Peter. 2011. "Rethinking Cities in Peruvian Amazonia: History, Archaeology and Myth." In *The Archaeological Encounter: Anthropological Perspectives*, edited by Paolo Fortis and Istvan Praet, 174–203. St. Andrews: Centre for Amerindian, Latin American and Caribbean Studies.

Heckenberger, Michael. 2005. *The Ecology of Power: Culture, Place, and Personhood in the Southern Amazon, AD 1000–2000.* New York: Routledge.

Heckenberger, Michael. 2006. "History, Ecology, and Alterity: Visualizing Polity in Ancient Amazonia." In *Time and Complexity in Historical Ecology: Studies in the Neotropical Lowlands*, edited by William Balée and Clark L. Erickson, 311–40. New York: Columbia University Press.

Heckenberger, Michael, Christian Russell, Carlos Fausto, Joshua Toney, Morgan Schmidt, Edithe Pereira, Bruna Franchetto, and Afukaka Kuikuro. 2008. "Pre-Columbian Urbanism, Anthropogenic Landscapes, and the Future of the Amazon." *Science* 321 (5893): 1214–17.

Iriarte, José, Mark Robinson, Jonas de Souza, Antonia Damasceno, Franciele da Silva, Francisco Nakahara, Alceu Ranzi, and Luiz Aragao. 2020. "Geometry by Design: Contribution of Lidar to the Understanding of Settlement Patterns of the Mound Villages in SW Amazonia." *Journal of Computer Applications in Archaeology* 3 (1): 151–69.

Lagrou, Els. 2019. "Learning to See in Western Amazonia: How Does Form Reveal Relation?" *Social Analysis* 63 (2): 24–44.

Lasmar, Cristiane. 2005. *De volta ao Lago de Leite: gênero e transformação no alto rio Negro.* São Paulo: Editora da Universidade de São Paulo.

Madsen, Peter. 2002. Introduction to *The Urban Lifeworld: Formation Perception Representation*, edited by Peter Madsen and Richard Plunz, 1–41. London: Routledge.

Maldonado-Torres, Nelson. 2007. "On the Coloniality of Being: Contributions to the Development of the Concept." *Cultural Studies* 21 (2–3): 240–70.

McMichael, C. H., D. R. Piperno, M. B. Bush, M. R. Silman, A. R. Zimmerman, M. F. Raczka, and L. C. Lobato. 2012. "Sparse Pre-Columbian Human Habitation in Western Amazonia." *Science* 336 (6087): 1429–31.

Mignolo, Walter. 2000. *Local Histories / Global Designs: Coloniality, Subaltern Knowledges, and Border Thinking.* Princeton, N.J.: Princeton University Press.

Morris, Craig. 1982. "The Infrastructure of Inka Control in the Peruvian Central Highlands." In *Inka and Aztec States, 1400–1800: Anthropology and History*, edited by George A. Collier, Renato Rosaldo, and John D. Wirth, 153–71. New York: Academic Press.

Morris, Craig, and Donald E. Thompson. 1985. *Huánuco Pampa: An Inca City and Its Hinterland*. London: Thames and Hudson.

Morton, Timothy. 2010. *The Ecological Thought*. Cambridge, Mass.: Harvard University Press.

Murra, John Victor. 1980. *The Economic Organization of the Inca State*. Greenwich, Conn.: Jai Press.

Oliveira, Roberto Cardoso de. 1968. *Urbanização e tribalismo: a integração dos índios Terêna numa sociedade de classes*. Rio de Janeiro: Zahar.

Overing, Joanna, and Alan Passes, eds. 2000. *The Anthropology of Love and Anger: The Aesthetics of Conviviality in Native Amazonia*. London: Routledge.

Pärssinen, Martti. 1992. *Tawantinsuyu: The Inca State and Its Political Organization*. Helsinki: Suomen Historiallinen Seura.

Pärssinen, Martti. 2021. "Tequinho Geoglyph Site and Early Polychrome Horizon 300 BC–AD 300/500 in the Brazilian State of Acre." *Amazônica: Revista de Antropologia* 13 (1): 177–220.

Pärssinen, Martti, Evandro Ferreira, Pirjo Kristiina Virtanen, Alceu Ranzi. 2021. "Domestication in Motion: Macrofossils of Pre-Colonial Brazilian Nuts, Palms and Other Amazonian Planted Tree Species Found in the Upper Purus." *Environmental Archaeology* 26 (3): 309–22.

Pärssinen, Martti, and Alceu Ranzi. 2020. "Mobilidade cerimonial e a emergência do poder político com as primeiras estradas conhecidas do oeste amazônico (2000 A.P.)." In *(I)mobilidades na pré-história: pessoas, recursos, objetos, sítios e territórios*, edited by Raquel Vilaça and Rodrigo Simas de Aguiar, 307–49. Coimbra, Portugal: Coimbra University Press.

Pärssinen, Martti, Denise Schaan, and Alceu Ranzi. 2009. "Pre-Columbian Geometric Earthworks in the Upper Purus: A Complex Society in Western Amazonia." *Antiquity* 83 (322): 1084–95.

Peluso, Daniela. 2015. "Circulating Between Rural and Urban Communities: Multisited Dwellings in Amazonian Frontiers." In "Indigenous Urbanization: The Circulation of Peoples Between Rural and Urban Amazonian Spaces," edited by Daniela Peluso, special issue of *Journal of Latin American and Caribbean Anthropology* 20 (1): 57–79.

Peña Márquez, Juan Carlos. 2008. "Mitú, cidade amazónica; territorialidad indígena." PhD diss., Universidade Estadual de Campinas.

Riris, Philip. 2020. "Spatial Structure Among the Geometric Earthworks of Western Amazonia (Acre, Brazil)." *Journal of Anthropological Archaeology* 59:101–77.

Roosevelt, Anna C. 1991. *Moundbuilders of the Amazon: Geophysical Archaeology on Marajo Island, Brazil*. New York: Academic Press.

Roosevelt, Anna C. 2013. "The Amazon and the Anthropocene: 13,000 Years of Human Influence in a Tropical Rainforest." *Anthropocene* 4:69–87.

Saito, Yuriko. 2017. *Aesthetics of the Familiar: Everyday Life and World-Making.* Oxford: Oxford University Press.

Santos-Granero, Fernando, ed. 2015. *Images of Public Wealth or the Anatomy of Well-Being in Indigenous Amazonia.* Tucson: University of Arizona Press.

Saunaluoma, Sanna, Justin Moat, Francisco Pugliese, and Eduardo G. Neves. 2020. "Patterned Villagescapes and Road Networks in Ancient Southwestern Amazonia." *Latin American Antiquity* 32 (1): 173–87.

Saunaluoma, Sanna, Martti Pärssinen, and Denise Schaan. 2018. "Diversity of Pre-Colonial Earthworks in the Brazilian State of Acre, Southwestern Amazonia." *Journal of Field Archaeology* 43 (5): 362–79.

Saunaluoma, Sanna, and Denise Schaan. 2012. "Monumentality in Western Amazonian Formative Societies: Geometric Ditched Enclosures in the Brazilian State of Acre." *Antiqua* 2 (1): 1–11.

Saunaluoma, Sanna, and Pirjo Kristiina Virtanen. 2015. "Variable Models for Organization of Earthworking Communities in Upper Purus, Southwestern Amazonia: Archaeological and Ethnographic Perspectives." *Tipití: Journal of the Society for the Anthropology of Lowland South America* 13 (1): 23–43.

Schaan, Denise, Miriam Bueno, Alceu Ranzi, Antonia Barbosa, Arlan Silva, Edegar Casagrande, Allana Rodrigues, Alessandra Dantas, Ivandra Rampanelli. 2010. "Construindo paisagens como espacos sociais: o caso dos geoglifos do Acre." *Revista de Arqueologia* 23 (1): 30–41.

Seeger, Anthony, Roberto DaMatta, and Eduardo Viveiros de Castro. 1987. "A construção da pessoa nas sociedades indígenas brasileiras." In *Sociedades indígenas e indigenismo no Brasil*, edited by João Pacheco de Oliveira, 11–29. Rio de Janeiro: Universidade Federal do Rio de Janeiro.

Severi, Carlo, and Els Lagrou, eds. 2013. *Quimeras em diálogo: grafismo e figuração na arte indígena.* Rio de Janeiro: Editora 7 Letras.

Vilaça, Aparecida. 2007. "Cultural Change as Body Metamorphosis." In *Time and Memory in Indigenous Amazonia: Anthropological Perspectives*, edited by Carlos Fausto and Michael Heckenberger, 169–93. Gainesville: University Press of Florida.

Virtanen, Pirjo Kristiina. 2012. *Indigenous Youth in Brazilian Amazonia: Changing Lived Worlds.* New York: Palgrave Macmillan.

Virtanen, Pirjo Kristiina. 2016. "Relational Centers in the Amazonian Landscape of Moving." In *Moving Places: Relations, Return, and Belonging*, edited by Nataša Gregorič Bon and Jaka Repič, 126–47. New York: Berghahn.

Virtanen, Pirjo Kristiina. 2017. "'All This Is Part of My Movement': Amazonian Indigenous Ways of Incorporating Urban Knowledge in State Politics." In *Creating Dialogues: Indigenous Perceptions and Forms of Leadership in Amazonia*, edited by Hanne Veber and Pirjo Kristiina Virtanen, 259–84. Boulder: University Press of Colorado.

Virtanen, Pirjo Kristiina. 2019. "Ancestors' Times and Protection of Amazonian Biocultural Indigenous Heritage." *AlterNative: An International Journal of Indigenous
Peoples* 15 (4): 330–39.

Virtanen, Pirjo Kristiina, and Sanna Saunaluoma. 2017. "Visualization and Movement
as Configurations of Human-Nonhuman Engagements: Precolonial Geometric
Earthwork Landscapes of the Upper Purus, Brazil." *American Anthropologist* 119:
614–30.

Viveiros de Castro, Eduardo. 2012. *Cosmological Perspectivism in Amazonia and
Elsewhere*. Manchester: HAU Masterclass Series.

Watling, Jennifer, Sanna Saunaluoma, Martti Pärssinen, and Denise Schaan. 2015.
"Subsistence Practices Among Earthwork Builders: Phytolith Evidence from Archaeological Sites in the Southwest Amazonian Interfluves." *Journal of Archaeological Sciences* 4:541–51.

CHAPTER 8

The Deep Roots of Southern Arawak Urban Imaginaries

Tales of Alterity in the Longue Durée

FERNANDO SANTOS-GRANERO

In October 1977, during a lively drinking party in the Yanesha community of Camantarmas, along the Palcazu River in Peru, one guest mentioned that he had recently shot a tapir but could not find its body. His remark moved Shecor, the party host, to tell us a story that left me much intrigued. He told of an old man from a neighboring community who had gone hunting at night and shot a tapir. Since the animal was too heavy, he went back home and told his sons to go retrieve the animal first thing in the morning. Next day, one of them went to the forest in search of the tapir. He did not find it where the old man said it was, but he found its tracks. He followed the tracks until he arrived at the mouth of a deep cave. Since the tracks went in, the young man entered the cave. Shortly after, a young woman appeared. She asked the hunter what he was doing there. After telling her that he was in search of a shot tapir, the woman revealed that the wounded tapir was her mother. She said that the cave was the abode of Moya'c, the Mother/Owner of Tapirs. Her mother had come here because there was a hospital where they could cure her. The man and the tapir-woman went deeper into the cave, until they reached the hospital. There the man saw an older woman lying on a stretcher, under bright lights, while doctors removed the lead shot from her body with shiny metal instruments. The story ended with the tapir woman releasing the young hunter after he promised not to tell anyone what he had seen.

When I heard this story, I was a second-year undergraduate student, and perspectivism—the Indigenous Amazonian conception that all living beings and objects were originally human and see themselves as human while viewing other beings as either animal predators or animal prey—had not yet been acknowledged as a crucial dimension of Indigenous Amazonian ontologies and worldviews, so I could make little of it. What stirred my imagination, though, was the fact that according to Yanesha people, tapirs had hospitals. I asked Shecor how was this possible. As if he were stating the obvious, he said: "Because they live in cities." Many years later, while doing my doctoral fieldwork, I obtained the same response when I asked about the dwelling places of *pocoy* people, water spirits who seek to seduce Yanesha people under the guise of attractive white-looking men and women. These supernatural beings, they told me, live in subaquatic cities—long and busy highways along the bottom of rivers.

Stories about underground or underwater cities also abound among the Ashaninka, Asheninka, Nomatsiguenga, and Matsiguenga, Arawakan speakers like the Yanesha, who likewise live along Peru's central Andean piedmont. The first three, composing what some authors have called the "Ashaninka cluster," occupy the center of this vast region, with the Yanesha and Matsiguenga living to the north and south, respectively (map 8.1). For the purpose of this chapter, I will call these five peoples the Southern Arawak.[1] Since members of this group belong to the same linguistic family, live in a similar environment, and have undergone parallel historical processes, they tend to share worldviews, cultural practices, and mythological themes. One such recurrent theme is that of supernatural or enchanted cities.

The Nomatsiguenga myth about Manitincaari, or Jaguar Lake, is a good example of this kind of narrative (Shaver and Ashby 1976, 97–101). The myth recalls the miseries suffered by Nomatsiguenga people when white colonists invaded their lands. The intruders not only expelled them from their homes, but also stole their children to keep as servants. It was in these circumstances that the spirit jaguars from Manitincaari came to their rescue. Under human guise, they told the Nomatsiguenga to come live with them in their underwater town. Tired of the white invaders' harassment, a group of Nomatsiguenga followed the spirit jaguars to Manitincaari. There, they were given new (jaguar) tunics and invited to live in the jaguar town, where they finally escaped from the greedy white people.

Most Southern Arawak narratives about enchanted cities, however, relate not to the masters/owners of animals or other spirit beings, but to the origin of white or Andean people. Several versions of this story have been recounted by Ashaninka, Asheninka, Matsiguenga, and Yanesha narrators (Varese 1973, 285; Kindberg et al. 1979, 3–4; Anderson 1985, 55–59; Baer

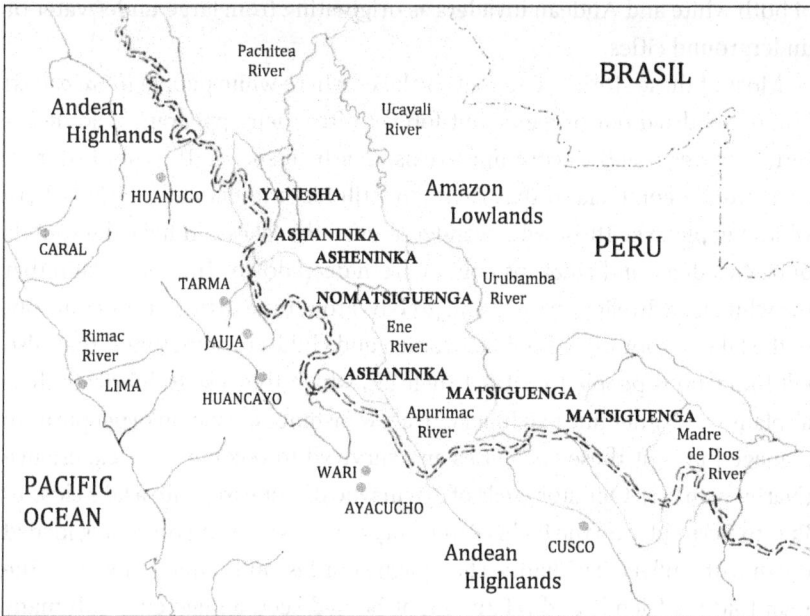

MAP 8.1 Location of Southern Arawak peoples and neighboring cities. The double line shows the boundary between Andes and Amazonia. Crafted by Fernando Santos-Granero.

1994, 157–58; Mihas 2014, 206–9; Santos-Granero 1991, 73–74). In most of them, the male protagonist (a man or a boy) hears sounds coming from the bottom of a lake or from beneath the earth: dogs barking, roosters crowing, cows mooing, guns firing, children laughing, or people splashing. Despite warnings against doing so, he sets out to fish for the underwater beings or excavate a hole to draw them out. After using different kinds of bait without success or digging a deep hole, the protagonist finally manages to fish or draw out a foreign-looking man. This imprudent action opens the doors for large numbers of white (or Andean) people to pour out from the hole or the bottom of the lake. Policemen, soldiers, and engineers come out in great numbers, mounted on horses or mules and heavily armed. Despite the local gods' and shamans' efforts to stop them, the invaders soon begin to kill native people and occupy their lands. The story ends with the white/Andean people's victory. They overwhelm the Indigenous inhabitants, and, at least according to some versions, thrive and proliferate after cutting off the head of the Indigenous god (Inca, Pachakama, or Yavireri) to appropriate his vital force. What is relevant here, however, is that the Southern Arawak conceive of both white and Andean invaders as originating from large underwater or underground cities.

Most of these stories state that the lakes where white people (*biracochas*) originated dried out or were shut forever after their appearance. Some assert, however, that they continue to exist (Narby 1989, 23). Thus, for instance, Asheninka people claim that there are still large underwater cities where white people live. Those who wander about such lakes can hear the sounds of trucks, dogs, and chickens coming from deep down. They also claim that the white lake dwellers are evil and greedy. From time to time, they come out of the lake to capture Asheninka women and children. Sometimes, they also kill Indigenous people to extract their fat, which they use to lubricate their airplanes and other fine machinery. In a few instances, Asheninka people have managed to visit these lake cities and survived to recount their experience (Narby 1989, 24). One story tells of a man who disappeared into a lake close to Puerto Bermúdez on the Pichis River, only to reemerge sometime later, loaded down with bullets, flashlights, champagne bottles, and canned tuna fish. The man told his friends and relatives that he had seen a huge city with many stores filled with all kinds of merchandise at the bottom of the lake. There was no one in the city, he claimed; that is why he had been able to escape alive.

As is the case in many other Indigenous Amazonian societies, Southern Arawak enchanted cities display all the trappings of large contemporary cities: buildings, streets, vehicles, highways, stores, and hospitals. These extraordinary places not only serve as models for the representation of extreme alterity, but also constitute the means by which Indigenous people convey their concerns about the nature of power and abusive authority. In this chapter, however, I am not so much interested in exploring the hermeneutics of Southern Arawak urban imaginaries, as I am in identifying the sources that inspired and shaped them. The fact that Southern Arawak contemporary stories of supernatural cities feature such modern conveniences as cars, stores, and hospitals suggests that they have taken contemporary Peruvian cities as their only model. This, as I intend to demonstrate, is not entirely true.

Adopting a reverse history approach, I analyze various instances of Southern Arawak urban encounters as reported in oral and written accounts or deduced from archaeological evidence. I begin with the narrative of a Yanesha leader who, according to living memory, was the first to visit Lima, Peru's capital, in modern times. From there I go back in time, searching for the earliest references indicating Southern Arawak acquaintance with cities and city dwellers, to pre-Columbian times and as far back as the Early Intermediate

Period (200 BCE–600 CE). I suggest that thanks to the intense interaction between Southern Arawak peoples—who, until recently, were in close contact with one another through long-distance trading networks, interethnic marriages, military confederations, and multiethnic villages—narratives of these urban encounters were widely disseminated among them, becoming the raw matter from which their urban imaginaries took shape and changed through time. Based on such a *longue durée* perspective, I demonstrate that Indigenous Amazonian peoples' fascination with, and distrust of, urban life may have deeper historical roots than we have previously thought.

Southern Arawak Urban Encounters

The following vignettes summarize seven Southern Arawak visits to Peruvian highland and coastal cities going back to the beginning of the Christian era. Most of these visits were to Lima, Cusco, and Wari (map 8.1). These were not, however, the only urban encounters reported in the documentary record.[2] In colonial and pre-Columbian times, they also visited regularly Tarma, Jauja, Huánuco Viejo, and a diversity of smaller citadels in the Jauja-Huancayo basin. If I have chosen to discuss these particular urban encounters, it is because they are the ones for which we have better information, especially concerning the visitors' impressions. Due to the long distances and difficult traveling conditions, these visits were exceptional events. For this reason, narrations of these urban experiences must have loomed large in the Southern Arawak imagination. Although as we go back in time the cities visited are increasingly smaller, they are still considerably larger than the dispersed, low-density villages to which the Southern Arawak were accustomed. This trait by itself would have awed them. However, apart from the size, design, and monumentality of these cities, what must have struck the visitors the most would have been the bizarreness and potentially violent nature of their inhabitants. This is, doubtless, the origin of Southern Arawak ambivalence with respect to cities and city dwellers.

1959 CE: 64 Years Ago

According to oral history, Berna Pascual Coronel was one of the first modern Yanesha leaders to visit Lima. His first trip to the capital, or at least the one he remembered most fondly, was the one he made in 1959. On that occasion, Peter Fast, a missionary-linguist working for the Summer Institute of

Linguistics (SIL), invited him to participate in the International Pacific Fair, to be inaugurated in Lima that October. The SIL intended to build a stand to display the institute's progress in the field of bilingual education, as well as an Indigenous house to exhibit native Amazonian peoples' lifeways. Fast invited Berna, by then chief of the community of Alto Yurinaki, to build the Indigenous house.

Berna traveled to Lima with his wife and two community members. Dressed in their traditional tunics and feather headdresses, the visitors caused a great sensation among the public attending the fair, to the point that even President Manuel Prado Ugarteche deigned to visit them. So great was the interest they stirred that the newspapers published Berna's picture (figure 8.1). The visitors were quite impressed. One of Berna's companions wrote, "Then we went to see a very large lake. It almost frightened us. We walked all around the city. There were all kinds of things and many cars, which almost ran us over. The streets along which we walked were very pretty. We saw many different things in Lima. There were many cables supported by trees going to the seat of government" (ILV 2004, 177). By then Lima had a population of around 1.4 million inhabitants and was experiencing its first big expansion thanks to increased rural immigration (Basadre 1983, 11:315). It was a bustling city, full of people, vehicles, and large buildings. The "large lake" that impressed the visitors was the Pacific Ocean, which features prominently in several Southern Arawak narratives of Lima (e.g., Kindberg et al. 1979, 10–11). It is, thus, probable that the model for the supernatural lake mentioned in the myths of origin of white people was the Pacific Ocean. This would make sense, since the Spaniards arrived from the Pacific Ocean and it was from its coasts that they advanced in their rapid conquest of the Inca Empire.

1914 CE: 109 Years Ago

In 1912, after the collapse of the rubber economy, the Asheninka, Ashaninka, and Nomatsiguenga joined forces to expel their former rubber *patrones* (bosses) and other white-mestizo agents present in the Pichis-Perené-Tambo region. Inspired by the words of Chief José, whom the rebels regarded as a world-transforming divine emissary (*tasorentsi*), the insurgents disrupted all traffic along the Pichis Trail, the mule track connecting the region with Lima (Santos-Granero 2018, chap. 3). Although the government sent troops to quell the uprising, they failed to defeat the rebels. By mid-1914, the sit-

FIGURE 8.1 Berna Pascual Coronel (*kneeling*), kindling a fire, surrounded by his wife (*far right*) and visitors at the stand of the Summer Institute of Linguistics, International Pacific Fair, Lima, 1959. *El Comercio*, October 8, 1959. Courtesy of Mary Ruth Wise.

uation had worsened so much that the region's authorities proposed to the government that the only solution was to arrest and execute, or exile, the entire Indigenous population.

By then, the Upper Perené region belonged to the British-owned Perené Colony (Barclay 1989). The colony produced high-quality export coffee in its own plantations and those of its European colonists. It depended, however, on the labor of the Yanesha and Ashaninka living within the colony for such heavy tasks as felling trees, opening new plantations, weeding, and harvesting. For this reason, when Víctor Valle Riestra, the colony's administrator, heard that the authorities had demanded the arrest and banishment of the region's Indigenous population, he was greatly concerned about how this would affect the colony.

To counter this initiative, Valle Riestra took with him a group of sixteen Ashaninka and Yanesha to Lima to show the public that they were "industrious civilized Indians" and ask the authorities for guarantees (Santos-Granero 2018, 62). The visitors, among whom there were one Yanesha and two Ashaninka chiefs, arrived in Lima after a gruesome three-day trip along mule trails, dirt roads, and railways. Their visit was a propagandistic success. Reporters interviewed the visitors to know their impressions of Lima, and their pictures appeared in the city's most important papers and magazines (figure 8.2; *La Prensa* 1914a, 1914b).

According to these reports, one thing that most impressed the visitors was the Presidential Palace, where President Oscar R. Benavides received and entertained them. Although the palace did not yet have the ornate Spanish plateresque aspect that characterizes it today, it was still a large and imposing building that occupied an entire side of the city's central plaza. Cars, introduced to Peru scarcely ten years earlier (Basadre 1983, 8:184), also impressed the visitors, especially after Valle Riestra drove them around the city to see its main sights. The cinema, with its moving images and extraordinary plots, also drew their admiration. However, José Carlos Mariátegui, the celebrated Peruvian radical, writing under the pseudonym Juan Croniqueur (1914) in the newspaper *La Prensa*, noted shrewdly that these "marvels and wonders are not enough to persuade the savages about the excellence of civilization." The visitors, he wrote, regard urban habits such as tight clothes and shoes as being too constraining, despise the city's comforts and gifts, and yearn to go back to their native forests. More importantly, he concluded, they show no intention of exchanging "the rustic simplicity of their savage life for the city's agitated and violent existence."

1746 CE: 277 Years Ago

Juan Santos Atahuallpa, an Andean mestizo, arrived in the heart of Asheninka territory in May 1742 with the aim of persuading the Southern Arawak to rise against the Spanish invaders (Amich 1975, 156). Shortly after, he con-

FIGURE 8.2 Perené Colony Ashaninka chiefs Zárate (*left*) and José Kinchori (*right*) and Yanesha chief Santiago López (*center*), visiting Lima, 1914. *La Prensa*, July 18, 1914. Courtesy of the Biblioteca Nacional del Perú.

vinced them not only to follow him, but also to join forces with their erstwhile enemies the Yine (Piro) and Conibo. After expelling the last Franciscan missionaries from Quimirí in August 1743, the rebels finally attained their goal of ridding the region of white people. During the following ten years, the Crown organized several military expeditions against the rebels, with little success. On one of these, however, General Llamas y Estrada attacked the former mission of Huancabamba, capturing sixteen Yanesha men, women, and children (Santos-Granero 2019).

On May 14, 1746, General Llamas sent the prisoners, accused of spying on behalf of Atahuallpa, to Lima for prosecution. They arrived more than a week later, after an arduous 250-mile (400-kilometer) trip on muleback. On the viceroy's orders, the authorities interned them in the royal prison, except for a sick prisoner who was sent to Saint Anne's Hospital. The criminal prosecutor interrogated the prisoners one by one. All of them insisted that they were Christian and had not had contact with the rebels. Since there was no proof to the contrary, the high court was forced to declare them innocent.

The accused spent most of their time in jail, so it is possible that they did not have the chance to visit Lima properly. However, they must have caught glimpses of the city on their way in and out, and while being transported within it. If so, the prisoners were probably the last Southern Arawak people to see Lima in its full colonial glory, for five months later, on October 28, a high-magnitude earthquake razed the city (figure 8.3). By then, Lima had a population of sixty thousand inhabitants (Seminario and Zegarra Díaz 2014, table 7). Not only was it a populous city but, according to Jesuit priest Pedro Lozano, it had "achieved the greatest degree of perfection of which a New World city was capable of, due to its sumptuous buildings, the many houses that adorned its straight streets, its ornate fountains, the height of its temples, and its large monasteries" (quoted in Seiner Lizárraga 2016, lxxiii).

Stories about this forced visit to Lima must have spread widely among the Southern Arawak. The visitors' accounts must have mentioned Lima's monumentality and many novelties but also the ghastly conditions of the royal prison, a place that, according to contemporary descriptions, was dark,

FIGURE 8.3 Panoramic view of the city of Lima, 1780. Fernando Brambila, *Vista de Lima desde las inmediaciones de la Plaza de Toros* (Madrid: Taller de Calcografía Nacional, 1780). Courtesy of the Ministerio de Defensa de España, Archivo del Museo Naval, Ms. 1726 (58).

cold, and humid, where prisoners were poorly fed and sheltered (Gálvez 1905, 59–60).

1637 CE: 386 Years Ago

In 1637, a group of Spanish adventurers entered the Andean piedmont east of the highland town of Tarma with the intention of finding the fantastically rich city of Paititi, of which they had heard so much. There are at least four fragmentary and biased accounts of this expedition and its results (Montesinos 1882, xxix–xxxi; Memorial 1986, 137–38; Córdova Salinas 1957, 231; Amich 1975, 45). These narratives suggest that Captain Pedro Bohórquez, with the authorization of Viceroy Jerónimo Fernández de Cabrera, led the expedition, while Francisco Montesinos, nephew of the Spanish chronicler Fernando Montesinos, was an important member of the party. After exploring Ashaninka and Yanesha territories, the expeditionaries returned to Lima, bringing with them six Southern Arawak paramount chiefs (*indios principales*).

The city's elite gave the Indigenous visitors a warm welcome (Montesinos 1644, fol. 31; 1882, xxix–xxxi). Fernando Montesinos lodged the Indigenous leaders in his house. The viceroy presented them with dresses of fine silk. Archbishop Fernando Arias de Ugarte entertained them in his magnificent palace. The Court's highest-ranking nobles vied for the visitors' attention and showered them with gifts. Even the judges of the high court and the Tribunal of the Holy Office, the dreaded Inquisition, took time to entertain the Southern Arawak paramount chiefs.

At the time, Lima had a population of around twenty-six thousand inhabitants and was one of the largest cities in the Americas (Pérez Cantó 1982, 384). In his "Description of the Indies," Reginaldo Lizárraga (1946, 49, 80) describes early seventeenth-century Lima as a checkerboard city with a large central plaza surrounded by spacious arcades, where all kinds of merchants and artisans gathered to sell their wares and services (figure 8.4). Fountains fed by the canalized Rímac River furnished water in its streets, plazas, and houses. Richly decorated churches and convents stood out in the city's skyline. Nonetheless, what most called the attention of the foreign visitors, according to Lizárraga, was the sumptuousness with which women dressed, as well as the lavishness of religious feasts and processions. The Southern Arawak chiefs could not have failed to notice these features.

After the visitors spent some time in the city, the viceroy ordered Francisco Montesinos to take them back to their land (Montesinos 1882, xxx; Memorial 1986, 137–38). Loaded with gifts, the six Southern Arawak leaders returned to Tarma accompanied by Montesinos, eight of his friends, and two Franciscan friars. When the group reached Tarma's piedmont, however, the leaders of the hinterland Ashaninka informed the expeditionaries that they were not welcome and should turn back. It is probable, though not sure, that at this point the six chiefs that came with Montesinos deserted the group. Disregarding the warnings, the expeditionaries continued their way deeper into Indigenous territory. As a result, on December 8, 1637, the interior Ashaninka ambushed and killed them all (Córdova Salinas 1957, 231; Amich 1975, 45).

1470 CE: 553 Years Ago

At the end of Inca Pachacuti's reign (1438–71), his son Tupac Inca Yupanqui undertook the conquest of the Amazonian peoples living northeast of Cusco at the headwaters of the Amarumayo, the present-day Madre de Dios River (map 8.1). Some chroniclers referred to these peoples by the generic ethnonyms Chuncho or Antis/Andes (Garcilaso de la Vega 1963, 317; Betanzos 1987, 131). Others were more specific, asserting that on this occasion Tupac Yupanqui subjected five Indian "provinces": Manaresuyo (Manari), Opatari, Guancavillca, Carabaya, and Guarmiauca (Santacruz Pachacuti 1968, 304). The first two of these—Manari and Opatari—were ancestors of the present-day Matsiguenga (Renard-Casevitz, Saignes, and Taylor 1988, 89–90). Tupac Yupanqui conquered some of these peoples by force; others he attracted through persuasion and the exchange of gifts.

Around 1470, after two years of fighting, Tupac Yupanqui went back to Cusco. He brought with him many Chuncho prisoners, but also a large delegation of Manari and Opatari allies. The new allies brought with them presents of parrots, monkeys, macaws, honey, and wax as a sign of vassalage or friendship. They also gave the prince large quantities of gold. Delegations of these peoples continued to bring presents to the Inca in Cusco and, later, in Vilcabamba, until the death of Tupac Amaru I in 1572 (Garcilaso de la Vega 1963, 318; Betanzos 1987, 135–36). The Manari and Opatari ambassadors must have been much impressed with Cusco, especially after a 125-mile (200-kilometer) trip going from the lowlands to an altitude of 11,150 feet

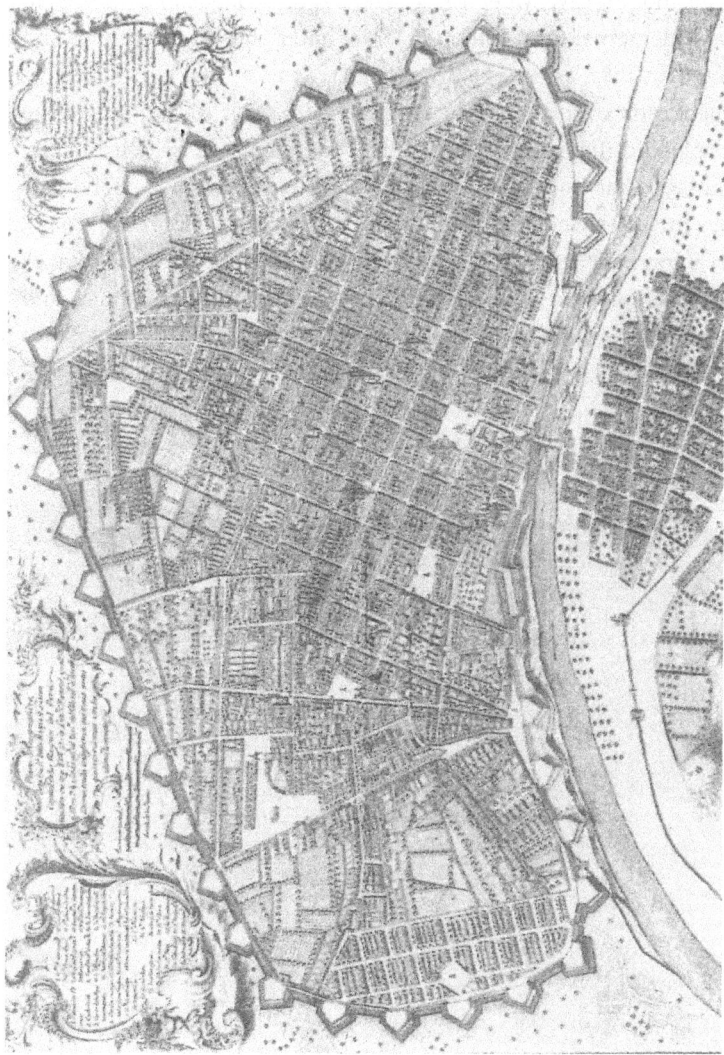

FIGURE 8.4 Plan of the fortified city of Lima, 1685. Pedro Nolasco Mere, *Plano scenographico de la Ciudad de Los Reyes, o Lima capital de los reinos del Perú* (Madrid, 1685). Courtesy of the Ministerio de Cultura y Deporte de España, Archivo General de Indias, MP, Perú y Chile 13bis.

(3,400 meters) above sea level. In previous years, Inca Pachacuti had rede-
signed and rebuilt the city to convey the empire's power and wealth. He had
desiccated swamps, canalized springs, and built new fountains to broaden
the city's plan and improve water access. He also razed large areas of the old
city to trace wider streets and construct larger and richer stone temples and
palaces (Betanzos 1987, 49–53, 75–79, 169–71).

The project took twenty years to complete (Betanzos 1987, 77), and the
result was splendid (figure 8.5). One of the first Spaniards to visit the city
reported, in 1533, that Cusco "was as big as they had been told . . . and that
in eight days that they were there they could not see it all" (Jerez 1947, 343).
Particularly impressive was Coricancha, or the Temple of the Sun (Betanzos
1987, 50). The temple was made of perfectly cut and polished stones, and
its doors and inner walls were covered from top to bottom with gold plates

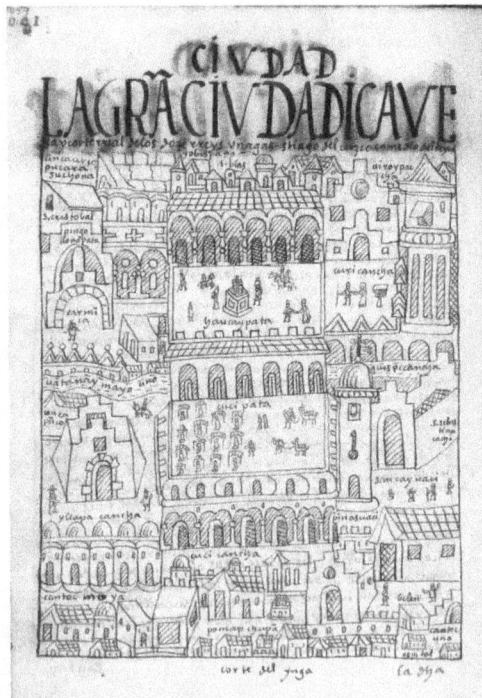

FIGURE 8.5 View of Cusco in Inca times, 1615. Felipe Guaman Poma de Ayala,
El primer nueva crónica y buen gobierno (1615). Public domain, posted to Wikime-
dia Commons.

(Garcilaso de la Vega 1963, 136–37). On the temple's main altar there was a large gold figure of the sun flanked at either side by the mummies of past Inca sitting on golden chairs. With a population of at least twenty thousand, and its many streets, buildings, plazas, and markets, Cusco must have presented an image that was hard to forget (Bauer 2004, 3).

The city, however, was also associated with the darker side of Inca rule. Joan de Santacruz Pachacuti (1968, 305) recounts that at the end of Tupac Yupanqui's reign (1471–93), a three-hundred-strong Opatari embassy arrived in Cusco loaded with presents of gold powder and nuggets for the Inca. That night a terrible frost burned all the crops to their roots. Locals blamed the catastrophe on the visitors. As a result, Tupac Yupanqui ordered his men to kill the Opatari and bury them ritually with their gold to appease the mountain gods. Since we know that the Opatari and Manari continued to visit Cusco with presents until the death of Tupac Amaru I, the last Inca, in 1572, it is possible that this story is somewhat exaggerated (Garcilaso de la Vega 1963, 319). Even so, there can be no doubt that the Southern Arawak were aware that just as the Inca ruler could be generous with his allies and tributaries, he could also dispose lightly of them for real or alleged offenses.

800 CE: 1,223 Years Ago

Although there is no documentary evidence of Southern Arawak connections with the Wari Empire, there is abundant archaeological data indicating the existence of uninterrupted relations between the Wari and the ancestors of the Ashaninka and Matsiguenga living along the Apurímac River on the Andean piedmont. The most recent data indicates that the Wari Empire emerged around 650 CE and ended around 1050 CE (Tantaleán 2013, 88). Some authors even argue that the Arawak expansion into the Andean piedmont facilitated the development of late prehistoric (c. 500–1500 CE) Andean highland polities such as the Wari by making accessible prestige tropical products such as feathers and coca (Wilkinson 2018). The empire's capital, also known as Wari, was located 9 miles (15 kilometers) from present-day Ayacucho, and only 100 miles (160 kilometers) from the Apurímac River and the Amazon region (map 8.1). Archaeological excavations have shown that during the empire's expansion phase, the Wari established several small outposts along the Apurímac, in areas between 1,800 and 2,130 feet (550 and 650 meters) above sea level (Raymond 1988, 1992). Javier Fonseca Santa Cruz and Brian S. Bauer (2013) and Enrique Meseth and colleagues (2015) confirm that Wari people had an important presence in the forested Andean piedmont. Given that this altitudinal zone is ideal for the cultivation of coca, archaeologists suggest that these outposts were founded to have ready access to coca fields.

Excavation of Wari tombs shows that coca was not the only product that the Wari obtained from the Amazon region. Other important tropical products brought from this region were hardwoods, cotton, hallucinogens, monkeys, exotic birds, and, especially important, feathers (Santillana 2000). The Wari produced some of these goods in their tropical outposts. Others, such as feathers, hallucinogens, and exotic animals, they probably obtained through trade with the ancestors of the Southern Arawak, whose expansion into the Amazonian lowlands was completed by 500 CE (Wilkinson 2018). This would have entailed some kind of understanding between the Wari and their Amazonian neighbors, as well as regular interaction between them.

Given that Wari, the empire's capital, was relatively close to the Apurímac Valley, it is more than probable that the ancestors of the Ashaninka and Matsiguenga visited it at least from time to time. The visitors would have found a large city spread over 4 square miles (10 square kilometers) and surrounded by a massive, 33-foot (10-meter) wall (Bulliet et al. 2012, 182). At its pinnacle, Wari had a population of between thirty thousand and seventy thousand people (McEwan and Williams 2012, 65; Isbell, Brewster-Wray, and Spickard 1991, 51). Built with uncut stones, the city combined administrative and ceremonial sectors with plazas, closed patios, merchant and artisan quarters, and elite residential areas (Schreiber 2012, 13). Some buildings were two or three stories high. Plastered with mud and painted white, they must have shone from far away under the highland sun as visitors approached the city. Wari's ceremonial sector, encompassing two large temples, one of them painted red, occupied an important part of the city and was the focus of most ritual activity. Festivities in these temples were probably the occasion to display the feather-covered garments and wall hangings for which Wari people are famous, and which Southern Arawak visitors would have recognized as being made with feathers collected by them (King 2012, 27–30).

100 CE: 1,923 Years Ago

There is archaeological evidence indicating that the connection between proto–Southern Arawak peoples and Andean urban centers predates the emergence of the Wari Empire. According to Donald W. Lathrap (1970, 74–78, 96, 135), there were two important Arawak migration waves from the Middle Amazon River to Southern Amazonia. The proto-Yanesha arrived to the Andean piedmont with the first wave, along the Ucayali-Pachitea River axis, around 3,600 years ago.[3] The proto-Ashaninka, proto-Nomatsiguenga, and proto-Matsiguenga arrived with the second wave, around 1,900 years ago, along the Ucayali-Tambo and Ucayali-Urubamba River axes (Lathrap 1970, 120–23).[4] Between 650 and 50 BCE, during much of the Early Horizon Period (900–200 BCE), the seminomadic pastoralists living in the Jauja-Huancayo basin had permanent exchange relations with the Amazonian peoples living along the eastern slopes of the Andes of Tarma—peoples that, as we have seen, were the ancestors of the Yanesha people (Browman 1975, 326). They traded Andean wares for coca, feathers, and other tropical products. By the time the first citadels emerged in this highland region, between 100 BCE and 600 CE, during the Early Intermediate Period, trade with the proto–Southern Arawak peoples was, therefore, well established (Mallma Cortéz 2018, 17). It is thus quite probable that the ancestors of the present-day Yanesha and Ashaninka occasionally visited the fortified cities of Auquimarca, Patan Coto, Coto Coto of Huánchar, and Coto Coto of Chilca, located in the provinces of Huancayo and Concepción, less than 95 miles (150 kilometers) from the Amazon region (Leiva García 2012, 46). These small cities contained hundreds of mostly circular, but sometimes rectangular, one- and two-story stone buildings, often surrounded by defensive walls.

Recent studies carried out by Richard Chase Smith (2004, 2011) in collaboration with Yanesha elders confirm the antiquity of these relations. Through the mapping of important landmarks (mountains, lakes, ancient roads, and buildings) connected to Yanesha mythical narratives, Smith and his team have demonstrated that the ancient Yanesha were knowledgeable of the wide land strip that crossed the Peruvian Central Andes connecting the Amazon with the Pacific Ocean. Although Smith's suggestion that the ancient Yanesha colonized the forested *yungas* region west of the Andes has still to be proven, there can be no doubt that their detailed knowledge of the Central

Andes could have only derived from hundreds, if not thousands, of years of traveling through the region.

Discussion

Documentary and archaeological evidence leaves no doubt that the proto–Southern Arawak were acquainted with urban centers since at least 100 BCE. It is possible, however, that their first encounters with urban dwellers took place much earlier. We know that in Peru urban life began with the emergence of Caral, on the central Pacific coast, around 5,000 years ago. The urban lifestyle inaugurated by Caral gradually spread throughout north-central Peru. At its peak, its area of influence encompassed eighteen river basins, including the tropical portions of the Upper Huallaga and Upper Marañón Valleys (Shady 2006, 60, 62). By the time the proto-Yanesha arrived at the Andean piedmont 3,600 years ago, Caral civilization had disappeared. However, its urban lifestyle continued throughout the Initial Period (1800–900 BCE) and, thanks to the cultural influence of the Chavín polity, flourished again during the Early Horizon (900–200 BCE). Given that transversal trading relations connecting the Pacific coast with the Andean highlands and the Amazonian piedmont across central Peru have been attested since the emergence of Caral, it is more than probable—although here we enter into the realm of the speculative—that the proto-Yanesha were acquainted with the Andean and coastal urban civilizations that followed Caral at least as early as 1500 BCE.

The antiquity of rural-urban relations in central Peru is in line with what we know about the archaeology of other continents and cultural areas. Gilles Deleuze and Félix Guattari (2000, 360, 428–29) have argued that there is increasing evidence that state societies, and with them cities, date back to the early Neolithic (c. 12,000 BCE) or even the late Paleolithic (c. 20,000–12,000 BCE). In their words, "It is hard to imagine primitive societies that would not have been in contact with imperial States, at the periphery or in poorly controlled areas. But of greater importance is the inverse hypothesis: that the State itself has always been in a relation with an outside and is inconceivable independent of that relationship." Following Ibn Khaldûn (2015), the fourteenth-century Arab philosopher and historian, Deleuze and Guattari (2000, 380) view this tense relation as one between city-states and nomad (tribal) societies, or, in their terminology, between the polis (the enclosed and ordered space of the city) and the nomos (the open and nondelimited space of wilderness). They claim that these two systems are not disconnected but coexist and compete "in a perpetual field of interaction." They presuppose each other not in evolutionary terms, with tribal societies preceding city-states, but in coevolutionary terms, that is, reciprocally affecting each other's development and shape. This suggests that city-states and tribal societies not only are mutually constitutive but model their respective identities by opposition to that of the other. It is thus not surprising that cities and city dwellers occupy such an important place in Southern Arawak mythologies. They represent the extreme Other and, as such, arouse both positive and negative responses.

On the positive side, Southern Arawak regard cities as sites of material wealth, abundance, and technological innovation. Cities constitute the expression of the Other's creativity, magic, and inventiveness, capacities that, according to Southern Arawak myths, belonged originally to them but were stolen by, or lost to, white or mestizo people (Varese 1973, 309–11; Villanueva and Trapnell 1976, 133–34; Santos-Granero 1991, 68–69). As a result, cities are full of marvelous or ingenious things: objects such as metal tools, gold statues, firearms, flashlights, cars, and trucks; extravagant foods and beverages like champagne and canned tuna; and new and practical conveniences and technologies such as hospitals, schools, stores, and movies.

Southern Arawak also view cities as monumental sites in which space is organized and used in radically diverse ways. They contain large public buildings (palaces, temples, and prisons) that stand out from the rest and can be seen from afar. They have broad open spaces (plazas, streets, and markets) where people meet in large numbers for social, religious, or commercial purposes. Their buildings, especially the public ones, are built with materials that are meant to last for many generations. They are decorated sumptuously. More importantly, cities often have facilities that make life easier: water canals, fountains, sewage systems. They even have "cable forests" conducting electricity to all corners.

Finally, Southern Arawak regard cities as important seats and sources of power. They are the dwelling places of lords, emperors, viceroys, and presidents, but also of grand priests, consecrated virgins, monks, and archbishops. The homes of these powerful people stand out due to their size and magnificence. They also differ due to the imposition of scripted forms of social exchange—strict rules of conduct, protocol, and etiquette—on visitors. Their large temples concentrate most religious activity, being the focus of complex and lavish collective rituals, sacrifices, and processions.

However, from a Southern Arawak point of view, cities are also fearsome places. They are overcrowded, noisy, and contaminated sites, full of busy pedestrians and aggressive conductors. Urbanites live an agitated and violent life, in which thefts and murders are common occurrences. They are constrained by their tight clothes and bizarre social habits. More importantly, city dwellers are greedy people, always in pursuit of material gain. They seek to impose their domination through lies and deceit, and do not hesitate to send their soldiers, police, and engineers to invade, measure, and colonize Indigenous lands. Although city rulers may make great displays of generosity toward their allies and friends, they can as easily turn against them depending on their whims. Worse of all, urbanites seek to deprive Indigenous people of their vital force by stealing their children, extracting their fat, and cutting off their gods' heads (see also Santos-Granero and Barclay 2011). Cities are thus the loci of despotic and abusive power, which finds expression in their prisons, army bases, and police headquarters.

Southern Arawak urban imaginaries have incorporated these positive and negative impressions. Being historical constructs, however, they have changed throughout time in consonance with transformations in the type and nature of Southern Arawak urban encounters. The earliest Southern Arawak narrative of fabulous Amazonian cities that we know of dates from 1665, when an Ashaninka captive of the Panoan-speaking Shipibo told Father Manuel Biedma (1981, 96–97) about a rich land ruled by a mighty king called either Enim, Pachacamac, or Gabeinca, Powerful Inca. The captive said that Enim was Lord of the Rivers. He lived in a sumptuous city called Masarobeni on the Ene River, facing another large city called Picha. Masarobeni was so big, he reported, that a person needed more than one day to get to know it all. It had high buildings and towers that could be seen from afar. Enim ruled over many "nations," from which he received all kinds of tribute. As a sign of his majesty and grandeur, he wore a gold diadem representing sun rays. He ate on gold plates, and his palace was decorated with large wall hangings made of colorful feathers he received as tribute from his many subjects.

The narrative of the fabulous Masarobeni, capital of the kingdom of Enim, combines elements from the Southern Arawak myths about the technological genius Pachacamac (Varese 1973, 309–11; Benavides 1986) with others from narratives about the foreign, wealthy, despotic divinity Inca or Enc

(Kindberg et al. 1979, 3–4; Mihas 2014, 46–50; Santos-Granero 1991, 73–74). It is more than probable that the Southern Arawak modeled the fabulous Amazonian city of Masarobeni on the Inca towns of Cusco, Tarma, and Huánuco Viejo, which we know they visited regularly in the fifteenth century. With the passage of time, the towers, gold diadems, and feather wall hangings of the older narratives changed into the hospitals, cars, and movies of more recent accounts, while the despotism of Inca rulers turned into the duplicity of conquistadores, viceroys, and presidents.

Ambivalent feelings concerning urbanites and urban life are not unique to Southern Arawak peoples, as the various contributions to this volume demonstrate. It is more than probable that all Indigenous Amazonian peoples living along the Andean piedmont of Peru, Ecuador, Bolivia, and Colombia had similar encounters with neighboring urban civilizations. The same is true of the peoples of the Greater Antilles, who displayed cultural practices and structures such as ball courts and ceremonial plazas that betray contact with Maya urban centers (Alegría 1983). We should not discard, however, the possibility that knowledge of urban lifestyles also derived, as Peter Gow (2011) has argued, from direct or indirect acquaintance with early prehistoric Amazonian urban settlements such as Santarem, Açutuba, Gavan, and Marajoara, which by AD 1000–1200 already exhibited the traits of central places or embryonic city-states (see also Heckenberger 2005, 132; Heckenberger et al. 2007, 200–203). Narratives of such urban encounters would have circulated together with myths, ritual practices, and prestigious trade goods along the many fluvial and interfluvial long-distance commercial networks that crisscrossed and interconnected the Amazon region (Lathrap 1973). If this is true, Pierre Clastres's (1998) assertion that Amerindian societies are "societies against the state" would not imply some Indigenous metaphysical capacity to foresee the state's future emergence but would derive from the very empirical fact that these societies have known, or experienced, the state's darkest facets since remote prehistoric times.

Notes

1. I exclude the Yine (Piro) people from this group because as Peter Gow (2002) has demonstrated, although also belonging to the Arawak linguistic family, they exhibit important cultural differences from their Arawak neighbors.

2. Other known Southern Arawak visits to Peruvian cities are: Asheninka to Lima, 1922 (*La Prensa* 1922); Ashaninka to Tarma, 1657 (Olmedo 1956, 70, 326);

Ashaninka to Lima, 1595 (Font 1965, 102); Opatari to Cusco, 1470 (Álvarez Maldonado 1906, 67); Manari to Cusco, 1576 (Acosta 1958, 250–51); and Yanesha to Huánuco Viejo, circa 1520 (Renard-Casevitz, Saignes, and Taylor 1988, 65). (Manari and Opatari were ancestors of the present-day Matsiguenga.)

3. Based on linguistic data, other authors suggest, however, that the proto-Yanesha, together with the proto-Chamicuro—and perhaps the proto-Panatahua—arrived along the Amazon-Marañón-Huallaga axis (Wise 2011). This, however, does not change my argument here.

4. The place of origin of the proto-Arawak, the dates of divergence of its various branches, and the migration routes these branches followed have been the object of much debate (Aikhenvald 2006, 447). There seems to be consensus, however, that the branching of Arawakan languages started around three thousand years ago and was completed by 500 CE (Heckenberger 2013; Wilkinson 2018). So, even if we accept that the divergence of the proto–Southern Arawak took place in later dates than those suggested by Lathrap (1970), the evidence suggests that Arawakan-speaking groups were already living along the piedmont of the Peruvian Central Andes by the time the first Andean citadels flourished in the Jauja-Huancayo region, between 100 BCE and 600 CE.

References

Acosta, José de. 1958. "Carta del P. José de Acosta al P. Everardo Mercuriano; Lima, 15 de febrero de 1577." In *Monumenta Peruana*, edited by Antonio de Egaña, vol. 2, 210–86. Rome: Apud "Monumenta Historica Societa Iesu."

Aikhenvald, Alexandra. 2006. "Arawak Languages." In *Encyclopedia of Languages and Linguistics*, edited by Keith Brown, 446–49. Oxford: Elsevier.

Alegría, Ricardo. 1983. *Ball Courts and Ceremonial Plazas in the West Indies*. New Haven, Conn.: Yale University Press.

Álvarez Maldonado, Juan. 1906. "Relación verdadera del discurso y suceso de la jornada y descubrimiento que hizo desde el año de 1567 hasta el de 1569." In *Juicio de límites entre el Perú y Bolivia*, edited by Víctor M. Maúrtua, vol. 6, 17–68. Barcelona: Imprenta de Henrich y Comp.

Amich, José. 1975. *Historia de las misiones del convento de Santa Rosa de Ocopa*. Lima: Milla Batres.

Anderson, Ronald J. 1985. *Cuentos folklóricos de los Ashéninca*. Vol. 1. Yarinacocha: Instituto Lingüístico de Verano.

Baer, Gerhard. 1994. *Cosmología y shamanismo de los matsiguenga (Perú Oriental)*. Quito: Abya-Yala.

Barclay, Frederica. 1989. *La Colonia del Perené: capital inglés y economía cafetalera en la configuración de la región de Chanchamayo*. Iquitos, Peru: Centro de Estudios Teológicos de la Amazonía.

Basadre, Jorge. 1983. *Historia de la República del Perú, 1822–1933*. 11 vols. Lima: Editorial Universitaria.

Bauer, Brian S. 2004. *Ancient Cusco: Heartland of the Inca.* Austin: University of Texas Press.

Benavides, Margarita. 1986. "La usurpación del dios tecnológico y la articulación temprana en la selva peruana: misioneros, herramientas y mesianismo." *Amazonía Indígena* 6 (12): 30–35.

Betanzos, Juan de. 1987. *Suma y narración de los Incas.* Madrid: Ediciones Atlas.

Biedma, Manuel. 1981. *La conquista franciscana del alto Ucayali.* Lima: Editorial Milla Batres.

Browman, David. 1975. "Trade Patterns in the Central Highlands of Peru in the First Millennium B.C." *World Archaeology* 6 (7): 322–29.

Bulliet, Richard W., Pamela Kyle Crossley, Daniel R. Headrick, Steven W. Hirsch, Lyman L. Johnson, and David Northrup. 2012. *The Earth and Its Peoples: A Global History.* Vol. 1. Boston: Wadsworth.

Clastres, Pierre. 1998. *Society Against the State.* New York: Zone Books.

Córdova Salinas, Diego de. 1957. *Crónica franciscana de las provincias del Perú.* Washington, D.C.: Academy of American Franciscan History.

Croniqueur, Juan. 1914. "Entre salvajes." *La Prensa,* July 19, 1914.

Deleuze, Gilles, and Félix Guattari. 2000. *A Thousand Plateaus: Capitalism and Schizophrenia.* Minneapolis: University of Minnesota Press.

Fonseca Santa Cruz, Javier, and Brian S. Bauer. 2013. "Dating the Wari Remains at Espiritu Pampa (Vilcabamba, Cusco)." *Andean Past* 11 (1). https://digitalcommons .library.umaine.edu/andean_past/vol11/iss1/12.

Font, Joan, 1965. "Misión y entrada de los Andes de Xauxa, 1596." In *Relaciones geográficas de Indias—Perú,* edited by Marcos Jiménez de la Espada, vol. 2, 102–5. Madrid: Ediciones Atlas.

Gálvez, Aníbal. 1905. *Cosas de antaño: crónicas peruanas.* Lima: Imprenta de "El Tiempo."

Garcilaso de la Vega, Inca. 1963. *Comentarios reales de los Incas.* Montevideo: Ministerio de Instrucción Pública y Previsión Social.

Gow, Peter. 2002. "Piro, Apurinã, and Campa: Social Dissimilation and Assimilation as Historical Processes in Southwestern Amazonia." In *Comparative Arawakan Histories: Rethinking Language Family and Culture Area in Amazonia,* edited by Jonathan D. Hill and Fernando Santos-Granero, 147–70. Urbana: University of Illinois Press.

Gow, Peter. 2011. "Rethinking Cities in Peruvian Amazonia: History, Archaeology, and Myth." In *The Archaeological Encounter: Anthropological Perspectives,* edited by Paolo Fortis and Istevan Praet, 174–203. St. Andrews: Centre for Amerindian, Latin American and Caribbean Studies.

Guamán Poma de Ayala, Felipe. 1615. *El primer nueva crónica y buen gobierno.* Copenhagen: Det Kongelige Bibliotek.

Heckenberger, Michael J. 2005. *The Ecology of Power: Culture, Place, and Personhood in the Southern Amazon, AD 1000–2000.* New York: Routledge.

Heckenberger, Michael J. 2013. "The Arawak Diaspora: Perspectives from South America." In *The Oxford Handbook of Caribbean Archaeology*, edited by William F. Keegan, Corinne L. Hofman, and Reniel Rodríguez Ramos, 111–25. Oxford: Oxford University Press.

Heckenberger, Michael J., Christian Russell, Joshua R. Toney, and Morgan J. Schmidt. 2007. "The Legacy of Cultural Landscapes in the Brazilian Amazon: Implications for Biodiversity." *Philosophical Transactions of the Royal Society of London*, ser. B, *Biological Sciences* 362 (1478): 197–208.

Ibn Khaldûn. 2015. *The Muqaddimah: An Introduction to History*. Translated and introduced by Franz Rosenthal. Abridged and edited by N. J. Dawood. Princeton, N.J.: Princeton University Press.

ILV (Instituto Lingüístico de Verano). 2004. *Pueblos del Perú*. Lima: Instituto Lingüístico de Verano.

Isbell, William H., Christine Brewster-Wray, and Lynda E. Spickard. 1991. "Architecture and Spatial Organization at Huari." In *Huari Administrative Structure: Prehistoric Monumental Architecture and State Government*, edited by William H. Isbell and Gordon F. McEwan, 19–53. Washington, D.C.: Dumbarton Oaks.

Jerez, Francisco de. 1947. "Conquista del Perú." In *Historiadores primitivos de Indias*, edited by Enrique de Vedia, vol. 2, 320–43. Madrid: Ediciones Atlas.

Kindberg, Willard, Ronald Anderson, Janice Anderson, and Larry Rau. 1979. *Leyendas de los Campa Asháninca*. Lima: Instituto Lingüístico de Verano.

King, Heidi. 2012. "Feather Arts in Ancient Peru." In *Peruvian Featherworks: Art of the Pre-Columbian Era*, edited by Heidi King, 9–44. New Haven, Conn.: Yale University Press.

La Prensa. 1914a. "Entre salvajes." August 19, 1914.

La Prensa. 1914b. "La vida entre los Campas y Amueshas." August 18, 1914.

La Prensa. 1922. "El Curaca Cubiro Churihuanti, jefe de diez tribus." March 31, 1922.

Lathrap, Donald W. 1970. *The Upper Amazon*. London: Thames and Hudson.

Lathrap, Donald W. 1973. "The Antiquity and Importance of Long-Distance Trade Relationships in the Moist Tropics of Pre-Columbian South America." *World Archaeology* 5 (2): 170–86.

Leiva García, Pavel Carlos. 2012. "Los Huancas del Intermedio Tardío de los Andes Centrales del Perú: una entidad sociopolítica compleja entre dos imperios." Master's thesis, Escuela Nacional de Antropología e Historia, Mexico.

Lizárraga, Reginaldo. 1946. *Descripción de las Indias*. Lima: Imprenta D. Miranda.

Mallma Cortéz, Arturo Luis. 2018. "El simbolismo del Tinkuy en la cerámica de la cultura Xauxa." Master's thesis, Universidad Nacional Mayor de San Marcos.

McEwan, Gordon F., and Patrick Ryan Williams. 2012. "The Wari Built Environment: Landscape and Architecture of Empire." In *Wari: Lords of the Ancient Andes*, edited by Susan Bergh, 65–81. New York: Thames and Hudson.

Memorial. 1986. "Véase en el Consejo de Indias el Memorial adjunto que se me ha dado en nombre del Capitán Don Andres Salgado de Araujo y sobre la conquista que propone se me consultará lo que se ofreze y parezieze." *Amazonia Peruana* 7 (13): 135–59.

Meseth, Enrique, Liang-Chi Wang, Sh-Hwa Chen, Jason C. S. Yu, and Michael Buzinny. 2015. "Reconstructing Agriculture in Vitcos Inca Settlement, Peru." *Irrigation and Drainage* 64 (3): 340–52.

Mihas, Elena. 2014. *Upper Perené Arawak Narratives of History, Landscape, and Ritual.* Lincoln: University of Nebraska Press.

Montesinos, Fernando. 1644. *Ophir de España: Memorias historiales y políticas del Perú. Manuscript.* Internet Archive. Uploaded July 9, 2017. https://archive.org /details/A332035/.

Montesinos, Fernando. 1882. *Memorias antiguas historiales y políticas del Perú.* Madrid: Imprenta de Miguel Ginesta.

Narby, Jeremy. 1989. "Visions of Land: The Ashaninca and Resource Development in the Pichis Valley in the Peruvian Central Jungle." PhD diss., Stanford University.

Olmedo, Antonio de. 1956. "Información de las misiones dominicas del Cerro de la Sal." *Revista del Archivo Nacional del Perú* 20 (1): 66–84; 20 (2): 317–340.

Pérez Cantó, Pilar. 1982. "La población de Lima en el siglo XVIII." *Boletín Americanista* 32:383–407.

Raymond, J. Scott. 1988. "A View from the Tropical Forest." In *Peruvian Prehistory,* edited by R. W. Keating, 279–300. Cambridge: Cambridge University Press.

Raymond, J. Scott. 1992. "Highland Colonization of the Peruvian Montaña in Relation to the Political Economy of the Huari Empire." *Journal of the Steward Anthropological Society* 20 (1–2): 17–36.

Renard-Casevitz, France-Marie, Thierry Saignes, and Anne-Christine Taylor. 1988. *Al este de los Andes: relaciones entre las sociedades amazónicas y andinas entre los siglos XV y XVII.* Quito: Abya-Yala.

Santacruz Pachacuti, Joan de. 1968. "Relación de antigüedades deste reyno del Perú." In *Crónicas peruanas de interés indígena,* edited by Francisco Esteve Barba, 279–319. Madrid: Ediciones Atlas.

Santillana, Julián. 2000. "Los estados panandinos: Wari y Tiwanaku." In *Historia del Perú: Culturas prehispánicas,* edited by Teodoro Hampe Martínez, 174–232. Barcelona: Lexus.

Santos-Granero, Fernando. 1991. *The Power of Love: The Moral Use of Knowledge Amongst the Amuesha of Central Peru.* London: Athlone Press.

Santos-Granero, Fernando. 2018. *Slavery and Utopia: The Wars and Dreams of an Amazonian World Transformer.* Austin: University of Texas Press.

Santos-Granero, Fernando. 2019. "Introducción: Autos de los indios chunchos remitidos por el Gral. Marqués de Menahermosa por sospecha de ser espías del rebelde Juan Santos Atahuallpa." *Amazonía Peruana* 32:257–59.

Santos-Granero, Fernando, and Frederica Barclay. 2011. "Bundles, Stampers, and Flying Gringos: Amazonian Perceptions of Capitalist Violence." *Journal of Latin American and Caribbean Anthropology* 16 (1): 143–67.

Schreiber, Katharina. 2012. "Una aproximación a las investigaciones sobre Wari: para-
digmas y perspectivas sobre el horizonte medio." *Boletín de Arqueología* 16:11–22.

Seiner Lizárraga, Lizardo. 2016. *Historia de los sismos en el Perú, catálogo: siglos
XVIII–XIX*. Lima: Fondo Editorial de la Universidad de Lima.

Seminario, Bruno, and María Alejandra Zegarra Díaz. 2014. *Las tendencias de largo
plazo de la desigualdad regional en el Perú, 1827–2007*. Lima: Centro de Investigación de la Universidad del Pacífico.

Shady, Ruth. 2006. "La civilización Caral: sistema social y manejo del territorio y sus
recursos; su trascendencia en el proceso cultural andino." *Boletín de Arqueología
PUCP (Pontificia Universidad Católica del Perú)* 10:59–89.

Shaver, Harold, and Betty Ashby. 1976. *Leyendas de los Campa Nomatsiguenga*. Lima:
Instituto Lingüístico de Verano.

Smith, Richard Chase. 2004. "Caciques chinchaycochas, funcionarios incas y sacer-
dotes amueshas: los caminos antiguos de Chinchaycocha hacia la Selva Central."
Cultura Andina 1 (3): 59–76.

Smith, Richard Chase. 2011. "¿Un sustrato Arawak en los Andes Centrales? la historia oral y el espacio histórico-cultural yánesha." In *Por donde hay soplo: estudios
amazónicos en los países andinos*, edited by Jean-Pierre Chaumeil, Oscar Espi-
noza Rivero, and Manuel Cornejo Chaparro, 219–54. Lima: Instituto Francés de
Estudios Andinos.

Tantaleán, Henry. 2013. "Hacia una teoría arqueológica del estado en los Andes pre-
hispánicos (II): los estados militaristas andinos." *Revista Atlántica-Mediterránea*
15:81–112.

Varese, Stefano. 1973. *La sal de los cerros: una aproximación al mundo campa*. Lima:
Ediciones Retablo de Papel.

Villanueva, Amelia, and Lucy Trapnell. 1976. "Todas las escopetas me van a mandar
los *tasorentsi*." *Amazonía Peruana* 1 (1): 133–34.

Wilkinson, Darryl. 2018. "The Influence of Amazonia on State Formation in the Ancient Andes." *Antiquity* 92 (365): 1362–76.

Wise, Mary Ruth. 2011. "Rastros desconcertantes de contactos entre idiomas y culturas a lo largo de los contrafuertes orientales de los Andes del Perú." In *Estudios
sobre las lenguas andinas y amazónicas: homenaje a Rodolfo Cerrón-Palomino*,
edited by Willem F. H. Adelaar, Pilar Valenzuela Bismarck, and Roberto Zariquiey
Biondi, 305–26. Lima: Fondo Editorial de la Pontificia Universidad Católica del
Perú.

CONTRIBUTORS

Natalia Buitron obtained a BA in anthropology and ethnology at the University of Siena (Italy) and trained in anthropology of learning and cognition (MSc) at the London School of Economics and Political Science, leading to the completion of her PhD (2017). She is now the Jessica Sainsbury Assistant Professor in the Anthropology of Amazonia in the Department of Social Anthropology and Fellow of Jesus College, University of Cambridge. Her current research connects Indigenous politics and political theory to explore the plurality of Indigenous sovereignties emerging from Amazonia. Her publications explore political subjectivities, village formation, and transformations in sociality and moral selfhood.

Philippe Erikson is lecturer (since 1996) and chairman of the Anthropology Department (since 2005) at Paris Nanterre University. He has spent three years doing fieldwork with Panoan peoples, namely among the Matis of western Brazil (since 1984), the Chacobo of northeastern Bolivia (since 1991), and the Cashinahua of Peru (since 2007). His research interests include comparative Western Amazonian social organization, material culture, cosmology, and body ornamentation. He is the author of *La Griffe des Aïeux: Marquage du corps et démarquages ethniques chez les Matis d'Amazonie*, also published in Spanish as *El sello de los antepasados: marcado del cuerpo y demarcación étnica entre los Matis de la Amazonía*, and editor of *La pirogue ivre: bières traditionnelles en Amazonie*. His numerous publications also include contributions in *Amazonía Peruana, Anthropozoologica, Campos, Current Anthropology, Journal de la Société des Américanistes, Journal of Latin American Lore, Journal of the Royal Anthropological Institute, L'Homme, Mana, Natural History, Scripta Ethnologica,* and *Techniques & Culture.*

Emanuele Fabiano obtained a PhD at the École des Hautes Études en Sciences Sociales de Paris in 2015. He is a member of the Laboratoire d'Anthropologie Sociale and the international work group Antropología Política Contemporánea en la Amazonía Occidental (Contemporary Political Anthropology in Western Amazonia). He has done extended fieldwork among the Urarina of Peruvian Amazonia, as well as in the Andean regions of southern Peru and Bolivia. He has investigated the anthropological, social, and political effects of extractive processes (timber and petroleum), and their effects at the ritual and cosmographic level. His recent investigations focus on the study of contemporary Indigenous Amazonian communities and their relationship with the state and local and international markets. In addition to his research in Peru, in 2017 he did three months of comparative fieldwork among the Emberá of the Darién region of Panama, with the support of a short-term fellowship from the Smithsonian Tropical Research Institute. He has been a recipient of a postdoctoral fellowship from the International Geography of Philosophy project funded by the University of California, Los Angeles, the University of Pittsburgh, and Rutgers University, and at present he is a postdoctoral researcher at the Centro de Estudos Sociais of the University of Coimbra.

Fabiana Maizza is assistant professor in anthropology at the University of Pernambuco. She obtained a PhD in social anthropology from the University of São Paulo (2009) and a master's degree from Paris Nanterre University. Her doctoral dissertation, based on extended fieldwork among the Jarawara of the Brazilian Amazon, analyzes the concrete and abstract ways through which Jarawara people deal with affine relations in a dangerous world in which all beings (human and nonhuman) constitute a potential threat for Jarawara life. Her current research focuses on the relations between humans and cultivated plants, as well as on gender relations among the Jarawara. She has published various articles on female agency, feminist politics of life, ecology and feminism, and human-plant relations. She is an associate researcher at the Amerindian Studies Center at the University of São Paulo, as well as at the Centre Enseignement et Recherche en Ethnologie Amérindienne, Paris Nanterre University.

Daniela Peluso is a cultural anthropologist whose current research focuses on Indigenous Amazonian communities and the anthropology of finance. She received her PhD in 2003 from Columbia University and is a senior lecturer in social anthropology in the School of Anthropology and Conservation at the University of Kent. For the last three decades, she has worked in lowland South America, mostly with the Ese Eja communities in the Peruvian and Bolivian Amazon, in close collaboration with native federations in various local efforts. Her publications focus on Indigenous urbanization, personhood, relatedness, gender relations, informal and environmental service economies, ethnogenesis, corruption and financial institutions. She assembled the dossier "Indigenous Urbanization: The Circulation of Peoples Between Rural and Urban Amazonian Spaces," published as a special issue of the *Journal of Latin American and Caribbean Anthropology*. She is on the board of the Society for the Anthropology of Lowland South America and the advisory board of People and Plants International, and she is an associate director of the Chacruna Institute for Psychedelic Plant Medicines.

Fernando Santos-Granero did undergraduate studies in anthropology at the Pontificia Universidad Católica del Perú (1980) and obtained a PhD in social anthropology from the London School of Economics and Political Science (1986). He has done extended fieldwork among the Yanesha of eastern Peru and historical research on the Indigenous societies and regional economies of Upper Amazonia. Since 1994 he has been a staff researcher at the Smithsonian Tropical Research Institute (Panama). His publications include numerous articles on Yanesha social organization, political leadership, shamanism, myth, ritual, and history. He has written and edited books on Yanesha philosophies of power, Amazonian regional economies, comparative Arawak studies, Indigenous forms of slavery, the occult life of things, and Indigenous notions of wealth and well-being. He has also made important contributions to the topics of leadership and power, landscape and history, people-making and bodyscapes, culture and language, kinship and friendship, knowledge and corporeality, and sorcery and modernity. His recent books include *Vital Enemies: Slavery, Predation, and the Amerindian Political Economy of Life* and *Slavery and Utopia: The Wars and Dreams of an Amazonian World Transformer.*

Pirjo Kristiina Virtanen, PhD in Latin American studies, is assistant professor and the head of Indigenous studies at the University of Helsinki. Her research interests include epistemological plurality, human-environment interactions, mobility, Indigenous research methodologies, and research ethics. She has worked in Brazilian Amazonia since 2003. Her publications include monographs, several edited books and articles on Amazonian Indigenous politics, leadership, urbanity, movements, digital technologies, youthhood, and biocultural landscapes, as well as Arawak historicity. She is the author of *Indigenous Youth in Brazilian Amazonia: Changing Lived Worlds* and co-editor of *Creating Dialogues: Indigenous Perceptions and Changing Forms of Leadership in Amazonia.* She is also an associated researcher at the Centre Enseignement et Recherche en Ethnologie Amérindienne, Paris Nanterre University. In addition to publishing on her research interests, she has co-authored various Indigenous school materials.

Robin M. Wright obtained his PhD at Stanford University (1981). Previously a full professor of anthropology at the State University of Campinas (1985–2005), he has since 2005 been an associate professor of religion and anthropology at the University of Florida. His principal areas of concentration are Indigenous religious traditions, traditional forms of healing, and the ethnology of the Americas. He lived and worked in Brazil for twenty years, during which time he conducted fieldwork in the Northwest Amazon. He has published widely in the areas of Indigenous shamanism, Indigenous Christianities, narrative traditions, religious movements, anthropological advocacy and Indigenous rights, and ethnology of the Baniwa of the Aiary River, northwest Brazil. Among his most significant works are *Historia indigena e do indigenismo no Alto Rio Negro, Cosmos, Self, and History in Baniwa Religion: For Those Unborn,* and *Mysteries of the Jaguar Shamans of the Northwest Amazon.* He has worked extensively with a Baniwa shaman for the purpose of recording and preserving shamanic knowledge critically threatened with disappearance. Most of his work has been digitized in the Archive of the Indigenous Languages of Latin America, through the University of Texas at Austin.

INDEX